STAR WARS

EPISODE III

The Making of
Star Wars
Revenge of the Sith

J. W. Rinzler

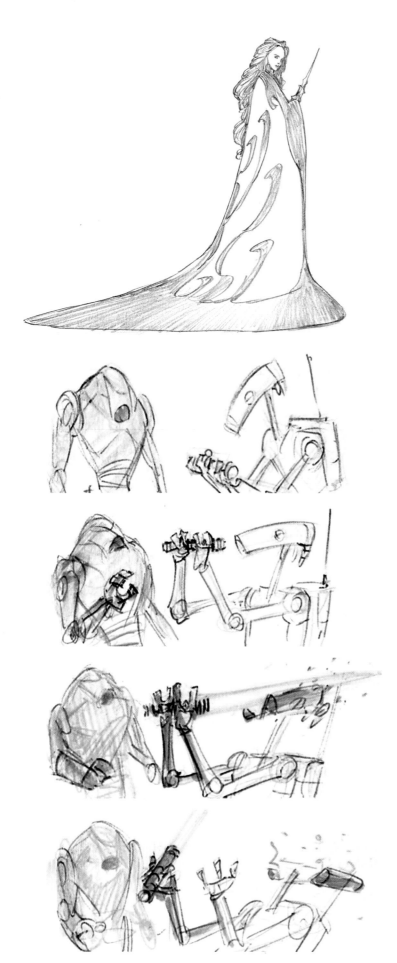

To Geneviéve, Sarah, & Judith

Photo credits: Keith Hamshere, John Knoll, Derryck Menere, Carl Miller, Tina Mills, Merrick Morton, Ralph Nelson Jr, David Owen, Paul Tiller, and Lisa Tomasetti, along with screen grabs from HD documentary footage by Tippy Bushkin.

First published in Great Britain in 2005

1 3 5 7 9 10 8 6 4 2

Ebury Press
Random House
20 Vauxhall Bridge Road, London SW1V 2SA

The Random House Group Limited Reg. No. 954009

A CIP catalogue record for this book is available from the British Library.

www.starwars.com
www.randomhouse.co.uk

ISBN: 0091897378

Printed and bound by Imprimerie Pollina S.A. in France – L20258

Papers used by Ebury Press are natural, recyclable products made from wood grown in sustainable forests.

EBURY
PRESS

Page 1: The Episode III teaser poster. Page 2: Industrial Light & Magic (ILM) composite image of George Lucas with computer-generated (CG) vehicles, planets, and creatures from Star Wars: Revenge of the Sith *(art directed by concept design supervisor Ryan Church; technical directed by Ryan Jones). Page 3: A Boga (lizard-creature) animation reference sketch by ILM lead animator Glen McIntosh. Page 4: (top left) Padmé with dagger by concept artist Iain McCaig; (left) sinkhole battle by concept design supervisor Erik Tiemens; (top right) hapless battle-droid storyboards by concept artist Derek Thompson; (above) Doodle "meeting sketch" of Nien Nunb by concept artist Warren Fu. Page 5: "Chicken-walker" by concept artist T.J. Frame.*

Contents

✦ Foreword

The *Star Wars* prequel trilogy has taken up more than my entire life for the last ten years. During the five years before George and I started work on it, during location shooting for *The Young Indiana Jones Chronicles*, I didn't live in the same place for more than two months at a time; in fact, my apartment in Prague had only a photo of a TV set cut out of a magazine taped to a wall. My daughters were playing with fluffy Yoda dolls.

But two things happened. In the extreme cold of a Jackson Hole, Wyoming, winter, George discovered that directing wasn't all bad. During our two-day shoot in December 1992–with Harrison Ford, who was playing a fifty-year-old Indiana Jones for an episode of *Young Indy*–George enjoyed himself so much that he decided he might direct *Star Wars: Episode I*. This decision didn't become final until 1993–the year digital technology came of age–but from that moment on, my life wasn't the same.

From 1995 to 2005, we've spent hundreds of millions of dollars, exposed millions of feet of film, recorded even more high-definition tape, shot over ten thousand setups, ate millions of catered meals, and drank literally thousands of bottles of wine in over a dozen countries. Now I have a permanent home with a genuine television and teenage daughters who lust after the real-life Darth Vader. Yet some things haven't changed: I'm working with essentially the same crew as the one I began with on *Young Indy*. I love working with them and shooting, and I love production. *This* book is a record of Episode III's entire production; *The Making of Star Wars: Revenge of the Sith* chronologically follows our story through its three-year cycle, and we've crammed into it as much as we could. I hope you enjoy it.

Rick McCallum
Skywalker Ranch, October 2004

✳ Introduction

The making of *Star Wars*: Episode III *Revenge of the Sith* really began when George Lucas first touched number 2 pencil to yellow legal pad in 1972. The following year, Lucas showed his treatment for *The Star Wars* to Alan Ladd Jr. at Twentieth Century Fox, who thought its author had potential. When an advanced print of Lucas's second feature, *American Graffiti* (1973), was smuggled onto the lot from Universal for Ladd's viewing–making it a true sneak preview–the deal was sealed. The contract between studio and writer-director was signed on August 20, 1973. The first *Star Wars* (1977) went on to become the phenomenon it still is today. Its sequels, *The Empire Strikes Back* (1980) and *Return of the Jedi* (1983), were also huge successes, and though Lucas directed neither, he was intimately involved with both, from the writing of the stories to the last frame of postproduction.

Following the completion of the trilogy, a period of non–*Star Wars* activity followed for Lucas–until he began the work that culminated with the theatrical release of the *Star Wars Trilogy Special Edition* (1997). The enormous posi-

tive reaction that greeted this re-release surprised everyone but the public, which had clearly been waiting to reappreciate these films. *Star Wars*: Episode IV *A New Hope* regained the title of the highest-grossing film ever, surpassing Steven Spielberg's *E.T.: The Extraterrestrial*. To mark the moment, Spielberg took out a page in *Variety* that showed E.T. crowning R2-D2 and the words "Dear George, Congratulations for renewing the most enduring motion picture in cinema history. Your pal, Steven."

Buoyed by his films' continuing popularity–and by the advances made in digital cinema–Lucas embarked in earnest on a vast ten-year project: the making of the *Star Wars* prequel trilogy. These films had actually been forming in his mind for some time, but Lucas had been patiently waiting until the technology was ready. Indeed, many of Lucas's companies–Industrial Light & Magic, the Computer Division, THX, and Skywalker Sound–had been working for years to advance the cause and techniques of digital tools. Nonlinear digital editing was one of his first major achievements. Lucas experimented himself with digital editing and visual effects, first with his TV series *The Young Indiana Jones Chronicles* (1992–94), then on the film *Radioland Murders* (1994), and finally with the *Special Edition*.

Above left: Producer Rick McCallum in the makeup department, Fox Studios, Sydney, Australia. Left: Concept art of Palpatine Leading Clone Troopers (or Rick's First Day of Production) by Church. Above: Hayden Christensen (Anakin Skywalker) in the Alderaan star cruiser (aka "Rebel blockade runner") corridor set in Sydney. Above right: Darth Vader's first complete costume fitting (Christensen, center) and from left: costume props supervisor Ivo Coveney, costume supervisor Nicole Young, author J. W. Rinzler, costume designer Trisha Biggar, CG artist David Weitzberg, and unidentified person. Right: (from left) George Lucas, president of Lucas Licensing Howard Roffman, and Rinzler review image printouts. Far right: "Alien costume 01 (Mustafar)" by concept artist Sang Jun Lee.

In Rick McCallum, whose collaboration with Lucas began on *Young Indy*, the director had found a producer whose independent-film mindset dovetailed perfectly with Lucas's documentarian work habits. McCallum helped recruit a core team of collaborators: production designer Gavin Bocquet, costume designer Trisha Biggar, and director of photography David Tattersall. The result of this confluence of people and technology was *Star Wars*: Episode I *The Phantom Menace* (1999) and Episode II *Attack of the Clones* (2002). The latter was also a historical milestone as it was the first film to be recorded digitally rather than on film.

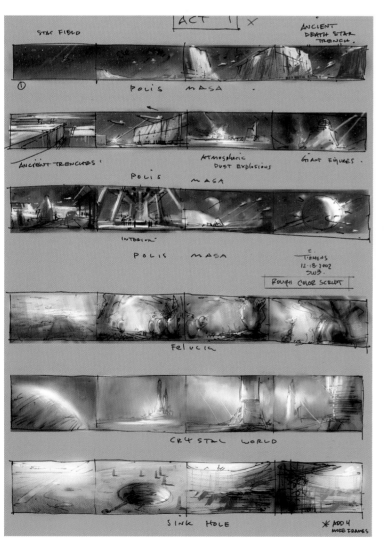

In spring 2002, although everyone knew that the third prequel and last *Star Wars* film would show how Anakin Skywalker becomes Darth Vader and how the Empire would crush the spirit of the Republic, no one knew exactly how these events would come to pass nor what they'd look like. No one–not even Lucas.

In the following pages, the reader will discover just how organically these events came to be. Not many writers have had the opportunity to witness up close every stage of the making of a film on an almost daily basis. For this, thanks–enormous thanks–go to George Lucas and Rick McCallum. Rick enabled all of it to happen, and George has graciously allowed three years of eavesdropping. During these years, I attended nearly every art department meeting, traveled to Sydney for the filming, attended dailies and animation dailies at ILM, watched George direct in the animatics department, sat in on editing sessions, observed the pickups at Shepperton Studios, and so on. It's been an amazing apprenticeship, and I've met incredible people–all of whom without exception have provided insights that will be found in the following pages. I only hope I've done justice to this great cast and crew.

The point of all this creative witnessing has been to write a book that gives readers the feeling that they were genuinely present in the art department, on the sets, in the dressing rooms, at ILM–and seeing things as they happened. Events, conversations, breakthroughs, and tensions have all been recorded as they occurred in real time, chronologically, with the same lack of future sight that existed at the time the events were recorded.

J. W. Rinzler
Big Rock Ranch, October 2004

Left: Rough color script by Tiemens. Above: Enhanced image of Swiss Alps taken during recce (scouting trip) for possible Alderaan locations. Right: Kit Fisto battle gear by Thompson.

 # Who's Who

Brad Alexander
Senior Animatics Artist, Skywalker
Ranch (SR)

Deborah Antoniou
Second Assistant Director,
Australia (Aus)/England (Eng)

Roger Barton
Editor, SR

Trisha Biggar
Costume Designer, Aus/Eng

Colette Birrell
Art Department Coordinator, Aus

Michael Blanchard
Postproduction Technical
Supervisor, SR

Gavin Bocquet
Production Designer, Aus

Jill Brooks
Visual Effects Producer, ILM

Ben Burtt
Editor/Sound Designer, SR

Ryan Church
Concept Design Supervisor, SR

Rob Coleman
Animation Director, ILM

Matt Connors
Head Scenic Artist, Aus

Ivo Coveney
Costume Props Supervisor, Aus

Fay David
Art Department Supervisor, SR

Dave Elsey
Creatures Shop Creative
Supervisor, Aus/Eng

Colin Fletcher
First Assistant Director, Aus/Eng

Brian Gernand
Model-Shop Supervisor, ILM

Nick Gillard
Stunt Coordinator, Aus/Eng

John Goodson
Concept Model Maker,
SR/Digital-Matte Department,
ILM

Ian Gracie
Art Director, Aus

Dan Gregoire
Pre-Visualization Supervisor, SR

Roger Guyett
Visual Effects Supervisor, ILM

Greg Hajdu
Construction Manager, Aus

Jonathan Harb
Digital-Matte Painting Department
Supervisor, ILM

Simon Harding
"B" Camera Operator, Aus

Phil Harvey
Art Director, Aus

Rebecca Hunt
Creatures Shop Supervisor,
Aus/Eng

Alex Jaeger
Concept Artist, SR/Art Director,
ILM

Stephen Jones
Production Supervisor, Aus

John Knoll
Visual Effects Supervisor, ILM

Euisung Lee
Senior Animatics Artist, SR

Janet Lewin
Visual Effects Producer, ILM

Jacqui Louez
Assistant to the Producer/Director,
Aus

George Lucas
Writer-Director, SR

Aaron McBride
Art Director, ILM

Rick McCallum
Producer, SR

Calum McFarlane
"A" Camera Operator, Aus/Eng

Fred Meyers
High-Definition Supervisor, ILM

Carl Miller
Director of Photography, ILM

Michael Mooney
Assistant Costume Designer,
Aus/Eng

Virginia Murray
Production Coordinator, Aus

Chris Neil
Dialogue Coach, Aus

Giles Nutggens
Director of Photography, Eng

Ardees Rabang
Assistant to the Producer, SR

Kathryn Ramos
Production Controller, SR

Denise Ream
Visual Effects Executive
Producer, ILM

Richard Roberts
Set Decorator, Aus

Peter Russell
Supervising Art Director,
Aus/Eng

David Tattersall
Director of Photography, Aus

Ty Teiger
Property Master, Aus/Eng

Jayne-Ann Tenggren
Script Supervisor, Aus

Erik Tiemens
Concept Design Supervisor, SR

Danny Wagner
Model Maker, ILM

Nicole Young
Costume Supervisor, Aus/Eng

Animatics Artists, SR
Dorian Bustamante
Eric Carney
Chris Edwards
Nathan Frigard
Barry Howell
Nick Markel
Hiroshi Mori
Greg Rizzi
Joshua Wassung

Concept Artists, SR
Robert Barnes
(and Sculptor)
T.J. Frame
Warren Fu
Sang Jun Lee
Stephan Martiniére
Iain McCaig
Michael Patrick Murnane
(and Sculptor)
Derek Thompson
Feng Zhu

Lead Animators, ILM
Scott Benza
Virginie d'Annoville
Tim Harrington
Paul Kavanaugh
Virgil Manning
Glen McIntosh
Jamy Wheless

Note: *For a complete list of cast and
crew, and many short biographies of
same, go to* **starwars.com.**

PART I

PREPRODUCTION

The Shadow Citadel
of Creation

PROLOGUE: The Digital Script

"Cinema started out as a part of vaudeville," says writer-director George Lucas. "They took out the magic act and they put in a film, because it was like a big magic act. 'Look! Right here on our screen—a giant train, moving right toward you!' That was a big event.

"Science fiction also came into its own at the beginning of the twentieth century, as it matured from Jules Verne to George Orwell and other writers, and while the literature of science fiction and fantasy became much more sophisticated, it was extremely difficult to translate those books into cinema.

"So when I did a fantasy film, we were really bumping up against the ceiling of technology all the time, which made it very hard. I'm a strong believer of cinema as cinema—not as a literary medium and not as a musical medium and not as a theatrical medium—but cinema as the moving image. And so I was able to design a fantasy film and push the limits of the medium of the cinematic form just a tiny bit. But what I really wanted to do was much grander and much bigger and much more outrageous—but I knew that I couldn't do that. I could only do so much with the technology I had.

"So I've always been pushing that technology. I've always been thinking, 'Wouldn't it be great if we could do this or we could do that!' But most of the time, you would get stopped. You couldn't do a movie with twenty thousand extras; you wouldn't even think of writing a scene like that. But now you can do it.

"Now you can pretty much do whatever you want. You're in the same arena that writers are in. If you can write it, you can film it."

Puppet Yoda (above) in 1980's *The Empire Strikes Back*; digital Yoda (top) from *Attack of the Clones* in 2002. Opening spread: Duel on Mustafar by Ryan Church.

Seven Planets for Seven Battles

CHOTT EL JERRID, TUNISIA
THURSDAY, SEPTEMBER 7, 2000

George Lucas and crew are on location for *Star Wars:* Episode II *Attack of the Clones*. It is the 53rd day of the shoot. On the list of today's scenes is one described as "PARTIAL," which means that some elements will be added later–in this case, five years later, for Lucas and producer Rick McCallum have decided to shoot a part of Episode III now in order to avoid making an expensive return trip later.

Built on the salt flat of Chott el Jerrid, near the towns of Tozeur and Nefta, the set is described as "TATOOINE HOMESTEAD (MOISTURE FARM)," and one of the day's props is listed as a "newborn baby doll," which the Call Sheet refers to as "A.N. Other." So, on a very hot afternoon, actor Joel Edgerton (young Owen Lars) and Breeden Phillip (Obi-Wan Kenobi's body double) are called on to pretend it's three years after the events of Episode II and that it's the moment in which Jedi Knight Ben Kenobi hands farmer Owen an infant Luke Skywalker. Owen is to keep Luke far away from the machinations of his corrupted father, Anakin Skywalker–who has become the terrible Sith Lord known as Darth Vader.

According to today's Call Sheet, this scene takes up only one-eighth of a script page–one or two shots in the film. Yet it will take Lucas three years, quite a bit of hard work, and the creative participation of thousands to create a context for this brief but poignant moment.

INDUSTRIAL LIGHT & MAGIC (ILM)
SAN RAFAEL, CALIFORNIA–APRIL 2002 (TWO YEARS LATER)

It's about one month before the theatrical release of Episode II. Following this morning's dailies, McCallum–sensing that something is in the air–suggests that concept design supervisors Ryan Church and Erik

From top: Breeden Phillip (Obi-Wan Kenobi's body-double) gives the infant Luke Skywalker to Joel Edgerton (young Owen Lars) for safekeeping in this Episode III sequence recorded during an Episode II location shoot. Producer Rick McCallum (left), director-writer George Lucas, and a familiar droid in Tunisia during a location shoot for The Phantom Menace *in 1997. Theirs is a working relationship that has lasted for more than fourteen years.*

Tiemens walk with Lucas among the nondescript buildings that house Industrial Light & Magic. After a few moments of chatting, as Church describes it, "George casually says to us, 'Oh, you guys, I want you to start thinking about seven planets–seven new planets that are completely different from each other–this is where the Clone Wars are happening. I just want you to think about that.' "

Church pauses while telling the story. "Well, this is something I've been thinking about since 1977, when I was kid, so I said to George, 'Oh, I think I've got some planets for you.' "

SKYWALKER RANCH (SR)
MARIN COUNTY, CALIFORNIA
THURSDAY, APRIL 25, 2002

The first Episode III art department meeting takes place a few days after Lucas's first instructions. Erik Tiemens, Ryan Church, art department supervisor Fay David, previsualization/effects supervisor Dan Gregoire, and producer Rick McCallum gather around a table to hear what Lucas has to say about the next *Star Wars* film–the last of the prequel trilogy and the third in the sextet.

Lucas's first story fragments are both embryonic and epic: Episode III will take place approximately three years after Episode II. At that time, the Clone Wars will be wrapping up, with seven battles raging on seven new planets. Each planet will have its own species, but the enemy armies will be made up of droids. Jedi Masters Kenobi, Windu, and Yoda are on different planets fighting for the Republic. We may see bounty hunter Boba Fett as a fourteen- or fifteen-year-old. We will visit Princess Leia's home planet of Alderaan; we may visit the Wookiee planet, Kashyyyk. And, Lucas says, because they've been at war for two or three years, vehicles need to be beat up, while clone troopers have added things to their armor to individualize it, based on where they've been fighting, similar to the way American troops did in Vietnam.

By meeting's end, Lucas has divulged just enough to provide the artists material to work on until the next gathering, and, for the next nine months, this will be the pattern. Indeed, for most of preproduction, the concept art department will be working blind–without a script–because

Anakin's Story So Far

A long time ago in a galaxy far, far away....

EPISODE I: THE PHANTOM MENACE

Anakin Skywalker is a nine-year-old slave living with his mother, Shmi, on the remote desert planet of Tatooine. One day while working in Watto's junk shop, Anakin encounters Qui-Gon Jinn, a Jedi Master and a great student of the living Force, who is traveling with Padmé Amidala, the young Queen of Naboo. Qui-Gon becomes convinced that little Annie is the chosen one—the being prophesized to bring balance to the Force. Annie's midi-chlorian count is staggering, and he can see things before they happen, which makes him the only human capable of piloting a Podracer. Consequently, Qui-Gon makes a wager with Watto: If Anakin wins the Boonta Eve Podrace, Watto will give him his freedom. Anakin triumphs and then bids a painful farewell to Shmi. Fortunately, he finds a new friend in Padmé.

Temporarily jubilant after his Podracing victory, little Anakin Skywalker (Jake Lloyd) sits on the shoulder of his would-be Jedi Master, Qui-Gon Jinn (Liam Neeson), and clasps the hand of his mother, Shmi (Pernilla August)...

Anakin's tutelage is tragically cut short, however, when Qui-Gon is killed by a Sith Lord named Darth Maul. The Jedi Master's dying wish is for his Padawan, Obi-Wan Kenobi, to take on Anakin as his apprentice.

EPISODE II: ATTACK OF THE CLONES

Ten years later, Anakin is an accomplished Padawan, though not yet a Jedi Knight. He's also a young man very much in love with Padmé. Because she is now a Senator targeted by unknown assassins, Anakin is assigned as her bodyguard—in part due to the influence of his political mentor, Supreme Chancellor Palpatine.

Hidden away at a Naboo lakeside retreat, Anakin and Padmé grow closer. But the young apprentice is tortured by nightmares in which his mother is suffering greatly. Padmé suggests that she accompany him to Tatooine to investigate. Once there, they discover that Shmi has married Cliegg Lars, a moisture farmer—and has been abducted by Tusken Raiders, the savage nomads who roam the desert wastelands. Anakin heads off alone to save her, but arrives too late: Shmi dies in his arms. Anakin gives in to his rage and slaughters the entire camp of Tusken Raiders, including its women and children. He returns to the Lars homestead and confesses to Padmé.

Shortly thereafter, Anakin receives an urgent message from his Master, Obi-Wan Kenobi, who is in danger on Geonosis. Padmé and Anakin decide to rescue him, but they, too, are taken prisoner by the rogue Jedi Count Dooku, leader of the powerful Separatists, who wish to secede from the Republic. Dooku decides to put them to death in the arena. Our heroes escape, however, and then lead a Jedi counterattack when reinforcements arrive.

Anakin and Obi-Wan pursue Dooku to a secret hangar, where he defeats them easily, cutting off Anakin's hand. But the most powerful of all Jedi—Master Yoda—arrives and saves them, forcing Dooku to flee.

On Coruscant, Dooku reports to his Sith Master, Darth Sidious, that all is going according to plan. Meanwhile, Anakin escorts Padmé back to Naboo, where, because it is against the rules of the Jedi Order, they marry secretly. Back on Coruscant, Obi-Wan, Jedi Mace Windu, and Yoda watch as thousands of clone troopers board Republic assault ships on their way to fight the Separatists in the Clone Wars....

...but a decade later, Anakin (Hayden Christensen) kneels at the grave of his mother, whom he was too late to save, while Qui-Gon's death has deprived him of his surrogate father.

there is no script, no treatment, no outline. "We never truly know what George is doing," explains McCallum, "but it's no different than Episode II, because we didn't know what he was doing on that one, either." Though this style of work begins in a relatively relaxed manner, there is pressure from the get-go. The costume and production design departments will need to begin building soon—the former in November, the latter in January—and that can't happen until Lucas signs off on finished concepts.

"Usually, no one would go off and spend millions of dollars without understanding what the very foundation of the film they're making is," McCallum adds. "But we break that very rule of film production. We do the reverse."

From the audience's point of view, the movies of the *Star Wars* prequel trilogy may seem to have a leisurely schedule, with three years to create each film. The reality is that each movie is enormously complicated. Not only does Lucas push people and technology to their limits, and beyond, but his schooling in the 1960s at the University of Southern California as an avant-garde documentary filmmaker-editor means that he makes his films in an unusual manner. Most filmmakers shoot a specific number of pieces and then turn them over to an editor with instructions on how to put them together. Lucas gathers material as would a documentarian, creating a massive crate filled with tons of pieces. Without instructions, he then slowly sorts through and assembles them with his editors, constantly revising, adding, and taking away as he goes.

This approach has significant practical consequences. One is the liberty of imagination it allows the concept artists, who begin unfettered by words. Another consequence is a more realistic, if longer, production schedule. "I'm shooting next summer for sixty days, and I shoot the following March for ten days, and I shoot that October for five days," Lucas says. "And then when I go to do the looping in London, I may shoot for a couple more

days—and it's in all the actors' contracts. It's in the budget. It's planned for. That's the way I make movies—as opposed to a lot of people who shoot the whole movie in one go and cut it all together, and then the studios say, 'Well what about this, what about that?'

"And so they have to call the actors back and they have to make new deals—but then the film's going over budget and everybody perceives it as being in trouble. And it's just silly. Why not just accept the inevitable at the very beginning? I started out as a documentary filmmaker, so I'm very used to shooting, cutting material together, going out and shooting some more, cutting it together, and creating it out of nothing. You have a vague idea of what your subject is going to be, but the actual story evolves as you deal with real people and real life. You don't quite know what you're going to get."

FRIDAY, JUNE 7, 2002

Light-years away from Hollywood, Skywalker Ranch is located north of San Francisco, on the far side of the Golden Gate Bridge. But from the style of its signage to its remoteness, the ranch has a single-mindedness and late-nineteenth-century aesthetic that align it more with the small towns along the sparsely populated northern California coastline than with the densely populated cities to the south.

Lucas bought the greater part of his property back in 1978, but construction wasn't complete until 1987, and only a very small part of the sixty-five-hundred-acre ranch has been developed. The ranch includes a few large houses, a Technical Center (which houses Skywalker Sound and the three-hundred-seat Stag Theatre), a fitness center, and a guest inn. The Main House was built to resemble a large Victorian manor, with walls of redwood burl, ebony, and rosewood.

The origins of Skywalker Ranch are multiple. Lucas has said that he is a "frustrated architect" and that he simply likes to build. Another motivat-

Inset: The Main House on Skywalker Ranch. Below: Episode III concept design supervisor Erik Tiemens painted this view of the Technical Building, where Skywalker Sound is located on the ranch. In order to keep his skills sharp and his vision active, Tiemens often sketches outdoors.

Thursday, May 16: *Star Wars:* Episode II *Attack of the Clones* is released.
Wednesday, May 29: *Attack of the Clones* passes the $200 million mark.

ing factor was his desire to create a place where filmmakers could work in a suitably relaxing environment–the inspiration for which can be traced back to Lucas's student days at USC and his early years working with Francis Ford Coppola to establish American Zoetrope. In fact, Skywalker Ranch is Lucas's second locale of this sort: the first was his own home, where at one time or another, throughout the 1970s, Walter Murch, Phil Kaufman, Michael Ritchie, and Matthew Robbins had offices. Today Skywalker Ranch is where the likes of Steven Spielberg, Clint Eastwood, James Cameron, and Robert Redford come to hone their films.

This is also where Lucas will work with his Episode III producer, concept artists, sound designers, and editors. As such, though it is a nonspeaking part, the atmosphere and design of Skywalker Ranch will have a major role in the making of the movie.

Within the art department, a trio of concept artists–Church, Tiemens, and Robert Barnes–have begun meeting with Lucas every Friday, a routine that will continue over the next year as they design and perfect the film's characters, cities, vehicles, and costumes. In a *Star Wars* film, nearly everything has to be built from the ground up, from control panels to

gloves to light fixtures, so the number of artists will increase as preproduction continues.

At today's gathering, Lucas examines photographs of exotic locales and interesting architecture, which are auditioning for the role of "planet." On the whole, though, he isn't inspired by anything shown. Church says, "He picked just a few things . . . I think he was saying, 'This has all been seen before.' George really pushed us a lot, but we quickly learned there were no drawbacks to being open with him."

Unused art from previous *Star Wars* films is also dusted off. The idea for a sinkhole planet originated in 1976, when legendary production illustrator Ralph McQuarrie first drew it, and Lucas approves it for this movie. "The idea is to have clone troopers rappel down into it," he explains. Lucas also likes Church's idea for a bridge planet, and says that Kashyyyk, the home planet of the Wookiees, will almost definitely be in the picture. An ice planet and a mining planet are considered, and Lucas proposes a ring planet.

They then examine artwork for "Mufasta," the volcano planet. Joe Johnston–a veteran *Star Wars* trilogy concept artist and now a director– recalls, "When we were doing *Star Wars,* I remember I had done a series

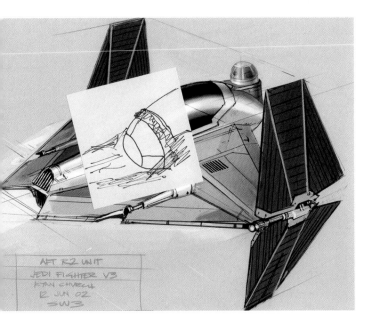

AFT R2 UNIT
JEDI FIGHTER V3
KTN CHURCH
12 JUN 02
SW3

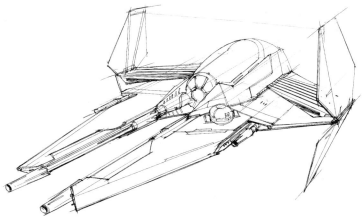

of sketches of Vader's home, and there was a sea of lava his house looked out on [. . .]. But before we got too far, George said we would save this for somewhere down the line."

"These are old, old, old. Mufasta's been around a long time," George says. "I've always had this set piece: the end between Obi-Wan and Anakin. I knew that's where this movie was going to end up. It's all this volcanic land, with lava shooting up, so it's almost monochromatic in its red-and-blackness. I've had that image with me for a long time."

Lucas ends the meeting by saying, "The first ten minutes are going to be a huge spectacle. You're not going to know what is going on, other than it's the Clone Wars." He also encourages the artists with what will become the guiding principle of this first conceptual art phase: "Now is the time to go way out there, to be as wild as possible!"

TUESDAY, JUNE 11, 2002

Within Lucasfilm resides the production company that makes the *Star Wars* films: JAK Films, Inc. (The name was formed from the initials of Lucas's three children: Jett, Amanda, and Katie.) The JAK art department is located in a beautiful, if somewhat cramped, attic on the grounds of Skywalker Ranch. The concept artists occupy about a quarter of a space that also houses the animatics department, a small photography studio, shelves filled with art reference books, a kitchenette, one sunny office atop a short flight of stairs, and two bathrooms—one with a bath-shower for those long nights, and another with a sign over the toilet that reads DOOKU'S THRONE ROOM.

A few of the walls are brick, as chimneys from fireplaces below make their way toward the roof. It can be a very light space, but some darker sections are lit only by luminous computer screens. Sculptures of spacecraft and aliens sit on many desks, while drawings, paintings, and photographs of characters and environments are pinned up on nearly all available wall space. At one end of the animatics department sits a great old cast-iron Verona stove manufactured by the Wehrle Company of Newark, Ohio.

At today's short meeting, another planet is approved as a concept: crystal world. Art department supervisor Fay David is just back from vacationing in Thailand, where she saw Bangkok's Episode II premiere—projected digitally. "That's good," Lucas says. "Because that means that all over the world, they're getting it." He goes on to say he had a somewhat contentious magazine interview about digital filmmaking. McCallum becomes incensed by what he hears and leaves to take care of a few things. A few minutes later, George asks, "Where did Rick go?" Fay points down the hall and says, "He stormed off that way . . ."

THURSDAY, JUNE 13, 2002

Production designer Gavin Bocquet, at producer McCallum's request, is making a "surprise" visit. When Lucas enters, Bocquet says, "Hello. I'm just passing through." However, Bocquet's voyage here—like many to come—has a twofold purpose: to give him an opportunity to see the design directions the film is already taking, and to remind everyone that production is out there, waiting . . . The meaning of Bocquet's visit, and future head-of-department pop-ins, is always clear to Lucas. As McCallum points out, "The one thing that George does deal with at a certain level is guilt."

Lucas and Bocquet quickly reminisce about how Episode II was supposed to be "smaller" than Episode I, but actually ended up being bigger in terms of the number of sets built. "Well," jokes Lucas, "Episode III will be 'smaller' still." Turning their attention to a Jedi starfighter concept, Lucas explains that the craft is transitional. They talk about its form, how the guns should work, how much they'll have to build, and how much of it will be digital. Rick says he'd like production to have three sets to design by November, but Lucas says that they won't "start these guys till March [2003]—six weeks is plenty." Rick would also like to have concept artist and key costume designer Iain McCaig—a veteran of prequels I and II—join the department by July, but Lucas asks, "What's he going to design—upholstery?"

Left: Tiemens's sinkhole planet, as inspired by Ralph McQuarrie's Crevasse City (inset). Above left: Superimposed on Church's June 12 Jedi starfighter concept are Lucas's sketched changes to the cockpit, which give it more of TIE fighter look in Church's revised sketch (above right). Right: In the Skywalker Ranch art department are (from left) Lucas, communications director Lynne Hale, McCallum, and production designer Gavin Bocquet.

The tenor of this exchange between Lucas and McCallum is typical of these preshooting months, but they know each other far too well to mistake the intentions of the other. Lucas will take the time he needs to write, and McCallum will continue to push for the time he feels production needs—but Rick is the first to point out that George always responds when he manifests a certain level of need. "With some directors, communication can be a problem because their egos get in the way. But George is more understanding—he understands the process. And he knows that I will never bug him until I really need the information."

As the meeting comes to an end, Lucas again exhorts the artists: "Expand our universe. Expand our weapons—push your imaginations." Turning to Bocquet, he estimates that there will be sixteen hundred visual effects shots for Episode III. Small talk turns to what exactly will push Anakin to the dark side. "It'll be Padmé," George says. "She'll get so angry at him for not picking up his socks."

R ick McCallum, the producer of the *Star Wars* prequel trilogy, is American but went to school in Europe. He returned to the United States to attend Columbia University, where he studied German, French,

and English literature. "It was after Vietnam and I didn't have to worry about getting drafted. I was finishing school and didn't know what to do." Although Rick at one time wanted to be a *nez* (nose) in the perfume industry, a summertime job as a part-time office assistant for filmmakers James Ivory and Ismail Merchant offered direction. "There was something immediate about the life of a film."

By the time he'd graduated, McCallum had worked on three Ivory-Merchant movies: *Savages* (1972), *Autobiography of a Princess* (1975), and *The Wild Party* (1975). He then had an opportunity to work for ABC News in Paris, where he discovered another dimension to production. "The assistant cameraman got very sick with food poisoning," Rick says, "so I had to help the cameraman that day—and I saw a whole other aspect of making film. I liked the set. I liked the adrenaline, the long hours, the connections you have with people. There were girls."

He knew now what he wanted to do for a living. Returning to New York City, he enrolled at the American Film Institute, where McCallum discovered that he had other talents. "I realized that my skills putting a short film together were better than my skills working with an actor. I found out that I could actually convince the crew to work for twenty-four hours. I got the locations easy. Then John Frankenheimer and I met. We got along very well and he hired me as an assistant director [on *The French Connection II* (1975), *Black Sunday* (1977), and *Prophecy* (1979)]. Then, when I was twenty-four, I met Dennis Potter."

Already a well-known scribe in his native England, Potter offered McCallum his first position as executive producer, on *Pennies from Heaven* (1981). "It was a huge financial disaster. It was such a disaster, I couldn't get another job." Seeing McCallum's predicament, Potter invited him to the United Kingdom, where

A Tiemens concept painting a gunship (above) and Mufasta (top), the volcano planet, which was originally envisioned by Joe Johnston (above middle). McCallum (top right) during the shooting of a Young Indiana Jones Chronicles *episode. Inspired by a* Star Wars Galaxy *trading card by Al Williamson (right), Lucas requests a lizard-dragon. Robert E. Barnes supplies a concept (above right) with Anakin astride the beast.*

the climate was much more to the expatriate's liking. "The experience was totally different from working in the studio system. And I said to myself, *Wait a second. Here I control my destiny.* In America, you don't. It's too power-centric. If I did a studio film and pissed off the star, I'd be off the picture in a second."

McCallum went on to produce Potter's *DreamChild* (1985) and executive produce his BBC TV series *The Singing Detective* (1986). He also produced director Nicolas Roeg's *Castaway* (1987) and *Track 29* (1988). It was on the set of *DreamChild,* which was being filmed at Elstree Studios, that Rick first met George Lucas, who happened to be visiting the nearby set of Walter Murch's *Return to Oz* (1985), which Lucas was executive producing. According to McCallum, George seemed almost envious of his small crew, because *Oz* was more of a traditional setup, with a relatively large crew.

As the years passed, McCallum became dissatisfied. "I made ten films in England and though they were all good, all of them were unsuccessful. By the time I was thirty-four, it was getting harder and harder to make the movies, to get the money, to get distributed—and that's when I met George again." Lucas was in London looking for a producer for his upcoming TV series *The Young Indiana Jones Chronicles,* and longtime associate Robert Watts reintroduced him to McCallum. "I said I needed someone that could do an American TV series, very fast-paced and difficult," Lucas explains, "and he brought these people in and one of them was Rick. He was just a great find. That's the way it works—it's just like casting." Rick, however, adds a caveat to the story: "I thought *Young Indy* would be an interesting transition from personal filmmaking to making something that was a little more commercial. Little did I know that George wanted to take a very commercial idea and do a very small, independent TV series."

The two went on to do *Radioland Murders* (1994), *Star Wars Trilogy Special Edition* (1997), and the first two prequels. Considering the enormous pressures of the business, theirs is one of the more durable director-producer relationships. "The great thing about Rick is he can do the impossible," George remarks. "If I say I don't want to shoot something tomorrow, or I want to do something else, he'll say, 'Okay,' work all night, move it all around—and it will get done." Rick describes their relationship as "nonverbal" and goes on to say, "Film is a director's medium. Television is a producer's medium. Working with George is a George medium. I have to be able to exhaust all the possibilities in my own imagination, and in everyone else's imagination, to achieve what he wants. And he needs someone like me to enable him to get it in the least dramatic way. Because he wants it easy, he wants it flexible. He wants to be able to do whatever he wants—at a cost that nobody else can compete with—because, at the end of the day, he's paying for it."

FRIDAY, JUNE 21, 2002

As usual, pre-visualization (or "animatics") supervisor Dan Gregoire is at today's meeting to get an idea of what's coming down the pipeline, though his department won't start working on the movie until later in the process. McCallum is in Japan this week for Episode II's premiere, and for talks with Fujinon and Sony on digital cameras and lenses.

Lucas begins by looking at new drawings and digital paintings that have been laid out on the table by Church, Tiemens, and Barnes. The latter is one of only a few to weather the entire prequel trilogy. But despite the long hours and stress, he's not complaining. "I had my own audio business after high school," Barnes says. "The resulting experience was so harrowing that I knew I had to do something that I loved for a living if I was going to be spending so much time doing it—and that's where design came in."

Going through the artwork quickly, Lucas makes comments and approves a half a dozen designs. Looking at one drawing of a round, metallic droid, he says, "Not enough character." He moves on to concept drawings from the previous *Star Wars* films—the last of the old art—and picks twenty-two of them.

Lucas then mentions that he'd like a lizard creature for Anakin to ride in the film. He's thinking of making it into a bronze statue that would be hoisted on top of the big rock that resides alongside the road to Skywalker Ranch B, which is nearing completion (Ranch B will be renamed Big Rock Ranch a few months later).

After the short meeting, Lucas mentions his imminent trip to Japan, where he'll join McCallum. "There's going to be seven hundred and fifty journalists."

"Does each one get a question?" Tiemens asks.

"If they do, I'm never coming back."

Concept design supervisors Erik Tiemens (*Forrest Gump,* 1994; *Star Trek: Voyager,* 1995) and Ryan Church (*War of the Worlds,* 2005) both attended the Art Center in southern California, and both labored at ILM on *Frankenstein*–a computer-generated film that was ultimately canceled–where McCallum saw their "fantastic" work. He consequently recruited them to help finish Episode II, and they've worked at the ranch ever since. Apart from Lucas, McCallum, and a few others, they will labor the longest on Episode III–more than three years. "One's Rembrandt," according to Lucas, "and one's Bierstadt"–Church and Tiemens, respectively.

"I remember on Episode II, when we were first bringing them on," recalls Fay David, "they had worked together on *Frankenstein,* so I think they had already established a rapport. They worked very, very well together. Ryan has a strong industrial design background and Erik brings to the plate a strong fine-art background, and I think the two complement each other."

about giving it up during his first year at Cal State Long Beach. "I had to make a decision," he explains. "Did I want to pursue aviation art or aviation as a pilot? It was winning a scholarship at Art Center that made the decision for me." Nevertheless, he kept up the piloting. "I was about to do my solo cross-country–I was probably weeks from taking my FAA exam– when *Star Wars* came along. One of the things that attracted me to *Star Wars* was the aviation side." Working with Lucas was another plus: "When I first met George, I was impressed with how down-to-earth and informal the meeting was.

"But when he says 'I want this or that'–it happens."

JULY 1 & 10, 2002

Despite working long days and nights on *Peter Pan* (2003) in Australia, concept artist Iain McCaig (*Terminator 2: Judgment Day,* 1991) is now dedicating his few spare hours to Episode III. He is also talking costumes via telephone with ILM artist Sang Jun Lee (*Men in Black II,* 2002; *The Hulk,* 2003), called Jun, who is, reportedly, thrilled at the prospect of working on Episode III. Jun will do some creature designs as a tryout; if George likes them, he'll be given more to do.

At the next two very short art department meetings, model maker John

Tiemens concurs: "I thrive off art history. Things get stale if you're self-referential. But you can drink from that cup–two thousand years of art . . . When I first met George, he showed me binders of what he likes in landscapes, and that put my imagination at full tilt. I've found that the more I've painted, the more of a rapport we've had. We don't have to talk it out."

Tiemens grew up in Santa Cruz, California. "I've liked drawing since I was a kid. It was just one of those things where the other kids stopped drawing and I didn't. I had a very perceptive mother in that she encouraged my talent. I was also very lucky to get a great art teacher, Katie Harper, at Santa Cruz High. In my senior year, she happened to know someone who was over at Games [Lucas's early video game company], back in 1987. So myself and a couple friends came up to the ranch and had lunch and a little tour. After that, I always thought at the back of my mind, *Wouldn't it be great to work here one day?*"

Ryan Church also started drawing at an early age–but was thinking

Goodson–another prequel veteran–shows Lucas a Jedi starfighter maquette, and freelancer Stephan Martinié're's crystal planet artwork is examined.

FRIDAY, JULY 19, 2002

The meetings are beginning to have a pattern. Digital paintings of environments and droids are pinned to three-by-five-foot foam core boards and lit by soft lights. Any work that can't be posted–models, artwork in binders, maquettes–is placed on a table directly facing the door through which Lucas always arrives. He reviews the table material first, then the boards.

Top left: Concept design supervisors Ryan Church and Erik Tiemens. The former created a Clone Wars scene on the bridge planet (above), while the latter painted a battle scene on the floor of a sinkhole (top right). The tank is based on a Joe Johnston Star Wars Trilogy *concept (middle right), which Lucas has reapproved for Episode III.*

Almost always dressed in a plaid shirt under a dark sweater, blue jeans, and white sneakers, Lucas uses two stamps while examining the artwork: OK and FABULOUSO (sic). The former is used to approve a concept for further exploration; the latter is used almost not at all. On *Attack of the Clones,* only a reported four works received FABULOUSOS–Lucas's shorthand for "Don't change a thing; I like it exactly the way it is."

In attendance today are Church, Tiemens, Goodson, David, and first-time attendee Jun. As usual, they are getting last-minute artwork printed and adding final touches to sculptures. Also as usual, there is a bit of tension as the door downstairs is heard to open and shut, the audio cue that Lucas is on his way upstairs. He enters the attic, and the meeting begins.

Goodson, who will be taking a short sabbatical to work on *Terminator 3* (2003), has made a small wooden model of the next-generation Naboo starship. Picking up the model for the new Jedi starfighter, which is looking more and more like a TIE fighter, Lucas gives it the final okay.

A few minutes later, McCallum comes in. "Any okays?" he asks.

"Lots of okays," George responds.

Accompanying Rick is a baseball-capped mystery guest, who draws curious looks from the group. When McCallum spots the approved starfighter, he asks if they'll need to put a real pilot in it. When Lucas answers yes, he asks Goodson to build a model of the cockpit, which will eventually serve as the basis for Gavin Bocquet's full-scale version.

"We're shooting already!" McCallum says.

New paintings include dramatic images of clone troopers rappelling down sinkholes, and after Lucas approves a few more pieces, Rick introduces Jun, who will be working primarily on costume concepts. "I come from South Korea," Jun says. "I drew as a kid, but my parents were not rich. In Asia, you need money if you're going to study art, so people were pushing me to learn computer programming, because you make more money doing that. In South Korea, if you're male, you have to go into the army; so I went into the army for two and a half years and thought about what I wanted to do–and decided to come here. I moved in 1995 when I was twenty-five. When I was a child, *Star Wars* really inspired me. The early *Art of Star Wars* books were very popular. So the first time I met George, I was really nervous, really dry in the mouth."

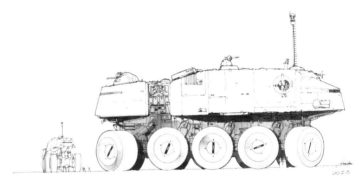

McCallum's mystery guest turns out to be Ron Fricke, acclaimed documentary filmmaker (*Baraka,* 1992) and cinematographer (*Koyaanisqatsi,* 1983; *Megalopolis*). It's been decided that the kind of material Fricke can gather for Episode III, by traveling to certain key locations and shooting them for use as background plates, will save time and, Rick says, add "the clouds George has always wanted."

The pace of the work is accelerating as the growing number of concept artists continue to work off the ideas Lucas provides. Conceptual researcher David Craig is also employed to unearth esoteric images, books, and films. "He's special, unbelievable–an artist in his own right," McCallum says of Craig.

The artists bounce off these and additional reference material supplied by the Lucasfilm Research Library. Lucas, in turn, is sometimes taken by the artists' designs. Essentially it's a series of inspirational melodies with the director-writer as conductor. Still, the unofficial deadlines are looming. By end of the year, most of the interior design concepts need to be finalized so that Bocquet and his team can start building in Sydney, Australia, where principal photography is scheduled. In addition, this time around Lucas and the concept art team are determined to have environments nailed down so that Director of Photography (DP) David Tattersall will have more to go on cinematographically, and not be stuck lighting for bluescreen without any reference.

Above all, there is a general feeling of excitement. For the artists, this film represents the culmination of all the creativity ever poured into the *Star Wars* galaxy.

FRIDAY, JULY 26, 2002

Lucas is running late. His son, Jett, has had a minor scooter accident. During the wait, conversation turns to the impending transition from Skywalker Ranch A to Skywalker Ranch B, where the business divisions of Lucasfilm will be moving in a month.

When Lucas enters, he explains the accident, saying that someone waved at Jett, who hit a speed bump while waving back. "I did the same thing once on a skateboard," Rick comments. "She was so beautiful, I waved, hit a manhole cover, and broke my arm."

Lucas turns to the business at hand, and approves Goodson's Jedi starfighter cockpit interior. He turns away from another more organic concept, saying, "I've never been a fan of bioships." Next he contemplates a drawing of a floating droid, then turns it upside down. "Now it's okay," he says and stamps it.

While reviewing paintings of planet environments, Lucas advises Tiemens and Church to "stay away from red, except for Mufasta." He also cautions against one rather dark painting. "That's what a regular movie would do. We have to be more careful," he says, going on to explain that most productions would use the shadows to save time (and money), lighting only the center of the set.

Next on the agenda: Jun's costume designs for the tentatively titled "lemur people." Though Lucas would like something "a bit more graceful," he okays a couple. "Two out of three," McCallum says, "not bad!" Lucas

---

Monday, August 19: Except for JAK, all of Lucasfilm moves from Skywalker Ranch into its new facility—Big Rock Ranch: a multistory Frank Lloyd Wright–style building.

FABULOUSO

OK

then turns to the conceptual lizard with Anakin on its back. "Work on the eyes," he suggests. "And add a plume, maybe, or a fan like a peacock's."

Afterward, he returns to the environments and–to everyone's surprise–grabs the FABULOUSO stamp and uses it on two paintings: one of the sinkhole planet and one of the crystal planet.

"When they draw something and George approves it," McCallum observes, "sometimes I have to quickly go to Rob [Coleman, animation director], and ask him, 'Can you do this?' And then–if it's feathers for the lizard–I might have to go back to George and say, 'Can we not make it feathers?' "

As art department supervisor, Fay David has to not only keep the department organized and hire freelancers, but also interface with George and Rick while fielding

queries and requests posed by the various production heads. "Fay is the backbone of the department," says Church. She is also the only woman in a predominantly male atmosphere, but says it's not difficult being the "den mom." "It's not just because she's smart," McCallum adds. "It's who she is–she's one of the key musicians in this jazz ensemble."

Fay David grew up in southern California, but because her father was in the navy they moved every couple of years. Her mother had a habit of waking her up in the middle of the night to watch John Wayne movies, like *The Sands of Iwo Jima*. Following her graduation from college, David moved to northern California and applied for a job at ILM. They were starting to ramp up for Episode I and needed production assistants. She was hired, and one of her first brief shows was Clint Eastwood's *Space Cowboys* (2000). A couple of years later, she applied for the art department coordinator position at JAK. After interviewing with McCallum and production controller Kathryn Ramos, David was hired for Episode II.

"You always hear that creative types are difficult to work with, but there were no egos," Fay says. "People were happy to share their ideas, and got along really well–and in very stressful situations. When you're under deadline, it's very easy to lose your temper, but that didn't happen once–instead, there was a lot of laughter coming from the back room."

From top left (counterclockwise): Lucas stamps a painting OK; Tiemens has a late-night discussion with concept researcher David Craig (right). "Nearly every day for ten years, George has been directing the designers," Craig says, "and they do drive the engine. Star Wars films are returning some of the storytelling to the designers"; art department supervisor Fay David, in addition to many other tasks, keeps McCallum abreast of all art department developments; concept artist Sang Jun Lee at work; a Church painting of the Wookiee planet Kashyyyk, partially inspired by McQuarrie's early work (inset); concept artist Feng Zhu and one of his droid concepts; two lemur creatures by Jun.

Friday, August 2, 2002

As these weekly meetings accumulate, Tiemens, Church, Jun, et al., are quite conscious of the learning process taking place. "George always goes for distilling the intent of the designer," Church says, "while the designer often becomes too engrossed in the details."

These meetings are also growing in attendance. Apart from the concept artists, there are often animatics artists, a representative from LucasArts (the video game arm of the company), and a documentary crew—between ten and twenty extra people on any given day—in a setting that is already cramped. After jump-starting this particular meeting—the artists thought he was going to arrive later in the day—Lucas explains that, to avoid repetition, the Wookiee environment shouldn't be like that of the Ewoks.

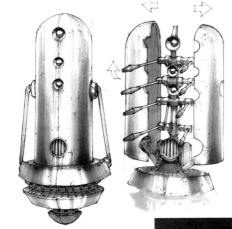

It's the final gathering before George leaves on his first vacation since starting work on Episode II three years earlier. McCallum departed for Croatia and Sarajevo, Bosnia, two days ago. As Lucas goes out the door, on his way to Canada, he turns and says, "This will be my last time off before three years straight on Episode III." In fact, during at least part of his vacation, he'll be working on the script for *Indiana Jones IV* (and he, like McCallum, has been working on the prequel trilogy nonstop since 1995).

The art department may have a seventh member. For a trial period of two weeks, Feng Zhu has been hired as a freelancer to execute some "hard-core industrial designs." "One day I got the call from Fay to do some test art. Droids," Feng says. "The assignment was to do a bunch of droids from different planets and then put them in front of George to see how he responds."

Friday, August 23, 2002

"Are we ready this time?" Lucas asks as he opens the door. It's 4 P.M. "You came too early last time," Fay says.

"Well, Jane [Bay, his executive assistant of twenty-five years] swears the meeting was for three [o'clock]."

It's a smaller group than last time, and the room is overheated. The first board is of droids; the second is more environments; the third is Kashyyyk, the Wookiee planet. Lucas approves a flying catamaran for the latter. He then recommends that they "try and get Alderaan to look a little more futuristic." As Lucas warms to the subject, he explains that "the environment's buildings should be culturally similar, but not completely unified"—because thousands of architects would've worked on them over the millennia.

The meeting breaks up as McCallum and Lucas sit down for a conference call with costume designer Trisha Biggar, in

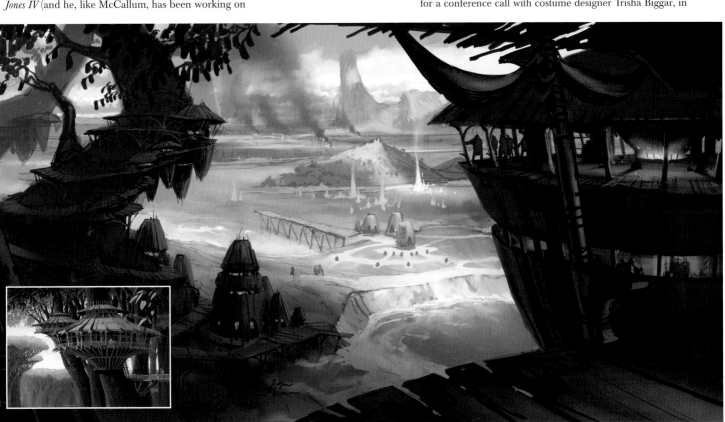

London, and Iain McCaig, in Australia. Like Bocquet's earlier visit, this call is somewhat designed to raise the specter of the script. Still, Lucas greets Biggar with, "Well, we can talk about the costumes, but it's hard to discuss the script. I know the story, but . . ."

Later McCallum points out that, while most directors work solely with a production designer, whose concept artists report back to him, Lucas prefers to work directly with the artists before attacking the script in earnest. "These preliminary visuals serve as inspiration for writing, more than anything else," he says. "But the minute George makes a decision in the art department, I relay that information to Trisha, Gavin, and David. The level of commitment to communication is tremendous. Without it, even at this early stage, the process would break down completely."

Although he predicts that the final script won't be completed for a year, McCallum reveals that principal photography is presently scheduled to start on Wednesday, June 25, 2003, at Fox Studios, Sydney, Australia.

FRIDAY, SEPTEMBER 6, 2002

Because a rhythm is developing among the artists and in their relationship with Lucas, the atmosphere is markedly more relaxed than at previous meetings. Individual artists are also developing their own internal rhythms. "Usually I drive back from LA [on Sundays] for five hours on Highway Five," Church says, "just sitting there listening to movie soundtracks, Wagner operas, and inspiring, beautiful music. I have a little tape recorder, and these whole images come into my head and I really get into it. So I just come in Monday morning, play it all back, and draw out ten or twelve ideas. The top six or seven make it to the end of the week. It's a great way to work."

On the table today are about thirty-five binders, labeled CORUSCANT, LEMURS, ALDERAAN, PADMÉ, MUFASTA, CORPORATE ALLIANCE, BRIDGEWORLD, KASHYYYK. Each is filled with art that has been approved for that world, species, or character. However, there are also folders marked MISCELLANEOUS VEHICLE/COSTUME/PLANET. The plan is to ask George to decide where these miscellaneous artworks fit into the movie, which represents another roundabout way of getting him to talk about the script.

When Lucas arrives, there's an initial discussion about the still-nameless ring planet; he says the main planet is made of gas and the ring architecture should be more of a "mishmash"—an international space station that each generation has kept adding to. Alderaan, he says, should be a Switzerland-like setting, but with cities—not villages—nestled among green alps: "An incredible technological event in the middle of the countryside. Very concentrated. Ultramodern."

He looks at a number of Jun's creature sketches and remarks of one, "I don't know what it is, but it looks good." As they sit down to discuss the folders, Lucas asks, "What's this?"

"Well, we were wondering if you'd like to organize these," Fay offers.

"No. We can look at them again, but that's it."

"Nice try," Rick chimes in.

FRIDAY, SEPTEMBER 13, 2002

Outside it's very hot, and in the art department an air conditioner is laboring very hard, making it difficult to hear. John Goodson is back, his stint on *Terminator 3* finished. He's been working at home on a larger-scale Jedi starfighter. It's a beautiful model, about a foot long and eight inches at its widest. Goodson has known since the age of five that he wanted to work in film—ever since watching an episode of *Lost in Space* and being sure that if he could open the back of his TV set, he'd be able to get a hold of the *Jupiter 2*.

Again, there's some confusion as to when the meeting is supposed to start. Depending on whether it was 4 or 4:30 P.M., Lucas arrives either twenty or fifty minutes late. Upon entering, he says, "Sorry," looks at Goodson's model, and quickly says, "That looks nice," then moves to the boards on the easel.

Jun turns off the air conditioner, and everyone's mood seems to improve. Lucas, however, finds the first conceptual interiors of Mufasta, the volcano planet, to be too much like those of the sinkhole planet. Once again, he emphasizes that the societies who build these respective cities would be dramatically different from one another; the architecture should reflect that. On the same track, he turns his attention to Alderaan, reiterating the importance of making the cities at least as big as New York, even though they're in a Swiss-style setting. To illustrate his point, he takes a black Sharpie and draws a huge tower upward over three vertically placed drawings.

Afterward, Tiemens and Church decide that they need to "push it further" and stop thinking too literally. Church says that when he first started working on *Star Wars,* its inconsistencies were often confusing; he couldn't understand how landspeeders still hovered even after being turned off. "Antigravity paint," he was told.

FRIDAY, SEPTEMBER 27, 2002

McCallum has invited Trisha Biggar and Gavin Bocquet to the meeting, as reminders that they're waiting in the wings. When Goodson comes in, Bocquet greets him warmly and remarks, "Every three years I see this man."

The number of artists has again increased, as two former freelancers—T. J. Frame and Feng Zhu (both from Los Angeles)—are now working in-house, the seventh and eighth members of the concept art team. Throughout this and almost every meeting, Feng will wear a baseball cap backward on his head. Frame has been brought in to work on environmental details. "I'd gone to school with T. J.," Church says. "Feng I knew from Art Center as well, and he'd always been really pestering me to get up here."

There's some concern among the artists that things aren't moving fast enough, but Trisha and Gavin aren't worried. The latter says that they got through Episode II and that this one will be fine, too. Bocquet and Biggar

A McQuarrie painting of Alderaan (above) and a Tiemens's version with fall colors (right). Alderaan was first conceived of by Lucas as being home to the Imperial prison, as described in his second draft of Star Wars *(1975): "The towering white oxide clouds pass, revealing the Imperial city of Alderaan. The magnificent domed and gleaming city is perched, mushroom-like, on a tall spire which disappears deep into the misty surface of the planet."*

Monday, September 9: Twentieth Century Fox and Lucasfilm announce that *Attack of the Clones* is coming to IMAX theatres in the U.S. and Canada beginning November 1, 2002.

have worked with Lucas and McCallum for more than a decade, and the mutual confidence of this core group more than offsets any worries about the schedule.

The door opens, Lucas walks in—and does a double take upon seeing Gavin. "I know nothing! Absolutely nothing," he exclaims. Church introduces T. J. and Feng, then talk turns once more to the Jedi starfighter.

McCallum arrives. "Oh, *hi* Rick. We haven't seen these gentlemen in so long," George wryly observes, nodding toward the guests. He then returns to the paintings while Trisha and Gavin sit on the table, the latter swinging his leg slowly back and forth. Once again Lucas is concerned about the similarity between cities. It's the biggest issue—he doesn't want audiences to be confused as to which city they're looking at. Meanwhile, Rick is urgently directing the documentary crew to change angles so that Gavin and Trisha are in the picture. Lucas says the next step is going to be nailing down what kinds of materials these civilizations are using.

"How do we rate their intelligence?" Church asks.

"I'd say they're all fairly sophisticated."

When Lucas gets to Jun's costume drawings, McCallum signals to

Biggar to move forward just as George, with his back turned to them, calls out, "Trish!" She goes up to the board and they discuss the real-world implications of Jun's sketches. Lucas approves almost all of them.

As the meeting comes to an end, there is some maneuvering as a second, more private meeting with Biggar and Bocquet is hastily convened. "They are observers," Lucas protests to McCallum.

"Just five minutes," Trisha says.

"The three of us," Rick adds, as he signals Fay to get more chairs for her office.

TUESDAY, OCTOBER 1, 2002

Veteran concept artist Iain McCaig arrives at the ranch. Tiemens and Church show him the binders filled with artwork the department has produced so far. "Boy, has the bar been raised this time," he says. "My work is cut out for me!"

While his family stays at home in Victoria, Canada, McCaig takes up temporary residence in Petaluma, a town of fifty-five thousand inhabitants about half an hour's drive through rolling hills from Skywalker Ranch (Petaluma is where Lucas shot nearly all of *American Graffiti*). McCaig first came to work in northern California in 1979. He opened a phone book and started calling production houses in alphabetical order. When he got to K, he called John Korty, one of the original Bay Area filmmaking mavericks and, coincidentally, a longtime friend of Lucas's. Korty hired McCaig, and his first job was to work on the trailer for Korty's *Twice Upon a Time* (1983), which helped persuade Lucas to become the film's executive producer. Eventually Iain went to work for Lucas himself, on Episode I. "George is really shy," McCaig remembers, "so for a year, he seemed uncomfortable around me. And then one day he just starts to relax. After that, he's a different person."

FRIDAY, OCTOBER 4, 2002

Because they work in fairly cramped quarters with no partitions, the artists often listen to music with earphones on to isolate themselves from one another. The result is that on any given day, it's usually quiet and meditative in the art department; craziness is reserved for the late nights.

When Lucas walks in, he remarks that there are a lot of people—and there are: Biggar, Bocquet, the doc team, and the concept art team. McCallum says, "We thought we'd start off slow."

"This is to try and get me to write a script," Lucas says.

"No . . . even I'm shocked," says Rick.

"There are so many people, no one can even hear what I'm saying."

Lucas notices McCaig, welcomes him, and hands him a blank piece of paper with an OK already stamped on it. "You can save it for a rainy day," he says, and Iain laughs.

Jun has created some high-tech costume designs for the people of Alderaan. "I think I'm going to make it a much more futuristic planet, much more elegant," Lucas notes, and gives three FABULOUSOS to Jun's work—startling the attendees and going some way toward finalizing costumes that Biggar can then begin to construct. Lucas says the key word for Alderaan is majestic. They show him a book on Switzerland, and, at the first photo spread, he exclaims, "That's Alderaan right there!" Pause. "Can we go there?" he asks McCallum. "Is it cheap?"

From top left: McCallum, Zhu, Jun, David, Tiemens, and Lucas study a John Goodson model of the Jedi starfighter; costume designer Trisha Biggar, concept artist Iain McCaig, and Lucas discuss Jun's costume designs for Alderaan; Tiemens, Lucas, and McCaig review sinkhole planet concepts. Right: Zhu, McCaig (with earphones), and concept artist Derek Thompson during a late night in the art department. Far right: a Padmé concept by McCaig.

The office of production controller Kathryn Ramos is down the hall from McCallum's. To get to his office, Rick must pass in front of hers. When the two first moved in, as Ramos tells the story, she positioned her desk so she could see when Rick passed by—in order to grab him. She is a fifteen-year veteran of the "Rick Wars," and knows that he can sometimes be difficult to nail down.

From behind her desk, Ramos also has a great view of the sun setting behind the now yellow hills. It casts a warm light over the ranch's grapevines, its red brick Tech Building, and Lake Ewok. In her spacious room hang two paintings: one of a young Tom Sawyer–esque boy who has taken off his shoes and is joyfully walking through the mud, and a second depicting an art deco–style maiden and armored knight. The two paintings are part of Lucas's collection and seem emblematic of his character and films.

Kathryn Ramos began working for McCallum at the BBC, while he was producing Potter's TV miniseries *Blackeyes* (1989). Rick had just fired his assistant, who was an old-timer at the BBC and highly respected. BBC stalwarts closed ranks and refused to provide a replacement—until Kathryn was drafted because she was the newest. During her half-hour interview with McCallum, she vainly tried to convince him that she had neither the necessary knowledge nor the experience for the job. Rick hired her on the spot.

Their first Lucasfilm project was *Young Indy*, which was going to be filmed all over the world. In her apartment, they, together, plotted out the complex location shoot, poring over atlases and almanacs spread over the kitchen table and floor. Their camaraderie continues today, as Rick will often come into her office to talk things over and make calls.

Per Episode III, Ramos says that they're about to open an art department at Elstree Studios, London, where Bocquet and supervising art director Peter Russell (*Indiana Jones and the Last Crusade*, 1989; *Gladiator*, 2000) will set up shop. She also reveals that Fox Studios, Australia, is booked: thirty buildings, all with different start and end dates. The longest-held will be Building 37, where the costume department will be lodged for fifty-one weeks. Without a script, production is obliged to hedge their bets, so some dates are solid, while others are written in pencil.

"We're trying to do this for a price," McCallum explains, "but we're building backward, designing a twenty-five-floor skyscraper without foundations. Do you know what it's like to budget a film without a script? That's what Kathryn goes through every day."

Unintentionally paraphrasing Indiana Jones, Ramos admits, "We're making it up as we go."

"Wouldn't It Be Cool If...?"

"Basically, I would tell them about a scene, an animal, or a character," Lucas explains, "and they would do a bunch of designs. I would okay some or modify or change them, and we build; we go to the next thing. And so, every week, they get more to design. Some of these guys are designing costumes; some of them are designing sets; some of them are designing props or cars. There's just a whole variety of guys up there, and each one does a different thing. And then I'm writing the script."

This is the big conceptual push. From mid-October 2002 to Day One of principal photography, life in the art department will hit its zenith in terms of quality, quantity, and hours. "It's like going to an art gallery opening every Friday," Tiemens says. "Here's ninety-nine new paintings for George to look at."

"It's the most fun I've ever had," Church adds. "Monday or Tuesday, we might go home at seven or eight in the evening; Wednesday, one or two in the morning; Thursday–all night." (Fortunately for these acolytes, the kitchen often sends up its leftovers.) "That was the magic hour," Church continues, "Thursday at 3 A.M.–the three-to-five stretch is the intense, focused work period."

"Here you're working on something you loved as a kid," T. J. says. "Everybody is supertalented and everyone has something to add to the mix."

As of October 18, 2003, three new artists have been added to this mix: Derek Thompson (creatures); Warren Fu (vehicles/environments); and Alexander Jaeger (environments), bringing their number to twelve. "I'd seen these *Art of Star Wars* books, but I'd never made the connection that you could actually make a living doing that kind of work," Fu says. "When I graduated from UC Berkeley, my friends told me about an internship at Lucasfilm. I didn't even know how to make a portfolio, so I just kinda put everything together in a folder and submitted it late. We had to sneak into my friend's office and use his mail machine to backdate it! I was rejected the first time, so this is icing on the cake being up here."

Echoing McCallum's metaphor, McCaig describes the department as a "jazz ensemble" in which each artist instinctively knows when to "step forward and take a solo" and when to merge back into the group, handing off characters and environments the same way musicians would a melody. "This is the biggest art department I've ever worked with," he notes. "And everyone is confident enough in their abilities so that we can jam the way that musicians do–and that's really rare."

"We wanted to make the art department a collective unit–and I wanted the guys to have fun," McCallum says.

Throughout this period, the one common thought voiced by those in the ensemble is: *Wouldn't it be cool if . . . ?* The next few months represents their unique chance to design a character, a weapon, a vehicle, or an environment that sticks– one that leaves a trace on one of filmdom's most celebrated sagas. "For the first part of the design process, it seemed like George was going from what we were drawing, rather than telling us what to do," Jaeger remembers. "A lot of what we did was what we'd really love to see in a *Star Wars* film. We'd draw it, present it, and see if he'd bite."

"George was always appreciative," Church adds, "and might say, 'Wow. Not for my movie, but that's a great idea.' We'd always try something out because–you've got George Lucas's eye, and not many people have that chance."

FRIDAY, OCTOBER 18, 2002
McCaig shows Lucas two paintings on his computer screen: one of Anakin Skywalker emerging from a volcano, burned but still standing, and another of Anakin on the back of a lizardlike mount. The first prompts Lucas to say that Anakin will probably be carried out of the volcano; the second prompts him to say that the lizard can run

---

*Right: A costume and hair style concept for Padmé by Warren Fu (*Artificial Intelligence: A.I.*, 2001; *Attack of the Clones*). "I was five years old when* The Empire Strikes Back *came out, and after I saw it, it was all over."*

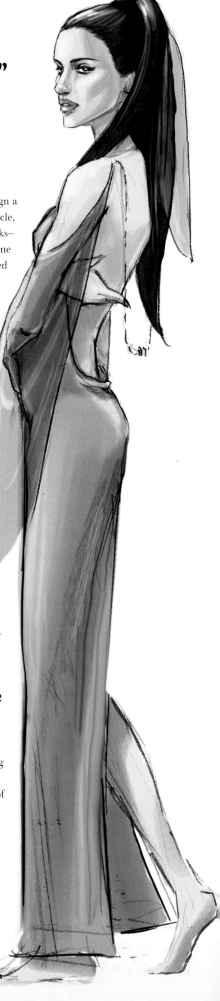

up walls and ceilings, which will enable them to create unique fight sequences.

He adds that Anakin won't be scarred till the very end; for most of the movie, he has to be attractive because Padmé is still "madly in love with him." For the first time, it is rumored that Padmé might die in this film. She may be seen last on Alderaan.

FRIDAY, OCTOBER 25, 2002

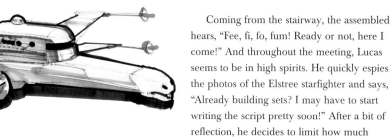

Lucas has sent the art department a list outlining which planets are important, their spellings (which often change), and their habitats:

```
Episode III Planets (Major)
Coruscant (city)
Naboo (garden)
Alderaan (snowcapped peaks)
Mustafar (volcano)
Dagobah (swamp)
Tatooine (desert)

Episode III Planets (Minor)
Cato Neimoidia (ring city around gas net) [Bad--Trade Federation]
Mygeeto (crystal) [Bad--IG Banking Clan]
Utapo (sinkholes) [Good--lemurs]
Kashyyyk (lake) [Good--Wookiees]
Seleucami (upside-down city/bridgeworld) [Bad--Techno Union]
Felucia (seaweed/coral) [Bad--Commerce Guild]
Polis Mazta (asteroid wasteland) [Good]

Planets (Not in Episode III)
Bespin (gas clouds)
Geonosis (red rock)
Kamino (water)
Hoth (ice)
Yavin Moon (fog/jungle)
Endor Moon (forest)
```

On the table are production photos from the Elstree art department, which is now open for business. Bocquet and his team have already produced a skeletal life-sized construct of the Jedi starfighter.

*Clockwise from top left: Derek Thompson (*Men in Black, *1997;* The Mummy, *1999), also an ILMer, had tried to join the previous concept art teams of Episode I and II–but finally made it on Episode III. Alex Jaeger (*Mission: Impossible, *1996;* The Perfect Storm, *2000) came up from ILM, and says that when Lucas is looking at his artwork, he feels a "little nervous; you can gauge sometimes by what he's been approving, whether yours are going to get picked or not." Concept artist Warren Fu is yet another ILMer. All the concept artists came to regard the heroic Horse Pilot (above, whose specially designed X-wing was created by Alex Jaeger) as their mascot. Actually a character from the* Star Wars *Expanded Universe, "Horse Pilot!" became the battle cry during late nights and inspirational design marathons.*

Coming from the stairway, the assembled hears, "Fee, fi, fo, fum! Ready or not, here I come!" And throughout the meeting, Lucas seems to be in high spirits. He quickly espies the photos of the Elstree starfighter and says, "Already building sets? I may have to start writing the script pretty soon!" After a bit of reflection, he decides to limit how much they'll build of the starfighter, commenting, "For God's sake, I don't need all that–" as he spots pre-viz supervisor Dan Gregoire coming down the hall: "You can do it, can't you?" he calls out, *it* referring to a digital extension of the practical cockpit.

Lucas then addresses the planet list, explaining that, if there are more than seventeen shots for any one environment, they'll need to build a set of some sort for that particular location. They'll need sets for the Jedi Council, Palpatine's office, probably the Senate, and they have a choice: either to return to part of Padmé's Episode II apartment or to create a new one. He also suggests reviewing *Return of the Jedi* and taking a look at Coruscant's plaza/park. Anakin and Padmé might have a love scene somewhere like that–but without greenery.

Suddenly Lucas divulges more of the story–the most since the very first Episode III meeting: At the end of the film, in a thirty-second wrap-up, Yoda will go to Dagobah, Obi-Wan will go with the infant Luke to Tatooine, and Bail Organa–with the infant Leia–will flee to Alderaan. Mustafar–whose name has now been changed from Mufasta–will occupy about twenty to thirty minutes of film time. Lucas is planning a lot of fighting there, about four to five scenes, and one "love scene."

Wednesday, October 23: Lucasfilm lends a copy of *American Graffiti* to a group of Petaluma girl scouts. Lucas shot *Graffiti* almost entirely in Petaluma, which is presently without a movie theater, so these intrepid scouts will be projecting the film onto a parking lot wall to create public support for the construction of a new cinema.

He has also altered the beginning of the film. Instead of starting with seven battles on seven planets, Episode III now opens with a huge space battle. Our heroes crash-land into a "bad guy's ship," perhaps Neimoidian, where there will be lots of "cliffhangers, from one near-death experience to another–*Indiana Jones and the Temple of Doom* aboard a ship." The ship might be breaking apart. He asks the artists to work on a "grand control room and a grand office." The heroes will be trying to rescue a kidnapped

character. For their escapades, he asks the artists to come up with dangerous situations, or what are generally referred to as "gags."

"Turbines?" Tiemens asks.

"Turbines are always good. Anything you don't wanna get near," Lucas says. He then reveals that Anakin and Count Dooku will have a huge duel aboard the ship. The entire opening sequence should last about twenty minutes.

As McCallum wanders around the periphery of the meeting, Fay David brings out a ship binder from which Lucas can select the kind of cruiser he wants. "We're out of our minds," he comments while flipping through the pages. "Making a movie where the bad guys win, and everyone dies, is not destined to be the most successful movie of all time."

After choosing a few vehicle candidates, he turns to Derek Thompson's images of battle-scene key frames, but puts on the brakes, saying, "I haven't gotten that far yet." As they take down one board to show the paintings pinned to the board behind it, there happens to be a completely blank board in-between. "It's a copy of the script!" McCallum says.

When the fully laden board of costume sketches is revealed, Lucas looks at a Photoshopped image of Anakin with a Mohawk, but says he prefers the longer hair worn by Obi-Wan and Qui-Gon. "Anakin's still a Jedi," he points out.

McCaig then mumbles something about Trisha needing to get started, and Lucas's response is similarly indistinct. Rick asks, "Is that a yes?"

"I don't know," George says, "I'm not sure what Iain asked. He's mumbling."

The upshot is that Trisha can start making costumes based on Jun's approved designs. McCallum is "ecstatic," for "production is finally beginning."

"I knew I wasn't going to get a script, but I had to keep them working," he explains. "Without a script, our priority then becomes: We know Padmé's in the film, we know she's going to be in her bedroom, and we know it's going to be night–so can we create a nightgown for her?"

October 28-31: Gavin Bocquet goes to Switzerland for a "recce," or location-scouting trip.

Monday, November 4: Production coordinator Virginia Murray opens the Episode III production office at Fox Studios, Sydney.

FRIDAY, NOVEMBER 1, 2002

ILM animation director Rob Coleman (*Dragonheart*, 1996; *Men in Black*) is on hand for the first time. Bearded and upbeat, he is the puppet master behind digital Yoda. Coleman is starting three months earlier than he did on Episode II, as he's been told that a few characters are far enough along in the approval process for him to come by and have a look–but he surmises that it's possible Rick is still throwing people at George to get him to write.

Indeed, when Lucas walks in and sees Coleman he does a double take, protesting, "What's he doing here? No animation! You can't come until June 24."

"I'll see you at the film's premiere," Coleman says.

But Lucas quickly offers that he may have to start writing "when reality hits."

"You said you've *been* writing," McCallum protests.

"I've been *thinking* about it."

Lucas does reveal a few more story details, saying that the opening space battle will be fought over Coruscant. Anakin and Obi-Wan in their Jedi starfighters fly into a Separatist cruiser, then split up as the star cruiser slowly breaks in half. Obi-Wan ends up on the bridge after a series of episodic cliffhangers, and manages to land the front half of the ship. Meanwhile, Anakin fights Count Dooku.

Anakin's longer hair is approved. While looking at a costume of a Mustafarian dressed in red, Lucas says, "We have to be careful he doesn't look like the Emperor." Somebody immediately connects the dots and says, "We have an Emperor this time!"

Earlier this week, when Lucas heard the news that Sicily's Mount Etna was erupting, he called McCallum and said that Ron Fricke should get over there and film it. Rick arranged for a local guide and the approval of the Italian government. JAK rented a camera from a company in Milan, and a Sicilian agent organized the hotel arrangements. Fricke flies out today, and will stay as long as necessary.

FRIDAY, NOVEMBER 8, 2002

A new environment is being explored: Polis Mazta, which has been conceptualized in three different ways across six paintings. According to Church, Lucas instructed them to create an asteroid wasteland, to consult 1960s NASA photos, and to include "space-suit guys"–a species that doesn't have much in the way of faces, based on nonutilized Episode II designs for a Kamino species. He hasn't specified yet whether they'll be good guys or bad guys.

Friday, November 8: On her return trip from filming *Cold Mountain* (2003) on location in Romania, Natalie Portman (Padmé Amidala) stops in London at Elstree Studios. There, they make a full-body cast of the actress in order to complete a custom-made dressmaker's stand, so Natalie won't have to be present for all of the fittings.

Clockwise from top left: Sketches by Tiemens of possible Naboo meeting places for Anakin and Padmé led to a concept painting; two McCaig conceptualizations of Anakin, one as he emerges from a volcano, and another more samurai-like, but Lucas would opt for longer hair. A Church concept of the asteroid planet, Polis Mazta. Before writing the rough draft, Lucas jotted down some undated notes, divided into three acts. His handwritten pages reveal that many of the final film's set-pieces are already in place.

31

Lucas examines paintings of Mustafar, a few of which show two Jedi in close proximity to boiling-hot lava. He observes that, "there is a certain reality about toast here—even in fantasy." Then he notices one where Thompson has shown Jedi using the Force to hurl lava at each other. Lucas notes that this represents a "good toast factor."

A series of drawings show Jedi being killed in combat on Mygeeto (crystal world), but Lucas objects—the Jedi will be "betrayed," not cut down in battle.

As conversation flows from one subject to the next, Lucas casually mentions that Episode III's principal villain could be a Separatist droid general—and everyone begins to take notes. McCallum leans against the wall to get a better look.

"I won't limit it at this point to a droid. It could be an alien of some

kind," George clarifies. "I'm not sure if I want him to be human. It's the Darth Maul. It's the Jango Fett, Darth Vader."

"Male, though?" Rick asks.

"I don't care. It's gotta be iconic. It's gotta be pretty evil," Lucas explains.

"Evil. Iconic. Got it," McCaig says.

"It's like, *Uh-oh! This is the bad guy.* Your first reaction is: *Scary.* But it also has to have a lot of personality and be very recognizable. He has to be able to do dialogue scenes."

"This is not a Sith, right?" McCaig asks.

"It's not a Sith."

"Age?" McCallum asks.

Wednesday, November 13: Ian McDiarmid (Supreme Chancellor Palpatine) is fitted for a costume at Elstree.

"Villains are ageless. He can't be young. Old people are scary. You can all get ahold of that and see if you can come up with a new iconic villain."

Rick pulls Iain aside, asking him to keep in mind a great actor or actress while working on designs. "Make that your number-one priority," he says.

"Work on the villain," Lucas reiterates as he leaves. "That's the next real assignment. Now I have to go to a business meeting." He pauses. "In the real world."

FRIDAY, NOVEMBER 15, 2002

George walks in, and Fay David points him toward two Separatist ship models. He likes them both, so he asks, "How many cheers for this one?" Moderate cheers. "And for this one?" Louder cheers. "You see? It's not hard to make decisions around here."

A board is then revealed that features the group's first attempts to create an icon of evil. "We all collaborated on the droid general," Thompson recalls. "It was one of the most exhilarating weeks, because we all got to attack one thing."

It becomes clear, however, that Lucas hasn't received what he wants just yet. He is quiet for about a minute, just looking at the various concepts, then, seemingly careful not to be discouraging, says, "The ones I like the most are . . . ," and stamps two for further research. He doesn't say anything negative, except for "Too ethnic, too *Alien*-ish . . ."

"Do you want to see more?" McCaig asks.

"Some of this is a little too devilish."

A Zhu painting of the duel on Mustafar puts into play Lucas's desire to have the fight and its environements in close proximity to the lava at all times.

"Full figure?" someone asks. "Could it be part droid?" someone else suggests.

"We need to see more articulation, so I know exactly what I'm looking at," Lucas responds. "And we have to be careful not to re-create Darth Vader, since he's showing up at the end of the movie." For those attending, this is a revelation–the first admission from Lucas that Darth Vader will definitely be in Episode III.

FRIDAY, NOVEMBER 22, 2002

This cold morning, anyone arriving at Skywalker Ranch would have noticed problems. A propane leak was discovered during the night, and repair people are everywhere. The artists have been evacuated. To keep warm, some of them are jogging the circuit around the grounds.

By the time the meeting is convened, it's a smaller group than usual: no ILMers and no animartists, except Dan Gregoire. Lucas arrives about half an hour late because of the leak. For the admiral's room, where Dooku confronts Anakin, George is concerned about how they'd actually shoot,

given the design. "This is the place where Dooku meditates on his grand schemes," Lucas points out, so he suggests they take out a column that would block his view of space.

"Could we do something that revolves?" Church asks.

"It's the executive suite. You gotta say to yourself, *If I had an office, this is what it'd look like*," Lucas says. "Remember: We can't go outside [into space]. Cinematically, it would be inappropriate. We have to stay inside the set."

Felucia (the plant planet) has been rethought based on microphotography. "This is good. Excellent," he remarks. Stamping the paintings, he continues, "If you go five miles, you run into this. This is odd. I like this. This is really odd. This is weird." He combines some landscapes, alters the scale of others, and says that, ultimately, the planet should have two basic areas: jungle and desert.

The next board has the next wave of Separatist general concepts. Warren Fu has conceived of a villain who catches George's eye. "Because my priority was environments, I didn't focus on the droid general until the end of the week–at the last minute," Warren remembers. "The morning of the meeting, I sketched one, which I didn't even like that much. But we put it out there, and George goes right up to it and says, 'That's the one.' I mentioned that the general might have organic eyes–George's eyes lit up and he said, 'Now that's interesting.' "

Monday, November 18: In Sydney, assistant costume designer Michael Mooney and costume supervisor Nicole Young start the costume department in Building 37. The accounting department opens temporary facilities in Building 28.

Left-hand page: Thompson, Zhu, and Church (top) prepare one of the boards featuring November 15's Separatist general concepts; Lucas and McCallum (below) during an art department meeting. Right-hand page: Fu's early sketches (below) for the new icon of evil led to his concept (with clenched fist, above) chosen by Lucas as the model for the droid general on November 22; on December 6, Fu presents the general with his bodyguards (top right), similar to the way Darth Vader arrives flanked by stormtroopers in A New Hope.

DROID GENERAL & HENCHMEN
W.FU 12/06/02
SW3

Moving on to the following concepts, Lucas studies some drawings by McCaig that suggest Padmé is sick while pregnant, and having terrible dreams–and remarks, "That's just because she was spending too much time with you!" But he then adds, "She does have a thing where she gives birth . . ."

"All right. Keep up the good work. The stuff was great, guys," he concludes. "I just have to figure out a movie to go with it."

FRIDAY, DECEMBER 6, 2002

Rick McCallum has returned from Sydney after a three-week trip, and has closed the next few art department meetings to nonessential personnel, knowing that the more intimate atmosphere will result in more decisions from Lucas. This, in turn, will yield more work for the somewhat starved-for-material production departments Down Under.

Sculptor Michael Murnane is here for the first time, the thirteenth member of the group. Eight lemur sculpts, four by Robert Barnes, four by the newcomer, sit on a table. Murnane (*Starship Troopers*, 1997; *Monkeybone*, 2001) worked on *Attack of the Clones* as a sculptor, but early in his career actually wanted to be an architect. "When I found out that architecture involved memorizing wood lengths and that sort of thing, I said 'Forget this,'" he recalls. "So I went to Long Beach State and studied illustration. I took sculpture, too–I took one class and almost changed my major, because I loved it so much. The

things I was trying to learn in two-D, you do it *live* with sculpture!"

When Lucas walks in and sees McCallum, he says, "I haven't seen you for a while–I didn't even know you were alive."

"I'm not," Rick replies.

They then try to show Lucas the same art binders as before, in the hope that he'll start to organize their contents. But Lucas would still prefer not to.

"Until I've started the script, it's hard . . . ," he says.

"Oh, God . . . ," McCallum moans.

"Take some aspirin," Lucas recommends.

"Aspirin? I need to freebase!"

George then looks over the lemur sculpts. He loves them and gives them all FABULOUSOS. Later, Murnane will explain that McCaig is pushing them to do sculpts that are character-driven, not species-driven.

They've added an Egyptian influence to Polis Mazta, the asteroid planet. Lucas muses over it for a while. "Okay. I'll buy that." While reviewing additional environments, he says, "The other film was low-key, twilight. I think we have to raise the sun up and go from sixty watts to a hundred twenty-five." In discussing Palpatine's costumes, he says, "I want to keep him where he was before. This is starting to look a little design-y."

"Working with George is a scary but exhilarating experience," T. J. Frame notes. "He comes up here and asks, 'Is it a good read?' He keeps it pure and honest. He makes sure that design is in service of the storytelling."

Tuesday, November 26: Nicole Young fits Christopher Lee (Count Dooku) for a costume at his home in London.

Lucas notices that he's running out of time: "Should I go for it?" he asks McCallum.

"Go for it," Rick says.

So George looks at another board and approves quite a bit.

"I haven't figured out if there's a correlation between more okays and not enough time," the producer observes, "but you're doing great."

After Lucas leaves, the tension and excitement dissipate—as they usually do—and an analysis ensues. Because of hints thrown out by Lucas that the script may be finished by Christmas, McCaig comments to the others, "We have two more weeks to be as outside the box as possible."

FRIDAY, DECEMBER 13, 2002

It's raining hard, and water is leaking into the art department. Once again, it's a smaller group. Earlier in the week, Lucas actually requested a copy of the infamous binders, so Fay David and her new assistant, Stephanie Lostimolo, made copies and sent them to his home, where he is now reportedly working on the script Mondays through Thursdays.

Lucas arrives ahead of schedule and approves two lizards, one male, one female. The doc team arrives,

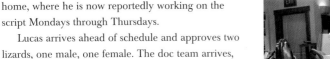

and he says to them, "I snuck up here early. You missed the whole thing. A song, a dance . . ." While looking at dress designs for Padmé, he asks the artists to avoid material that won't be good for hugs. "She's a victim in this one, but interacts with Anakin a lot."

Once again, without warning, he volunteers some key story points: "Mace we see more in the Jedi Temple—at this point, we don't see him out in the field, though that's subject to change. We see Bail Organa's wife, the Queen of Alderaan. She gets one baby. On Utapo, I have a big battle now. It's where Obi-Wan kills the [droid] general. So we'll need his henchmen. I'm thinking of doing a droid-dragon chase. I don't know how Obi-Wan is going to possibly win, but we'll figure out how to get out of it later."

Discussion focuses on what kinds of droids can do battle with a lizard-dragon. "Because it's a battle and Obi-Wan is chasing the general, the general will need a vehicle. It's gotta be a big fight. Lasers versus swords; lizards versus droids. Lots of speed, lots of chasing—*lots* of speed—jumping from one vehicle to another. Lizards getting killed, falling off cliffs, things like that."

McCallum then asks Lucas which Padmé costumes Biggar can get started on. "It's too early. I have to get an outline together," Lucas starts, but then adds: "She's in her apartment twice; she's in the Senate; she's on the landing platform." Cursory information—but enough for Rick, who calls Trisha afterward with instructions.

CHRISTMAS 2002

FOX STUDIOS, SYDNEY: After having had knee surgery earlier in December, McCallum arrives in Australia on December 20. Though some departments started weeks before, production begins full-scale operations the day after Christmas. Rick is now hiring an Australian crew, getting buildings organized, negotiating with Fox, purchasing equipment, setting up the wardrobe and art departments, and tackling anything that has a purchase order associated with it. "All of those things need sorting out," Kathryn Ramos says. "He happens to be a really hands-on kind of producer."

"What we're doing is controlling chaos," McCallum says. The way that's accomplished, he explains, is by having key personnel report any and all developments, so that—with Lucas's tacit approval—he can instantly act on that information. Together their communication creates the missing foundation, "because we're not going to find the more apparent foundation until we're well into postproduction—which makes for an interesting paradox."

SKYWALKER RANCH: It's now the ninth month of preproduction. "Back in August, I started writing this," Lucas says, "but the script starts to have its own life. Characters start to tell you what to do—and you end up with problems. By the third film, you have a lot of characters left over from before, and they're all running around yipping and yelling and saying, 'What about me?' And you have to solve these problems, because what you thought was going to happen isn't happening. I got far enough with the outline to realize that the bridge between Episode III and Episode IV still had them about fifty feet apart. So I had to disassemble Episode III and rethink it, to make it line up with Episode IV. When you actually put it down on paper and start doing it scene by scene—when you really start pulling it apart—you say, 'Well, I have to have a through-line. And I have to stick with it.'"

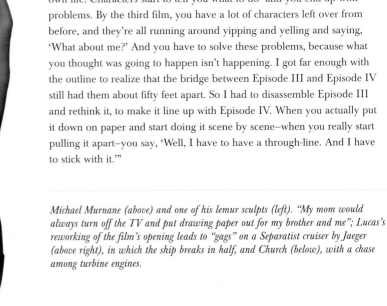

Michael Murnane (above) and one of his lemur sculpts (left). "My mom would always turn off the TV and put drawing paper out for my brother and me"; Lucas's reworking of the film's opening leads to "gags" on a Separatist cruiser by Jaeger (above right), in which the ship breaks in half, and Church (below), with a chase among turbine engines.

The Rise and Fall of Darth Vader

As Lucas's writing enters a new phase, work in the art department becomes more closely tied to the emerging script. And though the artists still engage in a great deal of free-flow conceptual creation, they're also very much involved in "detailing out" approved concepts, to the last cornice and control switch.

SKYWALKER RANCH (SR): FRIDAY, JANUARY 10, 2003

Bocquet is stopping by before flying to Sydney. He arrived on Wednesday, after his flight was delayed for nearly seven hours due to snow in London, and he's brought a few maquettes of Padmé's veranda.

Lucas walks in and asks, "Well, is the picture finished yet?"

He surveys a few Mustafarian busts, which he okays—one receives a FABULOUSO. The eyes are too human-like, however, so he requests a tweak. While looking at Mustafar command center interiors, he discusses how they need to be changed so the fight can begin there, then move outside to the volcano. Through the windows, he says, there should be "vistas that say this is bigger than something you see in other movies."

The look of the droid general is now approved; Warren Fu has given him a shield so he can defend himself against Obi-Wan. The next step is to make a sculpture of the villain. As for the Wookiees, Lucas says to keep them slim, so they're not like Ewoks. The Queen of Alderaan is fortyish, and Boba Fett will not be in the film.

He then turns to Bocquet and says, "I hear you have some questions for me. The answers are: 'No, no . . . never, never . . . I don't know.' " In their subsequent meeting, however, Lucas goes through the film scene by scene—with a huge disclaimer: "This is all subject to change."

A partial list of sets and characters include:

- Kashyyyk—Yoda, Wookiees, a 10-year-old Han Solo.
- Blockade runner from Alderaan—conference room and/or hallway—the same as the Vader hallway in Episode IV.
   - Coruscant rehabilitation center. This is where Anakin is assembled as Vader.
- Imperial Star Destroyer bridge. This is where the Emperor, Grand Moff Tarkin, and Vader look out into space and see the Death Star under construction.

Lucas approves "version 4" of Padmé's veranda, so now they can build that set in Sydney. As soon as the meeting adjourns, even though it's midnight in Australia, Bocquet phones McCallum with an update. "George always knows when he has to come through for us," Rick would say, while the next day Bocquet would tell starwars.com, "We're in a good position now, but if we're in the same spot in six or seven weeks, we might be a little bit nervous."

FRIDAY, JANUARY 17, 2003

Lucas's rethink of the script is becoming manifest to the artists—though they have yet to actually read it—as more and more links are estab-lished between Episodes III and IV. The bridge between the two is being buttressed, and the difficulty of writing that bridge is evident in many of Lucas's off-the-cuff remarks.

He shows up early, and once again the artists quickly pin the last of the paintings to the boards. Lucas notices that Biggar is present, and she asks, "How are you?" He responds, "Well, I promise you, this is the last time I'm doing this."

As they go through the boards, one of the new sets is unveiled: the rehabilitation center where Anakin becomes the mechanized Darth Vader. After his resuscitation, Vader is handed over to Governor Tarkin, who was played by the late Peter Cushing in Episode IV. Apparently there is some unused footage of the actor that can be cut into the new film. McCaig suggests digitally animating the lips, so Tarkin can be given some new dialogue, but Lucas shelves that issue for later.

He next reviews paintings of Palpatine's anteroom, studying them for a long time and then combining elements of three paintings. Lucas also reveals that Padmé will be pregnant throughout the movie, and, in the last of the Episode IV connections, asks that a peasant outfit be designed for a ten-year-old Han Solo.

"Trisha got maybe forty-five minutes with George," McCallum says in Sydney, "but it was enough to get a little more information and push us along."

FRIDAY, JANUARY 24, 2003

Lucas arrives and swaps the head of a sculpt of the droid general—whom Lucas has named Grievous—with the neck of another general sculpt.

McCaig has done additional illustrations of Padmé pregnant, which Lucas contemplates, slowly stroking his chin. He notes that Padmé has to be pregnant enough so that the audience has no doubt as to her condition, but not so pregnant that it becomes distracting. McCaig has also drawn Han Solo as requested, and Lucas approves the sketch.

The Mustafarian species has now officially been moved to Utapau (final spelling), and the lemur people removed from the film. "I was heartbroken when the lemurs were eliminated," Church recalls, "but that just shows how shortsighted I am. Ultimately, we have enough furry fighting things."

Bocquet and Lucas then retire for a private discussion, during which Lucas approves the building of more sets, including Palpatine's office and anteroom, the Polis Massa (final spelling) conference room, the blockade runner hallway, part of the Star Destroyer bridge, and part of Darth Vader's rehabilitation center. Once again, this information is immediately passed on to McCallum in Australia.

Monday, January 6: In Sydney, the art department opens for business in Building 48. The costume department starts in 44B (crowd costume storage), and costume props in 48 (depot). Art director Ian Gracie (*Pitch Black*, 2000; *Moulin Rouge*, 2001) and art department coordinator Colette Birrell (*Mission: Impossible II*, 2000; *The Matrix Reloaded*, 2003) start work today. Supervising art director Peter Russell and costume prop supervisor Ivo Coveney (*The Borrowers*, 1997; *Attack of the Clones*) begin on Wednesday.

Friday, January 10: The art department at Elstree Studios, London, closes its doors.

Far left: Darth Vader in the rehabilitation center, by Tiemens. Left: Lucas, flanked by Jun, Biggar, and McCaig. Above: Church's Alderaan starcruiser, aka the Rebel blockade runner (with Grievous's starfighter rising into it), is one of the many links between Episode III and IV.

39

Labels on image: SINKHOLE BOTTOM · GROTTO CHAMBER · SMALL TUNNEL · PASSAGE · SMALL CAVE · ROCK CLIMBING WALL · CAVE POOL LEVEL · LIMESTONE SHALLOW POOLS · UTAPAU · SW3·2·5·03·

FRIDAY, JANUARY 31, 2003

Tiemens has painted an interesting scene for Obi-Wan in an Utapau cave, based on a sketch by McCaig. Drawing on perceived parallels between the cave and the hollow tree in *The Empire Strikes Back*, where Luke confronts an apparition, Tiemens and McCaig have visually hypothesized that Qui-Gon Jinn might appear to Obi-Wan, instructing his former apprentice to go to Mustafar and stop Anakin.

When Lucas gets to the cave illustration, he asks, "What's that?"–indicating Qui-Gon. Before Iain can explain, he adds, "We never see the ghost of Qui-Gon; he's not that accomplished. He's able to retain his personality, but he's not able to become a corporeal ghost."

But the painting does give rise to another key story point: "We have a scene at the end. A funeral on Naboo. A casket is being pulled by horse-ish creatures. You can work on that."

"Where on Naboo?" Tiemens asks.

"Same place as the Episode I parade. This is the only shot on Naboo now."

The same day, Lucas's assistant Anne Merrifield finishes typing up his rough draft, which is shown only to McCallum. "We can't give the script to the department heads yet," Rick says. "Instead, I interpret it for them, because I don't want them to go too far down the line. It has to stay ephemeral at this point. There has to be enough information so they know what's going on and can plan, but not enough information so they lock something down–because everything is going to change."

Having toned down the other characters and the tempting tangents, Lucas can sum up the focus of the revised but still-evolving story in one word: *"Anakin."*

NOTE: This and subsequent summaries contain many scenes and much dialogue that won't be found in the final film. The purpose of these summaries is to show how Lucas assembles the story of Episode III slowly, over a period of years, piece by piece.

It is fifty-five pages and titled:

Star Wars Episode III: Revenge of the Sith

War! Evil is everywhere. There are heroes on both sides. Separatist terrorists have kidnapped Supreme Chancellor Palpatine, leader of the Galactic Senate.
General Grievous, commander of the separatist armies, has attacked Coruscant, the capital of the Republic, and has been driven back by the Jedi Commanders and their army of clones.
In the midst of the battle, two Jedi have discovered the starship where Chancellor Palpatine is being held captive and are attempting a rescue. . . .

ROUGH DRAFT SUMMARY: *The script's opening line belongs to OBI-WAN: "Flying is a job for droids, not Jedi." In their starfighters, OBI-WAN and ANAKIN weave their way among the ships battling above Coruscant. When OBI-WAN's vessel is crippled by buzz droids, he crash-lands into the Federation cruiser where PALPATINE is being held. ANAKIN follows. They fight off droids but are cornered by GENERAL GRIEVOUS, who greets ANAKIN as "the young hero of Bakura." ANAKIN and OBI-WAN communicate through hand signals, then whip out their lightsabers, cut a hole through the floor, and escape. However, they fall into fuel tanks, where they're surrounded by lethal, stinging jellyfish called "nitro fobos." ANAKIN and OBI-WAN escape through a vent and take an elevator to where they believe the CHANCELLOR is being held.*

LUCAS: "Obi-Wan always had a suspicion about Anakin. In the beginning, he didn't want Anakin to become a Jedi. He thought what Qui-Gon was doing was wrong. But the Jedi Council let Anakin in and they made him Obi-Wan's Padawan. Then, over the years, he lived with this kid—they fought together and they worked together, so they have a very strong bond now. So Obi-Wan is supporting Anakin because they're friends. He's been seduced by his closeness to the situation."

When the elevator door opens, droids capture OBI-WAN while ANAKIN escapes through the ceiling of the lift. OBI-WAN is brought to GRIEVOUS, and they fight on the ship's bridge. ANAKIN finds the CHANCELLOR, but is surrounded by droids. COUNT DOOKU arrives—or as he is now known, DARTH TYRANUS. They fight, cutting down the hapless droids and exchanging verbal slights:

```
            DARTH TYRANUS
I can feel your anger. Your hatred tells me you
      are not unfamiliar with the dark side.

              PALPATINE
Anakin, he was bragging earlier about how he
arranged to have your mother killed by the
              Tusken Raiders.

               ANAKIN
                You!

            DARTH TYRANUS
Yes, and now there is no escape for you,
           my young Jedi.
```

ANAKIN cuts off DOOKU's hand. PALPATINE orders him to kill TYRANUS, and ANAKIN slices off his head.

LUCAS: "Palpatine has told Dooku, 'I have somebody who I think will become a great Sith Lord and I think we can get him to join us. But we need to test him. So we're going to set up a situation where you fight him. If he gets the best of you, then I'll stop the fight and he'll have passed the test. If you get the best of him, then we'll let him go, and we'll let him stew for a few more years until he's ready.' But behind it, obviously, is Palpatine's real intention: If Anakin is good enough, Anakin can kill Dooku and become Palpatine's new apprentice. But he didn't tell Dooku that."

As the cruiser falls out of orbit, GRIEVOUS abandons ship in an escape pod. ANAKIN and PALPATINE join OBI-WAN and the former succeeds in landing what's left of the broken ship on Coruscant.

There, they are met by BAIL ORGANA, MACE WINDU, JAR JAR BINKS, and other Senators. When the main group moves off PADMÉ appears; she tells ANAKIN that she is pregnant and they embrace.

GENERAL GRIEVOUS retreats to the sinkhole planet called Utapau. He orders NUTE GUNRAY and the rest of the Separatist Council to Mustafar; he then speaks with DARTH SIDIOUS via hologram. GRIEVOUS questions his strategy but SIDIOUS councils patience.

On Coruscant, ANAKIN is awakened by a nightmare in which PADMÉ is consumed by flames. PADMÉ comforts him but ANAKIN worries her by stating: "My ability to use the Force is becoming greater than any Jedi. Soon I will control it . . . Maybe I wasn't destined to become a mere Jedi."

PALPATINE announces a reorganization: he would like ANAKIN to act as liaison between the Jedi Council and the Chancellor's office. The Council eventually accepts, with YODA speaking as a hologram.

When the meeting is over, YODA, who is on Kashyyyk, speaks with the spirit of QUI-GON JINN. YODA would like to know how the Jedi will be destroyed, but QUI-GON can't say because the Force is out of balance. Ten-year-old HAN SOLO then joins YODA.

```
              HAN SOLO
I found part of a transmitter droid near the
east bay . . . I think it's still sending and
           receiving signals.

               YODA
Good. Good. Track this we can back to the
source. Find General Grievous, we might . . .
```

HAN SOLO and YODA track the signal to Utapau. YODA informs the Jedi Council, and MACE decides to send OBI-WAN, along with thousands of clone troopers, to capture GENERAL GRIEVOUS.

On Utapau, GRIEVOUS and OBI-WAN fight; droids attack, and clone troopers weigh in. GRIEVOUS flees on his wheel scooter; OBI-WAN pursues on his lizard. After a breakneck chase, GRIEVOUS shoots the lizard from under the Jedi—but OBI-WAN cuts down the GENERAL.

OBI-WAN informs the Jedi Council of his victory, and MACE WINDU goes to see PALPATINE to negotiate a peace now that GRIEVOUS is dead. PALPATINE refuses. When MACE insists that the Senate decide whether or not to halt the war, PALPATINE attacks with "electric bolts" that emanate from his fingers. At PALPATINE's urging, ANAKIN cuts off MACE's sword hand. "MACE crumples, the blue rays engulfing his body. Finally, the Jedi leader falls silent."

The tremendous effort needed to generate the sustained lightning has transformed PALPATINE's face into that of DARTH SIDIOUS. With ANAKIN standing by, he orders the clone troopers to execute "Order Sixty-Six." On Mygeeto, KI-ADI-MUNDI is killed. KIT FISTO is killed on Saleucami (final spelling), PLO KOON on Cato Neimoidia, and AAYLA SECURA on Felucia. YODA is meditating and forewarned by the Force; he defeats the troopers sent to assassinate him.

On Utapau, OBI-WAN is shot off his lizard and falls hundreds of meters into a sinkhole. He swims underwater and emerges in a hidden cave. Two seeker drones emerge from the

Above left: Tiemens schematic of a hidden grotto within an Utapau sinkhole traces Obi-Wan's path to a possible meeting with his former Master, Qui-Gon Jinn (lower inset). Like Alderaan, Utapau existed long ago in Lucas's second draft of Star Wars. At that time, it was a stand-in for what became Tatooine on the script's opening page: "A vast sea of stars is broken as the warm amber surface of the planet Utapau emerges from a total eclipse . . . A tiny silver spacecraft races from behind one of the lifeless Utapau moons." Left, middle: Church's painting offers a close-up view of Obi-Wan's trek. Far left: One of the seeker droids that pursues Obi-Wan in the cave, by Thompson. Above: McCaig's Han Solo concept hypothesizes that the younger scoundrel may have been a slob.

water looking for him. OBI-WAN climbs into a hole and presses against the wall; a quick-moving nos monster streaks by OBI-WAN, swallows one of the droids, and pursues the other. OBI-WAN makes his way to a landing platform, where he commandeers a starfighter.

On Coruscant, PALPATINE completes his seduction of ANAKIN, who at first refuses to go over to the dark side—until the Chancellor makes a startling confession:

DARTH SIDIOUS
I have waited all these years for you to fulfill your destiny [. . .] I arranged for your conception. I used the power of the Force to will the midichlorians to start the cell divisions that created you.

ANAKIN
I don't believe you.

DARTH SIDIOUS
Ahhh, but you know it's true. When you clear your mind, you will sense the truth. You could almost think of me as your father.

ANAKIN
That's impossible!

DARTH SIDIOUS
Nevertheless, you must decide . . .

Thanks to promises of powers that would save PADMÉ from death, ANAKIN gives in to temptation. OBI-WAN and YODA return to Coruscant and the Jedi Temple, where they find a hologram that shows ANAKIN slaughtering the younglings. In the hologram, DARTH SIDIOUS enters, and ANAKIN kneels before him:

DARTH SIDIOUS
You are a Jedi no more, Anakin Skywalker. That life is no more. Today you begin your new life as Darth Vader, Lord of the Sith and bringer of peace and justice to the galaxy.

BAIL ORGANA arrives and informs YODA and OBI-WAN that PALPATINE has announced the formation of the First Galactic Empire. OBI-WAN wants to go after ANAKIN, but YODA counsels patience. BAIL and YODA flee to Polis Massa, while OBI-WAN makes an excuse to join them later. He goes to see PADMÉ and tries to persuade her to tell him where ANAKIN is, but she refuses,

---

Monday, February 3: In Sydney, production supervisor Stephen Jones (*Scooby-Doo,* 2002; *Peter Pan*) starts work, as does the assistant to the producer and the director Jacqui Louez (*Attack of the Clones; Good Luck Jeffrey Brown,* 2003).

Above left: Church concept painting of Palpatine and Anakin in the former's office. Above middle: T.J. Frame and animation director Rob Coleman waiting for Lucas's arrival. Above right: David, Coleman, and Lucas review very early CG animation on Coleman's laptop.

and he departs. PADMÉ then boards her ship with CAPTAIN TYPHO and her HANDMAIDENS.

On Mustafar, ANAKIN obeys SIDIOUS's orders and slaughters NUTE GUNRAY, POGGLE THE LESSER, and the rest of the Separatists.

PADMÉ arrives—but her entourage is gunned down by clones. As they close in on her, ANAKIN appears and calls them off. She pleads with ANAKIN, but he says she is either with him or against him. Just then OBI-WAN reveals himself—having sneaked aboard her ship. ANAKIN is enraged and, believing PADMÉ has betrayed him, Force-chokes her and then throws her against a wall. OBI-WAN and ANAKIN fight.

The old friends battle through Mustafar interiors and exteriors until,

Just as ANAKIN looks as if he has beaten OBI-WAN, the Jedi makes a quick move, cutting off ANAKIN's legs, and he tumbles down an embankment and stops near the edge of the lava. Suddenly, the Sith Lord bursts into flames and starts screaming.

OBI-WAN picks up ANAKIN's lightsaber and walks away. There is no dialogue. OBI-WAN rescues PADMÉ and takes her to Polis Massa. DARTH SIDIOUS rescues ANAKIN and takes him to Coruscant, where ANAKIN is operated on and made into the mechanical DARTH VADER.

On Polis Massa, OBI-WAN informs YODA and BAIL that PADMÉ is pregnant with twins. During the subsequent operation, the twins are saved but PADMÉ dies on the operating table. YODA tells them to send her body to Naboo. BAIL volunteers to care for the girl. OBI-WAN says he knows of a family on Tatooine who will take care of the boy while he watches from afar. YODA tells OBI-WAN that in his solitude he has training for him with "one who has studied with the Ancient Order of the Whills . . . Your old Master, Qui-Gon Jinn."

On Naboo, there is a funeral for PADMÉ. On Dagobah, a pod arrives, hurtling through the mist; after it lands, YODA emerges. As his ship nears Alderaan, BAIL ORGANA gives C-3PO and R2-D2 to CAPTAIN ANTILLES, telling him "to clean them up. Have the protocol droid mindwiped." "Oh, dear," C-3PO says.

On Alderaan, the QUEEN is presented with a baby girl. On Tatooine, OBI-WAN gives a baby boy to UNCLE OWEN.

On the bridge of an Imperial Star Destroyer, the EMPEROR, GOVERNOR TARKIN, and DARTH VADER look out into space, where they see the construction of the Death Star.

WEDNESDAY, FEBRUARY 5, 2003

Now permanently ensconced in Sydney (Oz), Rick McCallum, Gavin Bocquet, Trisha Biggar, and other production heads have set up regular communications with Lucas at his home via a videoconference link.

Tuesday, February 4: At a JAK-OZ videoconference, Isola Bella, Italy, is suggested as a location for the Theed funeral. Lucas says he'd need only a crowd there, no principals.

Wednesday, February 5: At the 2003 Empire Movie Awards in London, the Sony Ericsson Award for best scene of the year goes to Episode II's lightsaber duel between Yoda and Count Dooku. Christopher Lee accepts the award on behalf of himself and the Jedi Master, saying, "To you, his regards he sends."

They usually talk on Mondays and Wednesdays. Before each meeting, Bocquet e-mails production department artwork and costume photos to Fay David, who prints them out. Ryan Church then takes them to Parkway, Lucas's home, where the video call is placed to McCallum, Biggar, Bocquet, and whoever else is necessary, and the material is discussed.

"I would go down to his place two times a week with detailed artwork, presenting it to him, because he was working very hard on the script," Church recalls. "He's got a side nook, a writing room. It's lined with books, and he's got a writing desk. He has a cool teleconferencing system, so it was really like sitting in the same room with the guys from Australia. You could hold up an image to them. And George's kids are running around; he's extremely relaxed, shoes off. I learned a lot about making movies. He'd talk about how important it is to see the light on people's eyes."

Saturday, February 8: In the Presidio Park of San Francisco, California, ground is officially broken for the Letterman Digital Arts Center, future home of Lucasfilm Entertainment (Lucasfilm, ILM, and LucasArts).

Monday, February 10: Oscar nominees are announced. Rob Coleman, Pablo Helman, John Knoll, and Ben Snow are nominated for Best Visual Effects for *Star Wars: Episode II Attack of the Clones*. Gary Rydstrom and Richard Hymns at Skywalker Sound are nominated for Best Sound Editing for Steven Spielberg's *Minority Report*.

Above: Short Polis Massan sculpts by Murnane. Top and bottom right: Utapau cave dragon revisions by McCaig dated February 20, after Lucas found the February 7 concepts too rancor-like.

FRIDAY, FEBRUARY 7, 2003

Several artists have passed the night in the attic. Lucas arrives. "Well, hello, hello. Nothing today?"

"Polis Massa," McCaig replies, indicating a sculpt of an alien.

"It's good that he's short."

"You like?"

"I like."

They move on to the horses that will be pulling Padmé's coffin. "Horse things," Church says.

"Too horsey."

"Too horsey?"

"A horse is a thing that pulls a wagon . . . Sorry about that. I sent you in the wrong direction."

Looking at the Utapau cave dragon, Lucas says, "It reeks of rancor. Let's open up those imagination vaults."

Church suggests that Grievous might be able to breathe in space, which would give him an advantage over Obi-Wan, and Lucas thinks it's a good idea. Grievous could crawl out onto the hull of the space cruiser, then re-enter and escape in a pod.

At this meeting, for the first time and perhaps because he's reached a more comfortable place in his writing, Lucas starts directing within the art. He talks about what he's going to do with the camera and where he's going to pan. He goes into details, requesting visual bridges or combinations of images that will enable him to do what he wants with the camera. He designates exactly which paintings will be used for establishing shots, then consults a list, which he reads from: "Crystal world: Ki-Adi-Mundi. Field headquarters and a battle . . ." He stops and thinks. "You pan around, you end up here [pointing to a spot on a painting of the crystal world]. This would be damaged; as you pan in, this wouldn't be damaged . . ." Fay puts Post-its on paintings noting his directions.

Because there's an impending two-week lull without a meeting, Lucas gives them projects to work on, reading further from his list. "You might want to play with the ship pulling apart. Maybe do something upside down on the bridge . . .

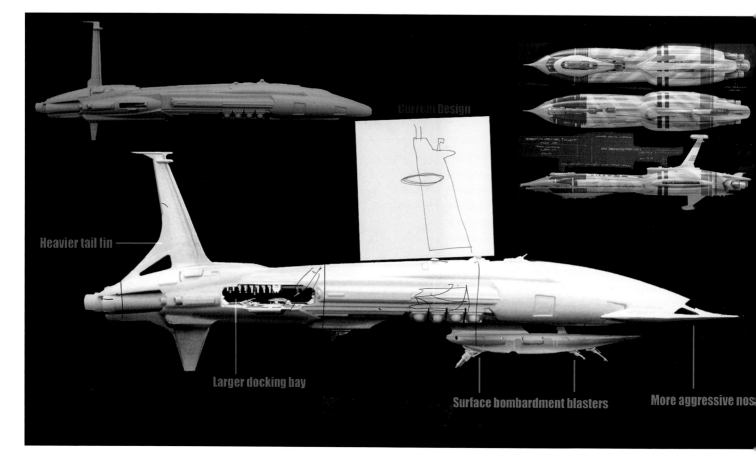

Heavier tail fin

Current Design

Larger docking bay

Surface bombardment blasters

More aggressive nos

When the ship crashes, there can be fireships pouring foam on it. We need a taxi ship for Bail . . ."

"All right, so have a good weekend. I gave you a few things to do."

"Dagobah?" Rob Coleman asks.

Lucas consults his paper. "It's not in here. A mistake. I'll have to put it in here." He confirms that there will be one shot of Dagobah, the same swamp as in *Empire*, and adds that we'll see a meteorite hit Polis Massa. It opens up, and Yoda walks out of it.

George leaves. Looking at the others, Coleman says, "That was a good one."

Friday, February 21, 2003–Day One Minus 19 Weeks

The countdown to Day One of principal photography has begun. Although there remain nineteen weeks, art department activity has begun to function very much with that one day in mind. The artists are now focusing even more on refining, and less on conceptualizing. Two more prequel film veterans are here today, perhaps to spur things on: ILM visual effects supervisor John Knoll and sound designer-digital editor Ben Burtt. Lucas hired Burtt way back in 1975 to create the original sounds for *Star Wars*. Burtt's work for *Revenge of the Sith* begins with his creation of videomatics, which will help Lucas visualize the movie's action scenes (Burtt will tackle editing and sound design in postproduction).

Rob Coleman is here, too, along with the others–and John Goodson, who says he's "glad to be alive" after surviving a car accident in which he broke his sternum. Lucas walks in and looks at some drawings of Jar Jar Binks. Someone asks, "Is Jar Jar in this film?"

"Does he have a tragic death scene?" Knoll asks.

"In this film, he's battle-hardened," Coleman points out.

Given a choice of Jar Jar costumes, George picks one that would cover most of the Gungan's body.

"You chose wisely," Coleman says, as that one will make animation easier.

Next are 3-D representations of the Separatist ship, which prompt Lucas to say: "I've redesigned the ship. It has more armaments on it, so it's clearly the most powerful ship out there . . . I've got a sequence where the elevator shaft is turned on its side–and [Obi-Wan and Anakin] run through it with the elevator chasing them. There's a sequence where the bridge turns over. Droids have magnetized shoes, but Obi-Wan doesn't. So he's running along the ceiling chasing them."

February 13: JAK-OZ videoconference–Attendees learn that the Kashyyyk meeting hall is "tricky." It will have Han Solo and Wookiees, and it will be almost completely digital.

Thursday, February 20: Lucasfilm and the Cartoon Network announce the creation of 20 three-minute-long animated shorts called *Star Wars: Clone Wars,* to be broadcast in late 2003 and early 2004. Helming this new series is Genndy Tartakovsky, the creator of *Samurai Jack* and *Dexter's Laboratory.*

Top: Lucas's sketch stuck onto Frame's cruiser concept indicates where the general's quarters should be (inset, Church). Right: Thompson (left) and McCaig launch into several weeks of intense sequential storytelling. Top right: Thompson's storyboards show an early version of the Dooku/Anakin battle, with the Jedi using the Force. Far right: Obi-Wan takes on Grievous's bodyguards–who have a nasty tendency to fight on even without key body parts.

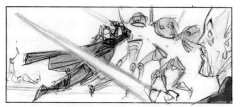

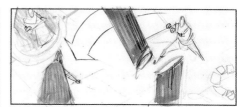

Lucas is going out the door when he notices Burtt: "Well hi, Ben! You lurking in the back?"

"Rick told us to come and lurk," Burtt says.

"Well, it's on again," Lucas says. "No script, but a lot of interesting ideas."

FRIDAY, FEBRUARY 28, 2003–DAY ONE MINUS 18 WEEKS

For the first time, McCaig, Jun, and Thompson—who has returned after a brief layoff—have been storyboarding, drawing out action sequences in panel-by-panel format.

After Lucas arrives, the storyboards are unveiled. "Without anything more than a few hints, we took a stab at it," McCaig says. In the drawings, the cliffhangers of the script's first twenty pages are laid out, interpreted, expanded. After studying one sequence, Lucas suggests that the Jedi lock a

door, then, in the ensuing explosion on the other side of the door, many droids could be blown up. As the concept artists and Lucas begin discussing in detail the storyboards, as story points are discarded and new ideas inserted, you can hear the film being made.

In the storyboards, Anakin finds Palpatine imprisoned in what looks like a Puritan stock that immobilizes his hands and head. Dooku arrives via elevator and advances upon Anakin. While dueling, Anakin acquires

---

Dooku's lightsaber, and Dooku uses dark side lightning. Palpatine tells Anakin that he must cut off Dooku's hands—he does so. Then he cuts off Dooku's head with a "full swing."

"Can he use Dooku's blade?" McCaig asks.

"Yes," Lucas says—which is followed by a collective "Oh yeah!" from the group.

But Lucas warns them not to get too detailed. "All we need is assemblages, then Dan [Gregoire] can get in there [with animatics]—otherwise these sequences are too cinematic for boards." In parting, he suggests, "I'd focus on the air battle first. We need to keep it edge-of-your-seat."

FRIDAY, MARCH 7, 2003–DAY ONE MINUS 17 WEEKS

Earlier this week, the pre-viz, or animatics, department officially started work. Led by Dan Gregoire, they are building assets—computer elements and models used in animations—and getting ready to tackle sequences.

Wednesday, March 5: JAK-OZ videoconference—Lucas advises that the Trade Federation cruiser generator room will have to be filmed in a tank of water. He confirms that C-3PO will have a gold finish throughout Episode III.

Friday, March 7: Production begins discussions with ILM on what will be needed on the sets to facilitate the computer-generated effects that will be added in post-production. JAK art director Ian Gracie asks visual effects supervisor John Knoll a variety of questions: what shade of white the rebel blockade runner should be, whether Jedi starfighters need windscreens, and so forth.

for generating two to three shots per day. As shots are finished, they're sent down to editorial, where Lucas approves, modifies, or disapproves them. Ben Burtt then works the approved shots into his videomatics, which use everything from concept art to photography to give the director an idea of how the scenes are developing.

At today's art department meeting, a model of a clone trooper starfighter, tentatively called a V-wing, sits on the table. There's also a sinkhole environment sculpt by Danny Wagner, who's here for the first time, making him the fourteenth member. Wagner started his career at a small effects studio in San Francisco. "The first movie we worked on was *Look Who's Talking* [1989] and my first job was making sperm, trying to

"I forgot my glasses," Lucas says upon arriving. "I can't see anything. Give me a stamp! I'll deny everything afterward." Looking over the new paintings of Mustafar, he thinks it might be funny if Obi-Wan and Anakin "jump and ride on the backs of some droids. I don't know if we want to get humorous in the middle of their fight, but we can go for it."

There is a new height chart for Wookiees, but Lucas finds that these Wookiees are too short, reminding everyone, "Chewbacca is seven foot four—but he's a *small* Wookiee. And in this film, their only companion is Yoda! All we'll see is feet. Yoda will be surrounded by feet."

FRIDAY, MARCH 14, 2003–DAY ONE MINUS 16 WEEKS

Heretofore static concept paintings and models are beginning to move, to take on life. The animatics department is designing shots using the art department's approved concepts, creating low-resolution animated three-dimensional sequences, or "digital storyboards." Their first assignment is the aerial battle above Coruscant. Each shot designer is responsible

Tuesday, March 18: Jimmy Smits (Bail Organa) is fitted for a costume in Los Angeles, California.

make them look goofy and funny. My first job at ILM was as a slime wrangler on *Ghostbusters II* [1989]. Hmmm . . ."

Top: Lucas, Tiemens, David (taking notes), and Jun. Middle: Handwritten evidence of Lucas's efforts to write R2-D2 into the script. His notes indicate dialogue between Anakin and the droid after the Jedi have crash-landed in the cruiser hangar. Bottom: At the request of property master Ty Teiger, set decorating coordinator Helena Donohue asks the archives department at Skywalker Ranch to send to the props department in Australia Vader's lightsaber and Luke's lightsaber from Episode IV for reference.

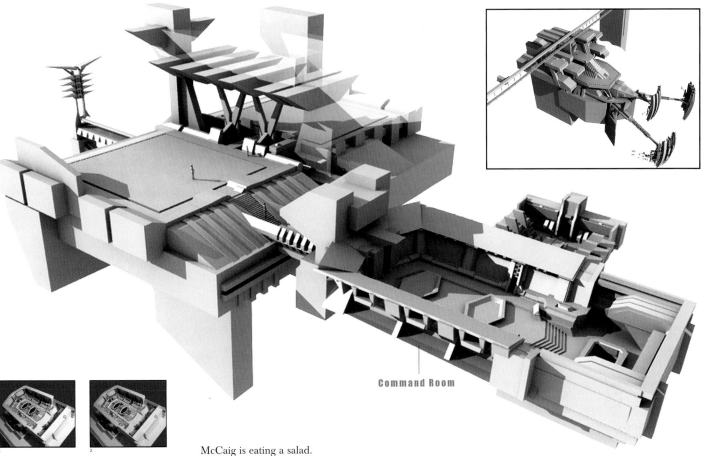

Command Room

McCaig is eating a salad. He says he's "exhausted" from doing storyboards, because it's like acting, creating a performance. When Lucas arrives, everyone seems to freeze for some reason. "What do we do now?" he jokes. As they review the V-wing model, someone asks, "Do the clones have Artoo units?"

"They're everywhere," Lucas responds. "Don't you have one in the back of your car?" Looking at the sinkhole sculpt, he says, "Make it big. Obi-Wan could climb out of there in two minutes. Don't be afraid."

He next studies Robert Barnes's in-progress sculpt of droid general Grievous. He observes that the only biological parts of Grievous are his eyes, brain, spinal cord–and that, perhaps, he has "a plastic sac for all of his organs." There is talk about how his earpieces could move to show emotion. During all this conversation, Barnes is in acute pain, which he explains later: "Generally, Thursday nights, everyone works late or all night. And I was on that pattern. One of those nights, my shoulder was cramping up until around two A.M.–when it stopped me in my tracks. It turned out I had two herniated disks in my neck. General Grievous just about killed me."

A moment later, in a rare instance, Lucas expresses mild frustration, as some paintings diverge from previously approved concepts. He emphasizes once again that clone troopers should look more beat-up and sport customized outfits–even to the extent, he says, of having written on their helmets the words FORCE YOU.

In Australia, McCallum says, "I'm a man without a script. Usually you get a script a year before production begins, and it's broken down, and

storyboarded, and costumes and sets are broken out; the actors are locked in to dates–but we don't have that. So everybody's taking the leap and focusing on what little information we get each week, which happens to be enough for us right now.

"We started set construction about two weeks ago, costumes have been pumping up, and the creature shop is just being set up. Everything is moving. We're heading for a destination, but we're not sure where we're gonna end up."

FRIDAY, MARCH 21, 2003–DAY ONE MINUS 15 WEEKS

Sitting with others in his office, Lucas delivers a short "state-of-the-script" report: "Well, I wrote a rough draft. It's really crude, but it basically gets the essence of the story down and the main beats of the film. I've also written about half of the first draft. Now I am going through, filling out and being more articulate. I still have elements, like Artoo-Detoo and Threepio, which I haven't really fit in everywhere. They're in one scene, but I haven't actually filled in their reality yet, because the film doesn't center on them. So I'm hoping to have the first draft done in two weeks. Then I'll start working on the second draft, and I'm hoping to get a third draft in before I have to go to Sydney–which means I'm going through a

Above: In a process used for various interiors, in order to give Lucas a more solid idea of what a set will look like and what camera angles he might have, T.J. Frame has digitally pieced together several conceptual artworks of Mustafar into 3-D artworks. Mustafar interiors consist of a command (war) room, conference room, landing platform, collection arms, and so on–but, thanks to these ensembles, draftspeople and model-makers in Australia are able to plan set construction (above left). Their early 3-D renderings of the "Mustafa" war room show several "set-build proposals"; the orange portions represent digital set extensions that would eventually be created by ILM.

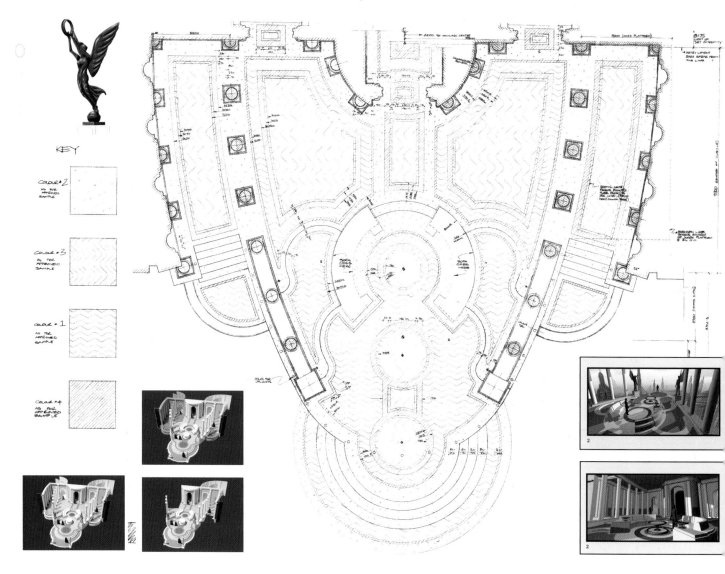

KEY

COLOUR #2
AS FOR
APPROVED
SAMPLE

COLOUR #3
AS FOR
APPROVED
SAMPLE

COLOUR #1
AS FOR
APPROVED
SAMPLE

COLOUR #4
AS FOR
APPROVED
SAMPLE

draft about every six weeks. Then I'll have it as best as I can—but I'm looking at the shooting very much as another draft."

When someone asks what his biggest challenge is going from rough draft to first draft, he responds, "What challenges me is what always challenges me."

"Which is?"

"Inertia. [laughter] Procrastination. I sit there with that page in front of me . . . I am very diligent about going to work at eight thirty every morning and leaving at six o'clock every night. But I can be chained to my desk and I still can't write it. I do it, you know, I do get it done; I actually write five pages a day. But left to my own reality, I would probably write a page a day. I force myself. It becomes agonizing to get those other four pages, otherwise—"

"You can't have dinner?"

"Well, I can't leave [laughter], so if I do four pages and I get onto the fifth page, I rationalize it: I've done my five pages."

Above: In March, the art department in Sydney begins working out the details of Padmé's veranda, from column styles and statue concepts (by Gert Stevens) to detailed blueprints with floor patterns. During videoconference calls, computer-generated representations enable Lucas and McCallum to decide how much of the set should be practical and how much digital. Church (right) and Tiemens (inset) created concepts of the Utapau windmills that McCaig had envisioned while sitting in a Vancouver airport.

FRIDAY, MARCH 28, 2003–DAY ONE MINUS 14 WEEKS

Everyone seems tired. Once again, many were up all Thursday night. Earlier this week, Fay David received a call from Lucas asking the art department to work on the windmill concept, as conceived by McCaig the week before, in which Obi-Wan and Grievous pursue each other through giant whirling blades. So McCaig, Tiemens, and Church have done passes on that idea, while Goodson has done a model for an Utapau vessel, which might become Grievous's starfighter.

"I like it," Lucas says, as soon as he arrives. "Should we put some guns on it?"

"We have some that pop up," Church points out.

When he comes to the windmills, Lucas says, "I actually gave this chase scene to Anne [Merrifield] to type up today. Obi-Wan loses his sword—he actually uses a pistol [against Grievous]—we haven't seen that before!"

After approving a few of the windmill paintings, he goes on to the next drawing. "What's this?" he asks.

"The glowing fungus room," McCaig replies, drawing the words out, knowing that this drawing is perhaps pushing Lucas's limits.

"I say, 'Nice try.' What's this one?"

"Glowing tube-worm room!" McCaig admits, and everyone laughs.

"Again, I say, 'Nice try.' "

FRIDAY, APRIL 4, 2003–DAY ONE MINUS 13 WEEKS

Another prequel veteran is visiting: stunt coordinator–sword master Nick Gillard. Wearing an *Indiana Jones and the Temple of Doom* dungaree crew jacket, the diminutive but steel-framed fight expert is accompanying Lucas on his rounds. "When Nick came here, he was waiting for four days," McCallum says, "before it was the right time for him to see George."

Lucas gives Danny Wagner's revised, much deeper sculpture of the Utapau sinkhole a FABULOUSO. To Gillard, Lucas explains, "This is where Obi-Wan and Grievous fight." He puts pins in the clay to show where action sequences are going to take place. Nick has already worked out on paper much of the fight sequences, but he's here to learn more about the various fight locales that have yet to be built.

Indicating an Utapau interior, Lucas asks, "What is this signage for?"

"Restaurant?" Church offers.

"Where is the restaurant? Show me more–how does the restaurant fit in here?"

"We can be a little more literal."

"Yeah, because eventually we have to say where they eat and shop," Lucas says and then goes into more detail for an unusually long time–it's clearly important the artists get this right for next week. He pokes holes in the ceiling of an Utapau interior to allow for shafts of light. "We have to figure out how the city falls together. It's slightly organic, but they have cars."

Tuesday, April 7: In Sydney, Nick Gillard starts the stunt department in Stage 4.

Saturday, April 12: DP David Tattersall and high-definition supervisor Fred Meyers conduct digital camera tests at ILM.

Lucas ends the meeting by saying that he wants Nick to speak with Dan Gregoire in animatics. "Have fun," he tells Gillard.

THURSDAY, APRIL 10, 2003–DAY ONE MINUS 12 WEEKS

As they have several times before, McCaig and Thompson are going to Lucas's home for a storyboard discussion. "We drove up to a big white house surrounded by cypress trees," McCaig remembers. "We drove through the double gates, past the main house, to an annex off to the right side. It's all beautiful redwood. You open the door and Lucas's office is like the deck of a ship, with what looks like a captain's poop deck at the end of a long room. That's his writing area. And today when Derek and I walked in with our boards, George was at the end of the room. His pencil was down and he was just sitting there with his head bowed. Then, looking calm and drained, he came down and said, 'I just wrote the end.' He had just finished the first draft."

FRIDAY, APRIL 11, 2003

Another longtime Lucas-McCallum collaborator from the *Young Indy* days, director of photography (DP) David Tattersall, is present. When Lucas arrives, he greets David warmly, "How ya doing!" and shows him various environments that he'll have to light.

Following last week's precise directions, the artists have created lots of Utapau interiors. "Utapau's starting to turn into a city," Lucas says. "I like this."

"David has to know what's going on," McCallum explains. "There's no way you can walk into this world unless you're constantly kept a part of it."

Above: Lucas's request for more Utapau-interior details results in Church's view of Obi-Wan's headlong pursuit through the sinkhole city of the droid general–whose vehicle began as a stand-alone monoped droid, but which was adapted for the general when the script required a vehicle as agile as the Jedi's steed.

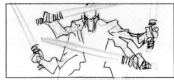

grab GRIEVOUS's fallen blaster and discharges it into the droid's guts. GRIEVOUS explodes from the inside out.

LUCAS: "I wanted it to be an alien who is mostly a droid, which is an echo of what Anakin is going to become. That was his job in the movie, and he needed to be designed in a way that was very compelling and very interesting to watch. Because he was the main action villain, we needed to create a special talent for him. So we gave him two arms that turn into four arms, which is a neat trick and visually very arresting."

The MACE/PALPATINE dialogue and fight are much more complex than in the rough draft. They fight and MACE knocks PALPATINE's lightsaber away.

> MACE
> You are well versed in the ways
> of the Jedi, yet you are no Jedi!

PALPATINE unleashes his lightning bolts. Both MACE and PALPATINE ask ANAKIN for help.

> PALPATINE
> I offer you knowledge, Anakin.
> Don't join their rebellion . . .
> I am your pathway to power.

LUCAS: "This is the point where Anakin has to make a decision. His rationalization is: 'Everybody is after power. Even the Jedi are after power.' Therefore, he thinks, 'They're all equally corrupt now. So which side am I going to be on? Do I align myself with Palpatine, who is a Sith Lord and who can possibly help me save Padmé? Or do I side with the Jedi and maybe lose Padmé?'"

MACE is winning, pushing the Sith Lord toward the window and his death. Just as MACE is going to force PALPATINE off the ledge, ANAKIN cuts off MACE's lightsaber hand. PALPATINE then blasts MACE with lightning that flings him out of the window to his death.

> *ANAKIN kneels at the feet of DARTH SIDIOUS.*

> ANAKIN
> I want the power to stop death.

From this point on, the script refers to ANAKIN as "DARTH VADER." PALPATINE then explains that he has a plan to wipe out the Jedi.

The first to receive Order 66 is CLONE COMMANDER BACARA (1138), and, this time, the list of Jedi who meet their end is more extensive. On Mygeeto, clones blast KI-ADI-MUNDI and SAESEE TIIN. On Saleucami, they kill KIT FISTO, BARRISS OFFEE, and ADI GALLIA. On Kashyyyk, MINA PODIA is gunned down—but YODA saves himself. On Cato Neimoidia, PLO KOON is blasted out of the sky, while an unnamed Jedi lies dead on the planet surface. On Felucia, AAYLA SECURA and QUINLAN VOS are silenced forever.

Sunday, April 13, 2003

Anne Merrifield has typed up the first draft, which bears today's date. A few artists are allowed to read it. "It's very dark—darker than you would think," Tiemens comments. Apart from being fifty-six pages longer than the rough draft, this version has the following changes and developments:

As they fly in their Jedi starfighters, R2-D2 now acts as ANAKIN's astromech; R4-G8 is OBI's. The two Jedi are also guided to the cruiser holding a kidnapped CHANCELLOR PALPATINE by the locator of Jedi Knight SHAAK TI.

The fuel tanks no longer have poisonous creatures; on the other hand, after they seal the hatch, a spark hits the fuel and the resultant massive explosion takes out the pursuing droids. Now it is R2-D2 who makes the elevator descend, separating the Jedi. OBI-WAN is captured by droids and led to GRIEVOUS—who kills a captive SHAAK TI before his eyes.

GRIEVOUS and OBI-WAN fight as the ship falls out of orbit, but now the droids magnetize so they can walk along the ceiling. GRIEVOUS escapes by breaking a window and crawling along the ship's hull into an escape pod. While fighting ANAKIN, DOOKU no longer claims responsibility for the death of ANAKIN's mother.

HAN SOLO has been eliminated from the film. It is now the CHANCELLOR who tells ANAKIN where to find GENERAL GRIEVOUS. PALPATINE also tells him more about the power of the dark side and the Sith Lord DARTH PLAGUEIS—who could keep life-forms from dying and who could communicate with midi-chlorians, influencing their creations.

On Utapau, GRIEVOUS reveals that he knows how to use lightsabers—and that he has four arms. OBI-WAN eventually rips off GRIEVOUS's stomach plate, revealing "the alien life-form's guts encased in a bag." OBI-WAN uses the Force to

STAR WARS EPISODE III
REVENGE OF THE SITH
by
GEORGE LUCAS

LUCASFILM LTD.

first
~~Rough~~ Draft
~~April~~ ~~March~~ 13, 2003
Revised April 13, 2003
92 Pages

THIS MATERIAL IS THE PROPERTY OF LUCASFILM LTD. AND IS INTENDED AND RESTRICTED SOLELY FOR USE BY LUCASFILM LTD PERSONNEL. DISTRIBUTION OR DISCLOSURE OF THIS MATERIAL TO UNAUTHORIZED PERSONS IS PROHIBITED. THE SALE, COPYING, OR REPRODUCTION OF THIS MATERIAL IN ANY FORM IS STRICTLY PROHIBITED.

Sunday, April 27: Hayden Christensen (Anakin Skywalker) arrives in Sydney to start training.

Above middle: The typed title page of an interim draft. This version, with Lucas's handwritten corrections, would become his first draft dated April 13. Top left: Thompson's early storyboards show how Grievous, with his four arms brandishing four lightsabers, might take on Obi-Wan aboard the Separatist cruiser.

And this time, after seeing the hologram of ANAKIN in the Jedi Temple killing the younglings, YODA announces that he will kill PALPATINE and that OBI-WAN must kill ANAKIN—and OBI-WAN objects. But YODA tells him it must be done: "The boy who was your apprentice, he is not."

YODA confronts DARTH SIDIOUS below the Senate. On Mustafar, PADMÉ and her entourage are attacked, but this time by droids, which ANAKIN destroys. PADMÉ confronts ANAKIN with what OBI-WAN told her—that he has gone over to the dark side—but ANAKIN claims to "have brought peace to the galaxy."

```
                    PADMÉ
        Obi-Wan was right. You've changed.

                   ANAKIN
          For the better. I have become
          more powerful than any Jedi
          ever dreamed of being [. . .]
        Together we will rule the galaxy.
```

LUCAS: "The thing that breaks Padmé's heart in the end is the fact that Anakin says to her, 'Come and join me. I have all the power now. I can rule the universe and you can do it with me.' So the idea of saving her life has become a minor issue. And that's when she says, 'Wait a minute. This is not what I want and you're not the guy I fell in love with!' "

Back on Coruscant, PALPATINE easily deflects YODA's attacks, and the latter barely escapes with the help of BAIL ORGANA.

PADMÉ dies on the operating table saying, this time, "He's not evil . . ." On Coruscant, after ANAKIN has become the mechanical DARTH VADER, he asks where PADMÉ is, and PALPATINE's line is new: "I'm afraid she was killed by a Jedi . . . she is no longer our concern."

"As I write the next drafts," explains Lucas, "there'll be a lot more cutting and pasting. Certain sequences will be right, and I'll just jump through them. The last thing that will be dealt with is the dialogue, because that you can change on the set or even afterward—you know, I'm not known for my dialogue. [laughs] I think of it as a sound effect, a

rhythm, a vocal chorus in the overall soundtrack. Mostly, everything is visual.

"What drove me to make these movies is that this is a really interesting story about how people go bad. In this particular case, the premise is: Nobody thinks they're bad. They simply have different points of view. This is about a kid that's really wonderful. He has some flaws—and those flaws ultimately do him in.

"The core issue, ultimately, is greed, possessiveness—the inability to let go. Not only to hold on to material things, which is greed, but to hold on to life, to the people you love—to not accept the reality of life's passages and changes, which is to say things come, things go. Everything changes. Anakin becomes emotionally attached to things, his mother, his wife. That's why he falls—because he does not have the ability to let go."

Diplomatic Cruiser
Sample Wall Section

Ref Image.

Ref. Image.

1.

2.

3.

4.

Left: Sheets like these are put together by the Sydney art department to show Lucas how early set construction of the Alderaan cruiser corridor replicates its appearance in the 1977 Star Wars. Dated April 8, panel 2 of the sheet shows, for scale, art director Ian Gracie next to Darth Vader. Above: Thompson's storyboards illustrate an early conceptualization of Obi-Wan's usage of a blaster against the insidious droid general.

OBI-WAN struggles to maintain control of his ship.

                    OBI-WAN
~~Split~~. *I want you to split off and take them from behind. I'll stay here as bait.*
                    ANAKIN
Are you sure?

                    OBI-WAN
~~Yes, I'm sure. Don't worry~~. I
can hold them off for a bit.

                    ANAKIN
A very little bit. ~~I'm fast, but
not that fas~~t.

                    OBI-WAN
Tower coming up... ~~split~~! *take off*

As they race toward a control tower on one of the Federation
Battleships, they fire at it until it EXPLODES. OBI-WAN
makes an abrupt turn to avoid the tower. ANAKIN accelerates
right into the explosion. The Droid Ships follow OBI-WAN,
blasting him with intense laser fire. He deftly maneuvers
around a large ship's superstructure, but the two Droid
Fighters stay on his tail.

                    OBI-WAN   *R4*
I'm running out of tricks ~~here~~!

WEDNESDAY, APRIL 23, 2003–DAY ONE MINUS 10 WEEKS

Starwars.com announces that Anthony Daniels (C-3PO), Kenny Baker (R2-D2)–and Peter Mayhew (Chewbacca)–will be reprising their respective roles in *Revenge of the Sith*. Mayhew hasn't appeared in a *Star Wars* film since *Return of the Jedi* (1983), so his return makes headlines worldwide. "I'm delighted to return as Chewbacca," he says. "I think his reappearance in this film is a fitting way to tie the whole saga together."

THURSDAY, MAY 1, 2003–DAY ONE MINUS 9 WEEKS

Lucas has requested an impromptu art department meeting. It's scheduled for 9 A.M., but he's late. At this point, the artists are under a fair amount of pressure. They're working now not only on general designs, but also on myriad design details for the Sydney art department, which is in the process of physically creating heretofore conceptual work. Many aspects of relatively sketchy paintings, such as columns, control panels, and chairs, now must become highly precise.

Lucas walks in, close to an hour late. "Here you go!" he says, tossing the first draft on the table. "There's a lot of cheating in there," he adds.

"'They fight,' things like that. It's a hundred and one pages. I was aiming for a hundred. I overshot by a half a page, but I'll fix that."

Fay David gets a call from Jane Bay. Frank Darabont, who is working on the script for *Indiana Jones IV*, is on hold. George leaves, saying, "Frank is a hard man to get on the line."

Taking advantage of the lull, a few peek at the pages Lucas has left on the table. "Oh, 'Obi-Wan passionately kisses Padmé!'" Feng jokes.

"The beast returns!" Lucas says upon reentering. "I think we need to add a face to the droid tri-fighter. So put a face on that turkey." As for Padmé's funeral procession on Naboo, he flattens her coffin.

"What's the time of day?" Tiemens asks.

"I think we could make it a twilight. I would avoid sunset. We could do it at dawn. We can also expose for the shadows, so they can walk into the beams of light."

After George has looked at the last piece of art, there is a pause. "Next week, I'll be back . . . ," he says, scanning the group. "I'm bringing in a guest director so I don't have to do this anymore."

Everyone is silent for a moment or two.

"Can you say who, or is it a secret?" Fay asks.

Friday, May 2: JAK-OZ videoconference—It's decided that the Polis Massa observatory where Yoda speaks with Qui-Gon will be completely computer generated.

Sunday, May 18: The Academy of Science Fiction, Fantasy, and Horror Films honors *Attack of the Clones* with two Saturn Awards in the categories of Best Costume (Trisha Biggar) and Best Special Effects (John Knoll, Ben Snow, Pablo Helman, and Rob Coleman).

JEDI CRUISER FRONT
RYAN CHURCH
3·APRIL·03
SW3

"Well, you'll see 'cause he's going to be here next week."

"All right . . . Wow!"

"Well, the fun part's over . . . ," Church says.

"I've done my part, so I'm bringing in a guest director. And all I have to do is sit back and watch it on television. [much laughter] It's easier than actually having to work for a living." Pushing his glasses up, Lucas adds, "I'll just see what he can come up with."

"Nice," McCaig says.

"Awesome," Church says.

"I've done pretty much everything I can do. All the sets are designed. All the people are cast. All the sequences are set up. It's up to Rick and the sword master," Lucas sums up, suddenly looking tired. "The director's coming in on Thursday, so I want to go through all this and show him everything that's here."

"Okay, we'll have a presentation ready," Fay promises.

"All right, I'm off to editorial," he says, leaving.

Church would later describe how he and the others spent the whole weekend wondering what Lucas was talking about, wondering if he needed to move back south—it was, he says, a "huge bombshell."

MONDAY, MAY 5, 2003–DAY ONE MINUS 8 WEEKS

In a basement suite of offices, Ben Burtt is at work on the videomatics: a hodgepodge of old film clips, temporary soundtracks, storyboards, stunt footage, and whatever else will work to create pre-principal-photography action scenes. Burtt's bureau is decorated with movie posters for *Sagebrush Trail*, starring John Wayne, and *Lo Sparviero del Mare (The Sea Hawk)*, starring Errol Flynn. On one wall are images from reels one through five of *THX 1138*.

Top left: Lucas's revisions to page two describe how the Jedi in their starfighters maneuver around a control tower. (Obi-Wan's astromech is here given the number R4-P17, which Lucas would later revise to R4-G8.) Top right: Church's painting of the battle over Coruscant has directional arrows to aid the animatics department. Church's Jedi cruiser (above), dated April 3, will be part of the opening space battle (OSB).

4.   7ft vertical opening

Today Ben is having a brief videomatics/animatics meeting with Dan Gregoire and senior animatics artist Euisung Lee. Gregoire starts by saying that the word from McCallum in Sydney is "more quantity, less quality." They then watch the opening space battle videomatics. Some shots aren't long enough, so Burtt has them add frames. When the cruiser crash-lands, Gregoire suggests that instead of Mace standing there waiting, he could arrive in a gunship. "Yeah, I'd entertain that," Ben says. "That way, Mace doesn't look like he was just going for a walk."

Lucas Licensing president Howard Roffman arrives and Burtt shows him the first ten minutes of videomatics–complete with music, sound effects, and voices (all provided by Burtt)–titled *Who Framed Binks?*

THURSDAY, MAY 8, 2003

The mystery guest-director turns out to be none other than Steven Spielberg. "Spielberg came to be involved in the animatics because we had new technology and I was talking to him about it," Lucas explains. "I said how great it was and I showed it to him. And his film had fallen out over the summer, so I said, 'We'll give you a laptop and we'll give you the program and I'll give you some scenes–and you can direct the scenes while you're just sitting by the pool.' He loves to do that stuff."

Spielberg tours the art department with Lucas, and they go over the script together. Though it initially sounded much more dramatic, what Lucas and Spielberg are doing is something they often do–collaborate– albeit, in this case, in a limited manner. "We have very, very similar sensibilities," George says.

FRIDAY, MAY 16, 2003–DAY ONE MINUS 7 WEEKS

Rob Coleman is here, along with the usual group, minus one: Iain McCaig's last day was May 9. Warren Fu and Alex Jaeger left some time before that. Today is John Goodson's last day. As the need for con-

Monday, May 19: In Sydney, drafting starts for the Alderaan cruiser conference room and other sets. Prefab construction begins on Stage 7 for the Mustafar conference room and the admiral's quarters. These two sets, among the largest, will take thirteen weeks to construct. On Stage 1, five weeks of construction on Padmé's veranda begins .

ceptual art dwindles, the inevitable downsizing of the art department has begun. On the table is a six-by-nine-inch birthday card reading, "Happy Birthday George! From the JAK Films art department."

Lucas shows up early. He conjures up the spirit of Spielberg by saying, "Our director's come up with a really good idea," which is for the battle on Mustafar: Obi-Wan and Anakin would end up on a large, burning piece of masonry on a lava flow, he explains. They'd have to stop fighting and, without speaking, start hacking off pieces with their lightsabers to create a path on which to jump to shore.

MONDAY, MAY 19, 2003–DAY ONE MINUS 6 WEEKS

ILM: ILM has been on the show now for about three weeks. Located in an industrial zone, its facility is a "rabbit warren," according to Coleman, who has been at ILM for ten years and who admits to still becoming disoriented "when they start punching new holes in walls." Made up of constantly reorganized interiors, lackluster cubes, temporary buildings, trailers, and makeshift work areas, ILM is all seemingly held together by the almost permanent squawking of a public-address system.

In the structure housing what will be the Episode III department, a big whiteboard posts projected schedules for the computer construction of characters and vehicles. The schedule is light for now, as most of the

"heavy lifting" won't begin till winter, when the department is fully staffed. As Coleman explains, the first stage is to build the skin, so the artists are divided into soft-surface/creature builders and hard-surface/vehicle builders. The next step is to create the "bones" or "chains" that move the asset. Then comes paint, and so on. It takes around six to eight weeks to fully realize a character or vehicle. ILM's first sequence, he says, will probably be the opening space battle. Theoretically, they should finish earlier this time–January 2005 for a May 2005 theatrical release.

Top: Dated April 9, the Sydney art department cyclorama of Palpatine's office complex reveals his office, waiting room, and antechamber. It also shows how Mace Windu and Palpatine measure up in the window where the two will have their showdown. Above: As of May 16, Palpatine's office set on Stage 7, after a couple weeks of construction. Above right: Coleman, Lucas, David, Wagner, Murnane, and Barnes examine the latter's lizard-head sculpt. Right: As of June 13, Padmé's veranda set on Stage 2 after several weeks of construction.

Rob's abode is small and dark; a bulletin board is covered with postcards, including one of John Lennon. Coleman reveals that he's having a hard time working up enough enthusiasm. On Episode I, he "just wanted to survive"; on Episode II, there was the creation of a digital Yoda to inspire him. But Rob describes Episode III as "having to climb Mount Everest–again."

FRIDAY, MAY 23, 2003

SR: In the art department, Burtt introduces to the artists editor Roger Barton, who's preparing for his long stint by studying the editing techniques Lucas used in Episodes I and II.

Lucas arrives, but, before he can start, the cell phone rings. Fay David says Jane Bay has Spielberg on the line. Lucas takes the phone and begins to discuss the DVD release of the *Indiana Jones* trilogy and *Indy IV*: "Hello. Sure. You're the boss. Uh-huh. I don't think we touched that or anything . . . No. We have a different point of view: you're more of a traditionalist; I'm more of an out-there kinda guy . . . That would be fine . . . I have to work all weekend . . . [Lucas begins okaying paintings while talking.] I like that idea. Well, that'll be the week before we start shooting–or how about the week after. Let me read it first. We have to agree, so we can be a united front . . . If anyone should know, you should know. . . . Well, I look forward to it. I'm excited about it. Okay. Bye-bye."

While they next study Mustafar fight storyboards, Thompson asks if it's okay for the duel between Anakin and Obi-Wan to shift back and forth in terms of who's aggressing whom. "They should reverse back and forth a couple times," Lucas agrees, "but Obi-Wan is the one who's come to kill him."

FRIDAY, MAY 30, 2003–DAY ONE MINUS 5 WEEKS

SR: Looking at a lizard sculpt, Lucas objects to the way the jaw closes. "If it doesn't look real, people don't buy it. Make yourself the dragon–become one with the dragon." Looking at some new takes on General Grievous, he rejects the new cape style with epaulets. He refers them back to Warren Fu's original, approved drawing, saying, "I really like this. This is moody, weird.

"That's it for me," he says, turning to Gregoire. "Did you have fun in LA?"

Gregoire has been traveling down south every so often to help Spielberg do his animatics for the Mustafar combat. "The first time I went down, I went with certain assets," Gregoire says. "I worked with Steven in the morning at his office at Amblin, and then George showed up. I showed Steven what we could do, and then those two kinda did their thing while I worked on the stuff that Steven had drawn out for me. The best approach we found was that I would 'drive,' instead of him actually moving the mouse around. Steven would draw umpteen sketches and then I would frame the shots and try to move the cameras around."

FRIDAY, JUNE 6, 2003–DAY ONE MINUS 4 WEEKS

SR: Lucas says to Coleman, "You did a great job with Yoda on MTV last night."

"Thanks. It was an incredible rush job."

"If you can do that, then you can do the whole film just as fast."

"That's what I was afraid of," Rob sighs. "I fell into your trap."

"You fell into it and now you can't get out of it," Lucas jokes. Turning to the others, he says, "We've got a new scene with Yoda and the Wookiees, with an AT-ST going through the water at night. I have a new ship, too. A Yoda escape pod for leaving Kashyyyk. The Wookiees pull the limb of a tree, and it comes out of the ground."

"We'll get on that," David says.

Looking at a strange vehicle, Lucas seems perplexed, so Church says, "It's really weird, built for droids."

"The only problem is, humans have to watch it," Lucas counters.

"That's it. We're back on schedule," he says as the meeting concludes. "And pretty soon, it'll start to make sense. Anne is typing [the second draft] now."

Saturday, June 1: At the Shrine Auditorium, Yoda receives an MTV Movie Award for Best Fight Scene for *Attack of the Clones*. In his acceptance speech—as created by animation director Rob Coleman, lead animator Jamy Wheless, cloth simulator Aaron Ferguson, and technical director Jean-Paul Beaulieu, and voiced by Frank Oz—Yoda says, "Hmmm...grateful am I this award to receive. To win, I did not expect. Promised myself, cry I would not." He then thanks George Lucas, Chewbacca, and others—but becomes angry when music cuts him off.

FRIDAY, JUNE 13, 2003–DAY ONE MINUS 3 WEEKS

SR: Today is the last art department meeting before principal photography begins. Present are Tiemens, Church, Jun, David, Thompson, Zhu, Frame, Gregoire, Wagner, Lee, Coleman, Barnes, Murnane, and Lostimolo. For Tiemens, Church, and David, it's been more than a year of intense activity. Although the three of them will continue to act as the art department, today marks the end of the major conceptual push. The remainder of the team will be broken up during the next few weeks, never to reconvene in such inspiring circumstances. "It was bittersweet," Tiemens recalls, while Church remembers, "My emotions were with the guys who were leaving."

Lucas arrives and starts by looking at Murnane's sculpts of the nos monster, asking, "Are we going to work on an eye for this guy?"

"The color for the eyes is this see-through, almost glaucoma eye...," Murnane responds, and Coleman adds, "They're reflective–he's gonna be in the cave and the lights from the droids will hit him."

"But it's good to get irises or something that give you a sense of direction," Lucas says. "Otherwise, it just becomes dead. It's hard to get him to act if you don't have eyes."

While studying Thompson's drawings of Yoda on a flying insect creature, Lucas hesitates, so the artist offers, "We were thinking on Kashyyyk that Yoda might have a local steed or something to bring his eye line up to the Wookiees."

"It's a possibility–but only during the escape," Lucas agrees. A few of the artists exchange pleased glances.

After reviewing the last piece of artwork at this last meeting, George asks, "That's it?"

"That's it. The last meeting," Fay says.

"All right, everybody happy?"

"Yeah, we're happy–are you happy?" a few answer simultaneously.

"Well, I'm done with my second draft–that makes me happy. Now I have to go write the third and fourth drafts–and get it done in two weeks!"

"Well, it's a long flight to Australia," Church jokes.

Lucas pauses before leaving.

"Have fun, guys. I'll come back with a movie," he says, adding to Coleman, "You'll come back with a headache."

Wednesday, June 4–Saturday, June 7: HD supervisor Fred Meyers conducts camera prep at Plus8digital in Burbank, California. Together they create a digital package that includes six lenses for production, a compact Cine Zoom lens for miniatures, tripods, matte boxes, HD monitors—in short, everything they'll need in Sydney except the cameras, which will be provided by Sony.

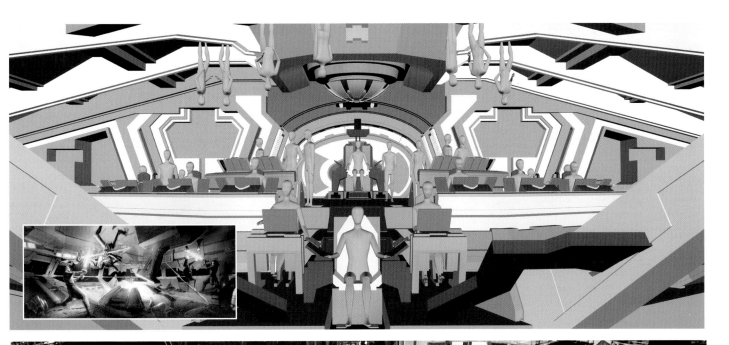

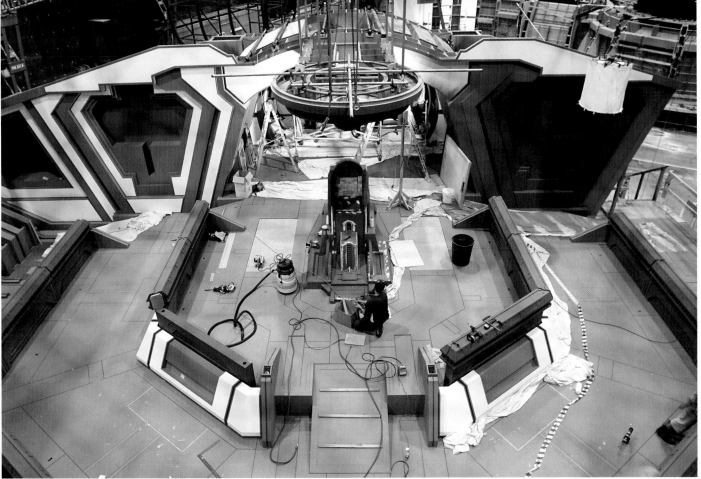

Saturday, June 7: Ewan McGregor (Obi-Wan Kenobi) arrives in Sydney; he starts stunt training the following Monday.

Wednesday, June 11: JAK-OZ videoconference—Lucas advises production that there's a new wet Wookiee scene, but says it may be difficult to accomplish. He'll discuss how to accomplish best with John Knoll, who has been counseling the use of a few "real" Wookiees.

Friday, June 13: The final JAK-OZ videoconference—In her notes to this last meeting, Sydney art department coordinator Colette Birrell writes, "Fay…that's it for teleconferences with George. SEE YOU SOMETIME IN THE NOT TOO DISTANT FUTURE! (Yeah baby!!!!)"

Top left: Six images of the last art department meeting, on June 13—Lucas exits the attic, traveling shortly thereafter to Australia. Far left: Yoda animation in preparation for his appearance on MTV. The artists worked in a "locked" room for six hours preparing the Jedi's acceptance speech, which consisted of about 3,500 CG frames. Above: On June 18, the Trade Federation cruiser bridge on Stage 1 after about five weeks of construction. Top: A Sydney art department CG shot shows how the set might look when battle droids walk on the ceiling—which scenario is further explored in a concept painting (inset).

"I'm starting to get one already," Rob says. "It's looking more and more like an animated movie."

"Well, that's what this is: Malleable film is called animation," Lucas says. "See you in September."

"Have a great time," Church says. "It was the best year of our lives."

"Well, the best is yet to come," Lucas says and closes the door behind him.

The 135-page revised second draft is dated June 13, 2003. In general, scenes have been refined; in preparation for shooting, they have been numbered. The major differences between this and the first draft are:

When OBI-WAN is hit by buzz droids, the emotional content is greater—ANAKIN insists on saving OBI-WAN, who is ordering ANAKIN to go on without him.

OBI-WAN and ANAKIN now both end up in the GENERAL's quarters. "This time we do it together," OBI-WAN says when COUNT DOOKU appears. However, COUNT DOOKU kicks OBI-WAN, who falls to the ground, unconscious. After killing COUNT DOOKU, ANAKIN insists on carrying the still-unconscious

OBI-WAN to safety, ignoring PALPATINE's orders to leave him behind.

Whereas in the earlier drafts ANAKIN dreamed that PADMÉ was falling into a pit of flame, in the second draft he sees her suffering in childbirth. She dies screaming, "Help me! Help, ANAKIN! ANAKIN, I love you. I love you."

A new scene with OBI-WAN, YODA, and MACE WINDU makes it clear that the Force is realigning and that a dark shadow surrounds the CHANCELLOR. Another new scene has MACE and OBI-WAN in a gunship accompanying YODA to a waiting Republic assault ship, which will take him to Kashyyyk. They discuss ANAKIN. OBI-WAN is confident and YODA says, "The chosen one, he is. Balance to the Force, he will bring." But MACE is skeptical and questions ANAKIN's loyalty to the Jedi Order.

In another new scene, PALPATINE insinuates to ANAKIN that OBI-WAN is meeting clandestinely with PADMÉ. The dialogue indicating that PALPATINE is responsible for ANAKIN's creation has been cut.

A new wordless shot has MACE, EETH KOTH, KIT FISTO, and SAESEE TIIN arriving at the Senate to arrest PALPATINE, "like gunfighters out of the Old West." ANAKIN enables PALPATINE to kill MACE and then bows before the Sith.

When YODA confronts the EMPEROR, he has the upper hand at first and quips, "If anything I have to say about it, at an end your rule is, and short it was, I must say."

During his duel with OBI-WAN, ANAKIN says, "This is the end for you, my friend. I wish it were otherwise. This is your last chance to join me." After OBI-WAN cuts off ANAKIN's legs, his tune changes:

                    ANAKIN
              Help me, Master.

Left: On June 18, Palpatine's office takes form on Stage 7, with recognizable details like the window that were worked out conceptually months before. Above: A Church painting of the duel on Mustafar, for which, Hayden Christensen (Anakin) and Ewan McGregor (Obi-Wan) prepare in Sydney, continuing to learn complex moves under the supervision of Nick Gillard on June 26 (inset). Right: Thompson's storyboards illustrate Jedi Master Shaak Ti's death at the hands of General Grievous aboard the Separatist cruiser.

OBI-WAN
Don't ask me, Anakin . . . you're evil.
You bring nothing but pain and
suffering. I can't help you.

ANAKIN
I hate you!

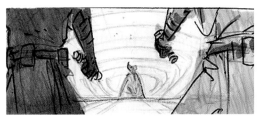

Later, it is clear that PADMÉ is dying of a broken heart.

MEDICAL DROID
Medically, she is completely healthy.
For reasons we can't explain, we
are losing her [. . .] She has lost the will
to live.

*And another key
exchange has been added:*

OBI-WAN
Do you think
Anakin's children
will be able to
defeat Darth Sidious?

YODA
Strong the Force runs, in the
Skywalker line.

*PADMÉ stays alive long enough to see
both children being born, and they're held
up for her to see. But she can "offer up
only a faint smile"—the smile Leia will
recall in Episode VI.*

*On Coruscant, when Darth Vader
regains consciousness, he asks:*

DARTH VADER
Where is PADMÉ? Is she all
right?

DARTH SIDIOUS
I'm afraid she died. . . .
It seems in your anger, you
killed her.

A low groan emanates from
VADER'S mask. Suddenly everything in the room begins to
implode, including some of the
droids. VADER screams, breaks
his bonds to the table, and
steps forward [. . .] VADER's
painful screams echo throughout
the center.

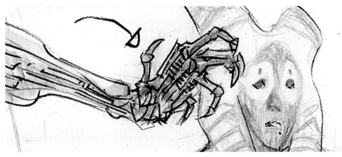

*The order of the end scenes has been
switched so that the last shot is now on
Tatooine: "OBI-WAN leaves OWEN and
the BABY, watching the twin suns set."*

**SYDNEY, AUSTRALIA: MONDAY, JUNE
16, 2003–DAY ONE MINUS 2 WEEKS**

On the lot of Twentieth Century
Fox Studios, housed within
Building 28's oval interior, the
Episode III production office is a
scene of concentrated action. Beneath
a ceiling that resembles a series of

inverted tepees, several assistants, drivers, technicians, and crew are tele-
phoning, faxing, e-mailing, walkie-talking, and just plain shouting. A *Return
of the Jedi* poster decorates one wall, and a *Phantom Menace* pinball machine–
its setting on UNLIMITED PLAY–resides next to the receptionist's desk.

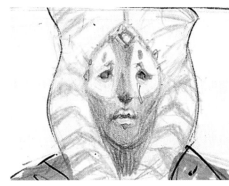

The northern wall of the office
area is divided into very plain, func-
tional work spaces that look out onto
a football field–sized quad. One of
these cubicles is McCallum's; another,
Lucas's. Their assistant, Jacqui Louez,
sits at a desk facing their work
spaces–essentially in
production's heart of
hearts.

Having arrived the
day before with his
family, Lucas is talk-
ing with script super-
visor Jayne-Ann
Tenggren about the
creation of a fourth
draft when Ewan
McGregor arrives.

"I know you!"
Lucas exclaims. "You're that suave
guy."

Before long, Lucas begins his
first extensive walkthrough of the
lot's seven stages and their work-
in-progress sets. With McCallum
and other department heads, he
arrives on Stage 7 to examine the
set of Palpatine's office. He looks
around, sips his coffee, and says,
"Home, sweet home."

He then talks things over, as
he will for each set, with Gavin
Bocquet. Much of their conversation is almost shouted as they
compete with the sometimes
enormous din of hammering,
sawing, and welding. McCallum
mentions that they have, this
time, a four-by-four-by-four
recording device, which gives
them higher resolution. Lucas
decides that they'll shoot a blank

plate, or "control take," of each set before shooting the actors, so they can digitally alter, or reproduce, each one in postproduction.

They then enter the set of the Alderaan space cruiser interior—an exact reproduction of the white corridor Lucas filmed back in 1976. "I love it," he says. "Maybe I could reshoot some of Episode IV. This particular set was where there was a lot of drama," he adds, referring to that film's last-minute, studio-decreed multiunit shooting. "The hardest part of these movies is that you get these great sets and you shoot on 'em for half a day—and then you have to destroy them and move on to something else."

Back in Building 28, Lucas goes over the shooting schedule with first assistant director (1st AD) Colin Fletcher. There are presently seventy shooting days scheduled, "but I'm sure there are things we can cut out," Fletcher notes. The two of them attack the schedule as if it were a riddle, puzzling out which set moves and costume changes they can eliminate to save time. "It's the hairdos that kill you," Lucas points out.

Next, he goes through binders of actors and actresses with casting director Christine King. Lucas is looking for handmaidens and other tertiary characters. He mentions that Keisha Castle-Hughes was incredible in *Whale Rider* (2002), but King says she's currently unavailable.

THURSDAY, JUNE 26, 2003–DAY ONE MINUS 4 DAYS

Lucas's fourth draft comes in at 129 pages typed. The differences between it and previous drafts are:

After ANAKIN kills COUNT DOOKU, PALPATINE says, "It's not the first time, Anakin. Remember what you told me about your mother and the Sand People." The story of DARTH PLAGUEIS has been augmented:

```
            PALPATINE
He became so powerful . . . the only thing
  he was afraid of was losing his power,
   which eventually he did, of course . . .
```

```
Unfortunately, he taught his
  apprentice everything he knew,
then his apprentice killed him in
         his sleep.
          (smiles)
  Plagueis never saw it coming.
It's ironic he could save others from
        death, but not himself.
     According to the legend,
   it was a power his apprentice
   found no value in. So the ability
    to save loved ones was lost
     with Plagueis "the wise."
```

As PADMÉ prepares to leave for Mustafar, she now forbids CAPTAIN TYPHO and her HANDMAIDENS from accompanying her, so their deaths on the Mustafar landing platform have also been cut.

And when ANAKIN lies dying, OBI-WAN's final words are new:

```
            OBI-WAN
You were the chosen one! It was said
    you would destroy the Sith,
   not join them. It was you who
  would bring balance to the Force,
   not leave it in darkness. You've
     become my brother, Anakin.
  I love you, but I won't help you.
```

"It's a downer," Lucas acknowledges. "The saving grace is that if you watch the other three movies, then you know everything ends happily ever after. Nevertheless, I now have to make a movie that works by itself, but which also works with this six-hour movie and this overall twelve-hour movie. I'll have two six-hour trilogies, and the two will beat against each other: One's the fall, one's the redemption. They have different tonalities, but it's meant to be one experience of twelve hours."

The last year has seen the written and visual creation of numerous and entire planets and civilizations, one iconic villain, one dragon-lizard, several Wookiees, and dozens of sleek starships. They've come into existence through numerous written drafts and thousands of images conveyed in drawings, paintings, sculpts, and storyboards. When principal photography begins, Lucas will move on to the real world of sets, a production crew, and actors, where much of this will be tested—and another draft of the script will be written.

From top down: Lucas with his key collaborators during the last days of preproduction at Fox Studios, Sydney, Australia: with McCallum; in the make-up department with Christensen (Anakin); in the art department with Gracie, Peter Russell, and Bocquet; in the creatures department with Rebecca Hunt and Dave Elsey; in the costume department with Biggar.

Top: (from left) First assistant director Colin Fletcher, DP David Tattersall, Lucas, and key gaffer Eddie Knight, in Sydney. Above: (from left) Dialogue coach Chris Neil, McGregor (Obi-Wan), script supervisor Jayne-Ann Tenggren, Natalie Portman (Padmé), and Lucas, during rehearsals.

Monday, June 23 to Friday, June 27: The veranda set is dressed and rigged.

PART II

PRINCIPAL PHOTOGRAPHY
The Moviemakers of OZ

PROLOGUE: The Crew

Twenty-seven years separates these two photos, the first (right) taken on the set at EMI Studios in 1976 (Mark Hamill as Luke, Lucas, Carrie Fisher as Leia, and Harrison Ford as Han) and the second—designed to mirror it—in 2003 on the set in Sydney (Christensen, McCallum, Lucas, Portman, and McGregor).

"When I did the first *Star Wars*," Lucas remembers, "I was confident primarily because of my inexperience. Now I'm confident because of my experience. When I did the first *Star Wars*, I was on my own in England, with a crew that was partly hostile, partly supportive. I made very close friends with the supportive part, and a lot of those guys went on to do the next two films. On these last three *Star Wars* films, I've been working with a group that I started with on *Young Indy*. So I have a lot of people who I've worked with for a long time—a talented, professional, experienced group—which makes everything easier, because even under the most stressful of times, this group is very good at working together."

The members of this core group are: producer Rick McCallum, production designer Gavin Bocquet, director of photography David Tattersall, costume designer Trisha Biggar, and financial controller Kathryn Ramos. Tattersall remembers that, way back in 1992, while shooting a scene for *Young Indy* on the grounds of a chateau in France, Lucas and McCallum were already talking of assembling essential personnel for the next *Star Wars* film.

This group would come to include those who began on either the *Star Wars Trilogy Special Edition* (1997) or *The Phantom Menace* (1999): animation director Rob Coleman, stunt coordinator Nick Gillard, visual effects supervisor John Knoll, supervising art director Peter Russell, property master Ty Teiger, script supervisor Jayne-Ann Tenggren, and others. "I really invest a lot of time trying to create the best atmosphere that I possibly can," McCallum says, "especially in my relationship with the people I work with. We've spent almost a lifetime together. Kathryn and I just celebrated fifteen years working together—to me, our lives are intertwined.

"The most sublime state of filmmaking is where everyone is interdependent," he adds. "No one person on the film can let anyone else down, because it has a ripple effect on the whole picture. It's incredibly collaborative—most people don't realize how collaborative it is, how intensely personal, how emotionally draining. You wake up at four-thirty A.M. and you finish around ten P.M. If you're not in the right physical and mental shape, you can go into a downward spiral."

✳ Shooting a Foundation

As the plane banks, travelers get their first glimpse of Sydney. "It's like San Francisco on steroids," Lucas would say. After weaving their way through customs and the tourist shops selling koala T-shirts, kangaroo dolls, and Aboriginal art, visitors to the Episode III set are usually met by a driver, who whisks them to Fox Studios, Australia.

During the twenty-minute trip on the left side of the road, travelers pass a variety of pubs, streets, residences, and a general decor reminiscent of London. Sydney was founded in 1778 as an English penal colony, but today it has the energy and optimism of a country not overwhelmed by its past.

Fox Studios is located on the city outskirts, adjacent to Sydney's soccer stadium and across from a large park. It has two arched entrances, one for the public and one for the crew. The former leads to a shopping area, playground, and multiplex. The latter leads to a kiosk staffed with good-natured guards. A hundred yards farther along, a second kiosk admits visitors into the heart of the studio: seven stages that will house Episode III's seventy-one sets, and about a dozen buildings that will house the supporting construction, props, costume, art, and creatures workshops.

Originally used for grazing cattle, and then as a fairground, these premises were converted to a studio in 1998. Yet the first film shot here—*A Daughter of Australia*—was back in 1922, and the studio's stages and streets bear the names of Australian film-industry luminaries: Chips Rafferty Lane, the Hector Crawford Stage, the Ken G. Hall Stage. But nothing ever hit these premises like *Star Wars*. A quick look around today reveals massive and continuous movement: trucks making deliveries, sets being painted, golf carts ferrying people. There are pylons, sacks of pebbles, metal girders, tents, cars, scissor lifts, props, and bicycles. The center of the studio is a tree-lined, hundred-yard-long grass quad, with wooden benches and many ibises—the Australian equivalent to the pigeon—on the lookout for crumbs.

"At the time Fox was considering starting a studio, I flew over to Sydney and met with the head of Fox, Kim Williams," McCallum says. "I was very reticent at first to shoot in a studio. I'd rather not have to worry about the film that's already in being late, or the film coming in behind you. It forces you into a situation that I didn't want our movie or George ever to be in. But after spending a week with Kim, I knew that he could deliver the studio—that it would be ready for us on time and that it was going to be a great place to work. He was such a decent man that I knew we'd have enough time on each side of our booking to be safe."

Lucas, McCallum, Hayden Christensen (*The Virgin Suicides*, 2000; *Life as a House*, 2001), Ewan McGregor (*Trainspotting*, 1996; *Big Fish*, 2003), Natalie Portman (*Cold Mountain*, 2003; *Garden State*, 2004), and many key cast and crew personnel arrived months, weeks, or days ago. "I've been here since the beginning of May," Christensen says, "getting in shape and learning the lightsaber fights."

"Hayden was here much earlier than I was," McGregor says, "but I had about three weeks of fighting, five days a week, for half-a-day at a time. It's much harder work now. On Episode I, I'd fight all day long, whereas now I'm like, 'Okay, guys, I think I've reached my limit.' It's repetition, repetition—but it's got to become fluid."

"I closed some of the actors' deals just days before we started shooting," McCallum admits. "I just didn't know how long we'd need them, until the script was done and the schedule set."

Indeed, the cornerstone of principal photography is the shooting schedule, which will be constantly revised as production gets ahead or falls behind. The keepers of this document are Lucas, McCallum, and 1st assistant director Colin Fletcher. Any changes they make have a butterfly effect on the whole production. Modifications are therefore immediately commu-

Previous spread: Padmé (Portman) and Anakin (Christensen) are the star-crossed lovers. Above: On June 25, gathered round Lucas are Mousy McCallum, assistant to the producer and director Jacqui Louez, Rick McCallum, and 2nd assistant director Deborah Antoniou. Below: The skyline of Sydney, Australia.

Fletcher is not the only one with questions, and so, a few days ahead of Day One, a technical read-through of the entire script takes place in the cafeteria, with all the department heads and key technicians present. As each scene is discussed, every foreseeable problem is tackled from a logistical point of view.

The evening before Day One, thousands of details are finally in place, and a giant machine is about to go into motion. Consisting of nearly a thousand crew members, many of whom just finished working on the two *Matrix* sequels, and literally tons of supplies, the machine's successful navigation of a projected sixty-three-day shoot will depend on the ability of its director and producer to keep the system moving, and to keep up morale while overcoming a variety of obstacles. With that in mind, McCallum is clear as to production's overriding priority: "There should be no hierarchy on the film, except that you have a writer-director who has an idea—and everything we do has to enable him to get to the purest state of realizing that idea. At the end of the day, that's what filmmaking is."

SHOOT DAY 1: MONDAY, JUNE 30, 2003

On today's Call Sheet, there is a note to the crew from McCallum and production supervisor Stephen Jones:

nicated to the 2nd and 3rd ADs, who create the Call Sheets that the actors and crew live by—as these list when and where everyone needs to be at any time of day.

Lucas and Fletcher have been poring over the schedule for the last two weeks. "George answered all my questions," Fletcher says. "We had about an hour a day. A lot of directors hate going through the schedule because it means facing reality, but George would just go through it as many times as I wanted."

Top: Christensen and McGregor arrived early in Sydney for their lightsaber boot camp: weeks of intensive training for the film's multiple duels, often with fencing double Kyle Rowling (middle). Above: During the technical read-through of the script in the cafeteria, Gillard, Knoll, Coleman, and Bocquet.

Dear Dudes and Dudettes,
Thank you for your hard work during preproduction.
We hope you know how much we appreciate everything you have done for the film. Have a great shoot.

Rick & Stephen

The Call Sheet also sets the stage for today, as it will for every day. The term *pt* indicates that only part of a scene will be recorded; the rest of that scene will be shot either another day or completed by ILM. Not every scene shot is listed.

NO. OF SCHEDULED DAYS: 63   SCHEDULED FINISH: Sept. 24
CREW CALL: 7:00
LOCATION: Stage 2
SET: INT. Elevator hallway—Federation cruiser
SCHEDULED SCENES SHOT: 5B (R2-D2 is ordered back to the ship), 11 (the Jedi squeeze through and seal the hatch in a main hallway), 14 (the seal holds when the explosion hits), 15 (they are attacked by wheel droids), 23 (Anakin & Obi-Wan step from the elevator), 16pt (battle takes place in the elevator), 27pt (Anakin with Obi-Wan over shoulder waits for elevator)

Though Day One Call sheet indicates that "crew call" is for 7:00 A.M., many of the crew and cast have arrived at 6:00 A.M. or well before, which will be the case for the duration of the shoot. In the cafeteria, a copious breakfast buffet is available starting at six, and many will fill up, since working days here are on average fourteen to fifteen hours long.

Lucas and McCallum arrive on the minimal set housed in Stage 2 just as daylight breaks outside. "I always love the first day–the energy, the

excitement," the latter exclaims. It is June Down Under–the beginning of winter–but still fairly warm. Lucas talks with visual effects supervisor John Knoll, who arrived about a week ago, and then spies a heater next to a chair with his name on it. "You'll need one in the next three months," a PA says, explaining that it will become colder and colder in these hugely empty stages.

As the crew prepares for the first setup, "sides"–bite-sized script pages for the day's relevant scenes–are distributed to Lucas, script supervisor Jayne-Ann Tenggren, and dialogue coach Chris Neil. Lucas asks that in the future they be delivered arranged in order of the scenes to be shot. He explains to Fletcher that he intends to cross out each scene as they finish it: "Believe me, it's very therapeutic."

Today's seven scenes are simple ones. For scene 23, all that Christensen and McGregor are required to do is exit an elevator, say a couple of lines, and walk off camera. When they arrive for rehearsal, Christensen is in his dressing gown and McGregor wears a sports jacket. They greet Lucas and prepare to block out the scene.

Note: A "take" refers to a single run-through of a scene or shot, which may be completed in one "take" or fifty "takes."

"The actors are on the set," Lucas announces to the crew, and the two shake hands with Fletcher. "Stand by to rehearse," Fletcher says. A bell rings, announcing that all extraneous work should cease and that no one can either enter or exit the sound stage. The bell also triggers a siren-like warning light on the stage's exterior wall.

"And . . . action!" Lucas calls out.

He then watches on a monitor as they rehearse. Immediately afterward, stand-ins Tom Maynard (Obi-Wan) and Peter Jackson (Anakin) take the actors' places.

"Basically, you rehearse with the actors so everyone can see what's going on," Fletcher explains. "The stand-ins watch what happens. The actors then get set up and complete their makeup while we start lighting the shot. We might get the stand-ins to go through the moves while we're lighting, so the cameras can rehearse. And when the lighting is complete and the actors are back on set, generally then we just shoot it."

At 8 A.M., they're ready for the control take. In a tradition dating back to the *Young Indy* days, McCallum operates the clapboard for the first shot

of the film. The bell sounds. "Here we go," Fletcher says. "Camera, speed, please."

"Okay, Rick, ready?" Lucas asks.

"V23," McCallum reads off the board. "Take one. 'A' camera . . ."

"And . . . action!" Lucas calls out.

"Good luck, everybody," Rick adds.

"Kick some ass! Let's do this in sixty days!" And begun, this shoot has.

"Beautiful," Lucas says after the control take. "Now let's try one with people."

The actors return from makeup in Jedi garb attended by Trisha Biggar, who is overseeing a couple of last-minute adjustments. At 8:26 A.M., they're ready for the first live-action take.

"Roll camera, roll sound," Fletcher requests. "And . . . action!" Lucas yells out.

After the take, McGregor informs Lucas that because he was situated behind the elevator door, he couldn't hear the word *action*. While crew fix that problem, Lucas reviews the scene with the actors, explaining that the Jedi are on the Separatist cruiser trying to find a kidnapped Chancellor–but

Above left: The ubiquitous heater always placed next to the director's chair. Above right: One of the flashing warning lights posted over stage doors. Left: McCallum performs his traditional clapboard duty. Above: Makeup artist Shane Thomas touches up Christensen as Lucas discusses scene 23 with McGregor.

they're aware that Count Dooku has baited a trap. "The trick part is the attitude," he says. "You don't have to be quite so serious about it. You *say*, 'It's a trap.' But your *attitude* is, *Noooo problem.*"

On the next take, Hayden's cloak gets caught in the door. On the following one, it is caught again. "Very good. Very good for the outtakes," Lucas says to Christensen. "Let's try one more—and lighten it up even

more." Take. Lucas walks onto the set. "I think we can go even lighter," he says to the actors.

The next take works. They're about to go tighter for close-ups, but Ewan's hair won't stay in continuity. Lucas asks Tenggren to intervene, but at that moment the actor gets his hair to obey. "All right! Nobody move!" he says, and they run through the scene without a hitch.

Later in the day, R2-D2 makes his first appearance. Cast and crew react visibly to his arrival, for the little astromech droid provides a physical link to the overall saga, and he reminds many here of their childhood experiences watching *Star Wars*. George remarks to Rob Coleman that the story of *Star Wars* is actually recounted by R2-D2 to the Keeper of the Whills, one hundred years after *Return of the Jedi. Journal of the Whills* is what Lucas titled his first outline of *Star Wars* back in 1972.

CAMERA WRAP: 19:10   SETUPS: 48   SCRIPT SHOT TODAY: 2m 28s
CATERING: Breakfast (140); lunch off-set crew (330); lunch on-set crew (351); afternoon tea (110).

SHOOT DAY 2: TUESDAY, JULY 1, 2003
LOCATION: Stage 2
SET: Federation cruiser interiors
SCHEDULED SCENES SHOT: 18B (Anakin climbs though hole in the ceiling); 21 (Obi-Wan fights droids)

Previous spread: Shooting on the Trade Federation cruiser hallway and elevator set. Top: 1st AD Fletcher with Lucas. Early versions of scene 16 called for the elevator door to be damaged in a Jedi battle with droids. Above: With droid wrangler Don Bies at the controls, R2-D2 prepares to make his entrance.

Outside, it's raining off and on. Inside, Lucas walks through the cool, dark stage interior until he arrives at the bright lights of the hot set. "I have a tendency to be a quiet person on the set," he explains. "I don't do a lot of yelling. I try to keep everybody happy and focused on what it is they're supposed to be doing, which is a challenge because there's always a lot of raw emotions on a movie set. But I've been doing this for so long that I've seen just about every crisis you can possibly imagine—and gotten through it.

"In working with the actors, I basically go over the scene with them and suggest what to do," he adds. "They know beforehand where we're going and what we're shooting. It's just a matter of getting that on tape. It's the same thing with the cameramen. I just assume we won't shoot till nine A.M., and then, after lunch, until three P.M., with forty-five minutes per setup. You have your wish list, then you have the realities."

His relaxed demeanor doesn't mean Lucas is unaware of the constant need for speed, as Fletcher remarks: "George sets himself challenges every day. What he's going to do, where he's going to be by lunchtime. He's like . . . incredible."

Today's scenes are again fairly straightforward. As the setups and the decors change, one thing about a set remains constant: the "video village"—a mobile command center that follows production everywhere. It's where Lucas watches two Panasonic TH-42PHD5 high-definition plasma wide-screen monitors that display in real time everything the two HDC-F950 Sony digital cameras record through their custom-built Fujinon lenses.

Seated beside him are Jayne-Ann Tenggren, Chris Neil, John Knoll, Rob Coleman, and ILM matchmove supervisor Jason Snell. All the village's equipment—monitors, tables, chairs, wiring—can be broken down and reassembled in a matter of minutes. The village is also where the most interesting conversations usually take place, and where McCallum comes to check on things. (He and his assistants remain in constant touch with on-set action via walkie-talkie).

"I was recommended by Francis Coppola, with whom I've worked on a number of movies," says Neil (*The Rainmaker*, 1997; *The Virgin Suicides*).

"The most challenging thing for me is coming in and trying to fit myself into the mix, to fill a role that hadn't been created on the other two films. It's a daunting task because you're dealing with the abstract and emotional world of artists and relationships."

"I'm advising George when questions come up [per visual effects]," Knoll says, "and answering questions that the [Sydney] art department may have. Jason Snell is getting measurements of camera positions and set measurements.

"But directing a movie is this really intense thing," he adds. "It's been described as being nibbled to death by ducks—and I don't want to be one of the ducks."

"The most important reason for *me* to be on set is to build a relationship with George," Coleman says. "We've collaborated before, so there's a history and a working relationship there—but a whole year goes by between Episode II and Episode III where I don't see him that much.

"It's also important for me to understand what George is thinking in terms of the interaction between an animated character and, say, Ewan McGregor. If I wasn't on set to hear a key piece of information, it could easily be a year before that little tidbit reaches me."

English-born Tenggren (*Sleepy Hollow*, 1999; *Road to Perdition*, 2002) has been at Lucas's side since *The Phantom Menace*: "The day that I flew up from LA to SF [to interview with Lucas], there was a terrific rainstorm and the plane was delayed for about three hours. Then there was a problem renting the car, so I arrived at Skywalker Ranch four hours late and was a complete wreck. I went in to see George, who looked a bit puzzled, because I really did look like a drowned rat. I said, 'Sorry, I was thwarted by the weather.' And he said, 'Well, what are you doing in this country anyway?' And we just hit it off. It was great. But it's only a good story because I got the job!

Top left: While shooting the June 30 elevator scenes, Lucas ("side" in hand) talks things over with McGregor and Christensen. Top right: The two Panasonic HD screens are plain to see in the video village. Middle top: McGregor (Obi-Wan) emerges from the ventilator shaft in scene 11. Middle bottom: Christensen (Anakin) and McGregor (Obi-Wan) are brothers-in-arms soon to fall prey to the dark side.

"I always feel that no matter what happens, George will always take the problem on board and come up with a solution," she continues. "There's never that fear element that the director will freak out. Whatever it is, good or bad, I always know I'm going to get a practical response—that doesn't always mean he's going to be pleased, but it means he's a real problem solver."

LOCATION WRAP: 19:57   SETUPS: 38   SCRIPT SHOT TODAY: 1m 25s

SHOOT DAY 3: WEDNESDAY, JULY 2, 2003
LOCATION: Stage 1
SET: INT. Padmé's apartment
SCENES SHOT: 69 (Obi-Wan and Padmé discuss Anakin),
71pt (Padmé tries to get the Senators on her side)

Today McGregor and Portman are doing their first scene together. As they wait, McGregor jokes to Portman about her character's amorous relationship with Anakin: "Yoda has become fiercely jealous," he says, and she laughs.

"Okay, here we go," Fletcher announces. "Roll cameras, please."

"It was so exciting to do substantive scenes with Ewan this time, because I respect him so much as an actor," Portman recalls. "He's really serious about the work, but he also lightens up the set."

"Get ready for rehearsal–as soon as we can, folks," Fletcher says, urging the crew on to the next setup. The following scene, in which Padmé rallies fellow Senators against Palpatine, is the first to include Anthony Daniels (C-3PO). In full costume, Daniels walks onto the set in his unmistakable manner. Seeing him, Lucas announces, "*Star Wars* has arrived." The two shake hands.

As the first few setups are completed, however, it is nearly impossible to hear the actors' voices, for the grating sound generated by C-3PO's costume whenever he moves drowns them out. Consequently, some takes are recorded without him. "I worry sometimes," Daniels admits. "People are in this really beautiful scene and I'm clanking through it, and I know they're going to have to replace everything they say."

LOCATION WRAP: 19:10   SETUPS: 38   SCRIPT SHOT TODAY: 2m 37s

SHOOT DAY 4: THURSDAY, JULY 3
LOCATION: Stage 1
SET: Int. Padmé's apartment
SCENES SHOT: 75 (Anakin questions Padmé about Obi-Wan's visit),
54pt (Anakin awakens in a panic and weeps)

Every set is attended to by dozens of technicians: grips, gaffers, makeup artists, and many more. Despite their number, which is relatively small for a film of this size, they make very little noise—which doesn't mean there isn't a lot of talking. It's just that everyone is whispering into their headsets. At any given time, there may in fact be at least twenty conversations going on without any two people actually standing next to each other.

One ongoing conversation has "A" camera operator Calum McFarlane giving directions to his crew, who operate the Techno crane on which is perched one of the two digital cameras. McFarlane always sits in or near the video village and is in fairly constant communication with Lucas. The director's desires to tighten up or pan are transmitted by McFarlane to his crew and into his own deft movements with the mechanisms that control the camera. "I don't think about the pedals and wheels," he says. "If you think about it, you're dead."

McFarlane's deadpan wit and calm will complement Lucas's, creating a nucleus of humor throughout the shoot. A second-generation Australian, McFarlane (*Moulin Rouge*, 2001; *The Last Samurai*, 2003) was given a camera when he was fifteen. His father said he'd pay for the developing if the teenager wrote down the exposures and shutter speeds. "I try and make the director and everyone look good," he says. "And there are people below me who are helping me out. The last thing I want is some poor bugger at ILM to have my face up on a dartboard, saying, 'My God, I've just spent the last few months cleaning up stuff he could've fixed in five minutes on the set.' "

Whatever McFarlane records is also being captured from another angle by Simon Harding's "B" camera, because Lucas uses two cameras on nearly every shot. Harding had been laid off in the United Kingdom some years before, so he took a Steadicam course and emigrated to Australia, where his

talents were welcomed by its nascent film industry. He describes working with Lucas as "fantastic" and wishes it would never end.

In the video village, while waiting, Lucas is describing his experiences during the making of Coppola's *The Rain People* (1969) to Chris Neil. A few yards away, they're putting on Anthony Daniel's C-3PO face. Droid supervisor Don Bies fastens together the two headplates that conceal him. "Don Bies did re-create the neck in a way that doesn't choke me," Daniels says, gratefully. "It used to be that I felt like Darth Vader was gripping me in every scene."

Bottom left: A typical formation in the video village—"A" camera operator Calum McFarlane talks with McCallum, Knoll, match move supervisor Jason Snell, and Lucas, as Neil studies the script. Top left: Another typical snapshot has Tenggren, Neil, Lucas, and Fletcher studying a scene on the monitors. Top right: While waiting to shoot scene 69 in Padmé's apartment, Portman and McGregor talk. Above left: "Star Wars has arrived"—Anthony Daniels (C-3PO) meets Lucas on the set (electrician Alex Laguna is in background), prepared for scene 71. Above right: Droid technician Justin Dix and Bies help Daniels get into costume.

McGregor is next to arrive on set. "I've had a couple of moments on Episode III that have taken me back to when I was a child watching *Star Wars*," he says. "And they've been both with Anthony Daniels, with See-Threepio. I don't think I was in a scene with him in the other two. When I was on set with See-Threepio, I really remembered what it was like to be six or seven and watching these films. And I felt the excitement of being in them, you know–now."

Later that afternoon, McCallum and Lucas are discussing the last scene of the day, a shot that has Anakin and Padmé in bed. The audience will

When Christensen arrives, Lucas shows him where on the bed he'd like him to sit when he awakes from his nightmare: "You pop up and throw the sheets back." To Portman, he says, "It's like when you were sleeping with the bugs crawling all over you [in Episode II]. But now you've got a big bug sitting next to you."

LOCATION WRAP: 20:15   SETUPS: 37   SCRIPT SHOT TODAY: 3m 10s

see only the back of her head, but Hayden has asked for Natalie to be present–it's an emotional moment for Anakin, who's having terrible nightmares, and the actor feels her presence will add to his performance.

It becomes a race against time to get the last shot: "I have forty minutes left. I have to shoot the scene. It's going to be very tight," George says to Tenggren.

Top: McGregor and Daniels share a scene together on Padmé's veranda. Above left: Back in June, costume props supervisor Ivo Coveney working on Darth Vader's helmet and breastplate–acoutrements that Anakin Skywalker will soon be needing, as his dreams (in scene 54) push him toward evil (above right). Above middle: Lucas discusses a scene with Portman and McGregor. Above, far right: Bocquet in the Sydney art department, and with art director Phil Harvey and Russell on the set. Right: Lucas frames a shot for "B" camera operator Simon Harding and McFarlane.

SHOOT DAY 5: Friday, July 4, 2003

LOCATION: Stage 2

SET: Int. Padmé's veranda—Coruscant

SCENES SHOT: 66 (Padmé wants Anakin to ask the Chancellor to stop the fighting)

This is the fourth day on the veranda. "The Padmé set was like the kind made for MGM musicals," Jay Laga'aia (Captain Typho) recalls. Of course, beautiful sets like this one were conceptually born back in the art department of Skywalker Ranch, but they've been brought into three-dimensional form with the aid of multiple disciplines in Sydney: set decorating, props, construction, paint, fiberglass, and others. All of these departments—about four hundred people strong—are overseen by the head of the JAK Australia art department: production designer Gavin Bocquet.

"In theory, being the head of the department, I supervise everything—*in theory*," Gavin says. "But of course, there's a whole hierarchy of delegation and so many good people on the ground. I'm very interested in the technical drawings, so I'm very much in-hand with all the draftsmen, but when it starts to be the building side of it—particularly on a film of this size—then the art directors who are looking after those sets will be the ones on the ground checking on a daily basis that the details are right."

The art department is located in Building 48 at the far eastern end of the lot. It's a hangar-like locale, where a Jedi starfighter, airspeeder, and couches sit downstairs. One room is entirely dedicated to blueprints, hundreds of which hang from racks. Upstairs, in a U-shaped series of rooms, are the draftspeople, CAD technicians, model builders, and art directors.

"Production designers and art directors all have this blind faith that everybody is doing their job properly," Bocquet says, "but to write a textbook about it would be

hard. Our scheduling and budgeting amounts to hundreds of thousands of dollars—and yet there is no book on film budgeting. Generally, you have a ballpark figure, say sixty thousand dollars. And then the construction manager and Ian [Gracie] and Peter [Russell] will break that down into how many carpenters and how many painters and how many nails. And it's amazing how close very often the ballpark figure is to the final one. I suppose that justifies experience. But I find it fascinating—and frightening—if you step back from it."

The son of a bank manager, Bocquet says that his "benchmark film" was *2001: A Space Odyssey* (1968), which he saw thirteen times. Another big influence was Gerry Anderson's work (*Thunderbirds Are GO*, 1966). After studying product design at the Royal College of Arts in London, he was put in touch with production designer Norman Reynolds, who was working on *Return of the Jedi*. Gavin was hired and helped on Jabba's skiff, among other things.

Years later—after working on many films, including Steven Spielberg's *Empire of the Sun* (1987)—he returned to the Lucas fold when McCallum needed someone for *Young Indy* who, in addition to being a top-notch production designer, was also familiar with Czechoslovakia. Lucas and McCallum had opted to film much of the TV series there, and Bocquet's employment was sealed thanks to his experience in Prague working on Steven Soderbergh's 1991 film, *Kafka*.

"Basically the global control of all of the art department is down to Gavin," Peter Russell says. "Directly below Gavin is the main art department, set decoration, and props. Gavin takes concepts and works them up into viable set proposals, which are then handed down through myself or the other art directors [Ian Gracie and Phil Harvey]

every little thing. And it goes on for three years solid, nearly every day of the week, hundreds of questions every single day. It never lets up. A friend of mine once said in every shot of a movie, there's a thousand ideas—and that's true actually."

"It is a very big machine," Ian Gracie agrees. "We have in excess of sixty-seven sets, which is a lot to rotate through seven sound stages. And George and Rick are very much aware of how much it takes to make a movie, so we have to be frugal. We try to double up on sets and re-use pieces just to make life a little easier and cheaper. Half the job of the art department is to not only make it look good, but to make it fiscally viable."

"Most films are road movies: They're on location, they're contemporary," McCallum sums up. "Or if they're period films, they use period locations. But everything in the *Star Wars* universe has to be built. There's no place you can go and rent a *Star Wars* prop—it's just a different kind of filmmaking."

Back on Stage 2, "B" camera operator Harding is using a Steadicam for a scene that starts out with talk about Anakin and Padmé's unborn child. "I'm having a hard time shifting from the baby to the politics of the scene," Portman says, but Lucas assures her it's okay.

Later, Lucas, McCallum, and Fletcher go over the shooting schedule. McCallum still thinks they can finish in less than sixty days. In the darkness behind them, only C-3PO's luminous eyes are visible.

LOCATION WRAP: 20:03   SETUPS: 20   SCRIPT SHOT TODAY: 2m 55s

SHOOT DAY 6: MONDAY, JULY 7, 2003
LOCATION: Stage 2
SET: Int. Padmé's veranda—Coruscant
SCENES SHOT: 116 (Anakin tells Padmé of the rebellion and leaves for Mustafar)

Over the weekend, Samuel L. Jackson (Mace Windu), Peter Mayhew (Chewbacca), and Ian McDiarmid (Palpatine) arrived in Sydney. On set, Jackson greets Lucas, who gives him a hug. "It's good to be here," Jackson says.

to our eight draftsmen—and they're the backbone of the department; they're the guys who actually do the mileage. Up until then, it's all sketches; from then on, it can be measured, priced, budgeted, and painted. Next, you do an overall assembly drawing and up to twenty subsequent drawings for detail."

Of course, the director is consulted at each stage. "I guess I've been accused of being a micromanager," Lucas says, "but as far as I'm concerned, that's what making a movie is all about. I'm really responsible for every single detail on the picture. I work with a lot of very talented and creative people, but I have to make sure that it's exactly what I want it to be, because it's so critical that it look natural and fit into the environment. So I have to spend a lot of my time answering questions and making decisions about

Top left: Coleman, Knoll, Bocquet, and Russell in the Sydney art department. Middle left: Lucas and Bocquet study a maquette. Above left: A concept painting of Padmé's veranda by Tiemens—this painting is part of the visual script, whose purpose is to act as a lighting and reference guide throughout production; it contains paintings by the Skywalker Ranch art department for every scene in the movie (for more information, see page 222). Above: A tender moment in Padmé's apartment. Right: Portman (Padmé) in the green cut-velvet robe.

"Welcome home," Lucas replies.

While Christensen and Portman rehearse, Lucas and Jackson talk. "Did you get in this morning or last night?"

"Saturday. I've played two rounds of golf already!"

"Well, we're at it again," Lucas says.

"To be back at Fox Studios, among the army of people that create what all the fans know as *Star Wars* is pretty wonderful," Jackson would later add. "For many, this will be the height of my career–the one thing that peo-ple will never forget–because it'll be part of some-thing way bigger than anything else I've done. I actually tend to forget how really enormous this process is and what a gigantic family feeling it is. When you come together at lunchtime, every-body knows everybody. You look outside and there's a football game going on, and there are people standing around talking, and there are people riding on bicycles, and there are peo-ple gathered together who have known each other for a very long time."

On the set, Christensen and Lucas are discussing Anakin's temperament when he returns to Padmé's apartment after slaughtering Jedi at the Temple.

"Do you think there's more or less a sense of urgency?" Christensen asks.

"You're full of adrenaline because, one, you've spent the whole night killing people, and, two, the situation is not good: The Jedi Council has tried to overthrow the Republic," Lucas replies. "That's news to everybody. Take a little bit of time with that. When you say, 'I will not betray the Republic'–that's your rationalization. So you're very strong on that."

Lucas then talks to Portman about Padmé's thoughts: "You're saying, *This is* not *the guy I married.*"

Speaking of Anakin's warning to Padmé, George suggests, "When you get to 'You need to distance yourself,' I'd take that a little slower."

"So it's almost threatening," Hayden agrees.

"Yeah–and the slower you take it, the more threatening it becomes."

Back in the video village, Knoll tells Lucas that on-set personnel have assured him that an impending set change will take only a few moments. Ian McDiarmid joins them. "Hi, Ian. How are you doing?" Lucas says. "Welcome to the picturesque veranda." He then walks to the set and says to Christensen, "Make sure it's personal. It goes up and down. Take a few beats [pauses] in there."

"You understand where my instincts are coming from," Christensen says. "I'm trying to give it sort of a monotone."

"Yeah, but a monotone isn't right. You're emotional here. You've made a decision–but you don't know if it's the right decision . . . There's always this good in you, and this little part is always asking, *What am I doing?* Even at the very end. That's what makes you turn and kill the Emperor."

Christensen nods in agreement.

"At this point, you're not completely cold. The point where you become numb and flat is when you say, 'I hate you' to your best friend," Lucas continues, adding, "That last take was really good."

"Sure."

"I spent the whole weekend rewriting the scene with you and Palpatine, where you turn. I've added some more to that. I've stretched it out and given you a little more to go on in terms of him pulling you in."

"Nice."

"Anyway, I know we can do this."

Returning from the set, Lucas tells McDiarmid about the rewrite, noting that Jayne-Ann will give him the new dialogue. He explains that the scene now has more justifications for Palpatine's behavior. "You're just misunderstood," George says.

"Of course," Ian smiles.

LOCATION WRAP: 19:10   SETUPS: 35
SCRIPT SHOT TODAY: 3m 21s

SHOOT DAY 7: TUESDAY, JULY 8, 2003
LOCATION: Stage 2
SET: Int. Padmé's veranda–Coruscant
SCENES SHOT: 140 (Obi-Wan tells Padmé that Anakin has gone to the dark side)

On the veranda set, the actors are having difficulty. "Oh, I just want to get through it," Lucas says mostly to himself, after the third mistake. McGregor asks if they could stop a moment so he can collect himself. After the next take, the scene is finished without error and Natalie gives Ewan a hug.

Meanwhile on Stage 4, Jackson is rehearsing his lightsaber battle with Nick Gillard and the swordsmen. They go back and forth repeating the moves on a wide, long red carpet marked with masking tape. Dressed in a

black T-shirt, dark blue sweatpants, and a baseball cap, Jackson goes through the moves in slow motion. "Even your defensive moves are attacking," fencing double Kyle Rowling says to Jackson.

"Nick and I have been talking about this for a couple of years," Jackson says. "And he has graciously been trying to figure out a really spectacular [light]saber battle for me to do. He's combined a lot of different styles, so that it looks very good and it travels well. The fight actually makes me dominant, it makes me vulnerable, it makes me sneaky. Nick is always trying to find things that make Mace at ease yet lethal. The fight that I'm doing here, I had to learn pretty quickly. I had to learn some ninety-seven moves in two to three days, and then learn to speed them up *and* learn to move."

Stunt coordinator-sword master Nick Gillard was born, grew up, and still lives in Brighton, England. "My father was in the navy, so I was sent to military school when I was twelve," he says. "They dropped me off but I quit that school. There was an advert in the newspaper for riders for a circus, so I went along. I did trick riding and we also ran a medieval jousting tournament. My parents came to take me out, but my mum realized I was

having a good time, and it was keeping me off the streets. I was there from twelve to probably twenty, but I went into the stunt business when I was eighteen. We got called at the circus to go and work on a film, *The Thief of Baghdad* [1978]. That was it for me. We got good food. It wasn't money or anything–it was the food.

"I was on the set of *Jedi*; I had just become a stuntman," Gillard recalls. "Mark Hamill actually wanted me to double him, but it didn't happen. In England, to be a stuntman or -woman, you have to be an instructor in six sports just to get on the register. You have to have a fighting one, a gymnastic one, a trampoline one, a water one, and a horse-riding one. You have to be category ten in skydiving. And then you do five years probation where you can only work under a stunt coordinator, a full member. And then you do another three to five years where you can coordinate yourself but not others. It all goes before a committee each time, and they work out when you've gained enough experience."

Back on set, Ewan and Natalie continue. Portman is becoming appropriately emotional as Obi-Wan tells her character that her husband has done terrible things. After one take, she immediately asks, "Can we go again?" in an effort not to lose the moment.

After subsequent takes, Lucas says, "I'm happy. I got two different good takes. Our work here is done."

LOCATION WRAP: 19:45   SETUPS: 24   SCRIPT SHOT TODAY: 2m 42s

---

Previous spread: A panoramic view of the veranda courtesy of John Knoll. Above left and middle: Lucas discusses with Portman and Christensen an emotional scene. Concept artist McCaig has this to say about Padmé's tragedy: "You have a person who began so naive and idealistic. And here she is at the end of her life still idealistic. She believes her love can redeem Anakin—even at the end, she believes it." Above right: Christensen (Anakin) with his friend and fight instructor Nick Gillard.

SHOOT DAY 8: WEDNESDAY, JULY 9, 2003

LOCATION: Stage 2, Stage 3

SET: Int. Padmé's veranda

SCENES SHOT: 55 (Anakin tells Padmé about his dream)

After this scene wraps, the veranda will be destroyed, decimated in a few hours, whereas it took the construction department more than seven weeks to make it.

"The veranda was tricky," construction manager Greg Hadju says. "Nothing's straight and square on *Star Wars*. It really stretches the carpenters, particularly. A couple of the foremen are good mathematicians and really understand practical geometry and the development of arcs. We've managed to track down some books and have them republished for us, too. After Episode II, they said, 'When's the next one happening, 'cause we've never done such a complicated job and we've never had our skills stretched like this.' They all live for *Star Wars* basically."

In the creatures department building, Peter Mayhew is having his first fitting in the new Chewbacca costume. Under the care of creatures shop creative supervisor Dave Elsey and supervisor Rebecca Hunt, it's here that all eight Wookiee costumes are being made, averaging twelve weeks each. Indeed, it takes a week of ten-hour days for one person to add the black hair to one particular Wookiee suit. The twenty or so craftspeople working here also fabricate Neimoidians, Mon Calamari, casts of Darth Sidious, and

so on. Tacked to one board are dozens of ears to choose from. In a box rests baby Luke Skywalker, whose seams are clearly visible.

"When I was a kid, all I used to do was watch horror movies," Dave Elsey recalls, "which made me what I am now: a maker of monsters. It was only my parents pointing out that it's actually not doctors that make monsters, but the makeup people. So I said, 'Great. Now I know what I want to do for the rest of my life.'

"So I'm in charge of the actual creating of the things–making them, sculpting them, painting them, sticking them on, and implementing things–and Becky [Rebecca Hunt] makes sure that I do that on time and on budget."

After they finish putting his head on, Mayhew does his characteristic head tilt and stands up, towering over the technicians. "We're going to need a stepladder for on-set checks, aren't we?" one technician notes. Mayhew flexes his biceps and says, "The Wookiee is back."

In the video village, Lucas is saying, "If I'd taken the prequel trilogy to a marketing company, Episode I would have started here [with Episode III]–and Episodes II and III would've been about Darth Vader killing people. But in the end, I wouldn't be able to write movies like that."

On this occasion, because there's ample time, Lucas continues with his perspective on the *Star Wars* saga: "If you see them in order, it completely twists things about. A lot of the tricks of IV, V, and VI no longer exist. The real struggle of the twins to save their father becomes very apparent,

whereas it didn't exist at all the first time [audiences saw Episodes IV, V, and VI]. Now Darth Vader is a tragic character who's lost everything. He's basically a bitter old man in a suit. 'I am your father' was a real shock. Now it's a real reward. Finally, the son knows what we already know.

"It's a very different suspense structure. Part of the fun for me was completely flipping upside down the dramatic track of the original movies. If you watch it the way it was released, IV, V, VI, I, II, III—you get one kind of movie. If you watch I through VI, you get a completely different movie. One or two generations have seen it one way, and the next generations will see it a completely different way.

"It's extremely modern, almost interactive moviemaking. You take blocks and move them around, and you come out with different emotional states."

LOCATION WRAP: 19:45   SETUPS: 21   SCRIPT SHOT TODAY: 2m 49s

SHOOT DAY 9: THURSDAY, JULY 10, 2003
LOCATION: Stage 5
SET: Int. Jedi Temple—council chambers
SCENES SHOT: 62 (Anakin is approved as the Chancellor's representative)

Left: Peter Mayhew returns as the Wookiee Chewbacca; prosthetic make-up/fabrication technician Kristelle Gardiner (right inset) checks on things in the creatures department in building 48. On July 9, as word spreads throughout the studio that Mayhew is in full costume for the first time, many visitors come to pay their respects—including a familiar astromech droid. Alas, the two will have to wait nineteen "story years" to meet again on film, as Episode III has no scenes with them both. Above right: Lucas studies the Jedi Council layout.

The Jedi Council set, which seems at once familiar and larger than it appears on screen, has been built on a raised platform. In fact, many of the sets are built that way, which allows for more things to happen around and under the construct, and for the bluescreen to be evenly lighted.

Alien Jedi arrive and take their places for rehearsals. Lucas walks from one to the other, greeting the Council. "You found your old chair," Lucas says to Jackson.

"Everyone quiet, please!" says Fletcher, who, at one time, with all these aliens about, might have felt bewildered. "At first I didn't know the *Star Wars* language," he admits. "People were talking about 'Neimoidians'—and I just didn't know what they were. So I went out and got some of the *Star Wars* books, and went through them to understand."

Lucas looks over the composition of the Council members and has one alien change chairs. Jackson asks whether, when Anakin arrives in the room, he can point Anakin to a seat. Lucas agrees that it'd be a good idea.

"Is there someone I'd be addressing in particular?" Hayden asks.

"Yoda, Ki-Adi-Mundi, or Mace—the senior triumvirate," Lucas answers.

During the first rehearsal, Christensen paces to show Anakin's displeasure with the Council. But Lucas explains, "You can't really wander around while you're arguing with them. It's more West Point."

LOCATION WRAP: 20:30   SETUPS: 44   SCRIPT SHOT TODAY: 3m 59s
TRAVEL: Christopher Lee (Count Dooku/Darth Tyranus) flew Auckland-Sydney.

SHOOT DAY 10: FRIDAY, JULY 11, 2003

LOCATION: Stage 7
SET: Int. Palpatine's private office
SCENES SHOT: 59 (Palpatine and Anakin discuss the Jedi Council)

Anthony Daniels has walked over to the makeshift editing suite on the second floor of Stage 2. In a bare room with standard office furniture and a few computers, editor Roger Barton has called up C-3PO's scenes on the Avid for Daniels to study and then overdub. "Pardon me, my ladyship, is there any way I might be of service?" he intones. For each line, Daniels does a few readings till both he and Roger are satisfied. Sometimes, they add a joke. "George will kill me!" Anthony predicts.

"George occasionally lets me fiddle with the lines, because every actor becomes an expert in their own role," Daniels explains. "But I wouldn't want the responsibility he has on these movies. I've realized that if he walks by and doesn't acknowledge you, it's not that he's being rude, it's just that his head is full of a whole universe—some of which is about to crash."

Meanwhile on the cavernous Stage 7, Christensen and McDiarmid are

rehearsing the scene in which Palpatine appoints Anakin to represent him on the Jedi Council. Lucas reflects out loud that he could've filmed the rehearsal: "I could have done it all in one shot this morning and we could've saved a day."

"Well, you're keeping people employed," McFarlane says.

Scene 59 is long on dialogue, and, at the end of a long day, they do another take. "That was brilliant," Lucas says. "I'd say we got it."

There's applause, and Lucas walks over to Christensen and McDiarmid. "There were shades of different performances that I like. Two takes were very good," he says. "I'll see you guys tomorrow to figure out next week's work. The marathon week." Lucas and Christensen hug goodbye. The cast and crew seem happy with the way the second week of principal photography has gone—a level of comfort has been established.

Lucas shakes David Tattersall's hand. "You did a good job."

"Are we rehearsing tomorrow [Saturday]?" David asks.

"Yes, probably ten to one."

LOCATION WRAP: 19:45   SETUPS: 29   SCRIPT SHOT TODAY: 2m 55s

SHOOT DAY 11: MONDAY, JULY 14, 2003

LOCATION: Stage 7
SET: Int. Palpatine's private office
SCENES SHOT: 94 (Palpatine revealed as a Sith Lord)

"Let's hold the work." Fletcher requests. The warning bell sounds. "This is a long scene, everybody, so find a place that's comfortable. No movement on the stage," he adds.

"And . . . action!" Lucas calls out.

McDiarmid and Christensen, Emperor and Jedi, circle each other as they converse. Cut. Lucas reviews with the two how he wants the scene blocked. Take. The director asks for more surprise and more energy from Christensen—more incredulity—as he discovers that the Supreme Chancellor is in reality a Sith Lord. Looking off the set, Lucas spots McCallum and Bocquet, who is waiting to ask how many chairs he wants in the opera box.

"George suddenly invented an opera scene," Bocquet says. "So we needed a theater box, and we literally had a day. So we took three of the chairs out of Palpatine's red office and did a quick repaint job, changed the back, and added fabric—all the things we could do in, like, four hours.

Even in the world of multimillion-dollar filmmaking—thanks to the early days of dressings, greeblies, and old aircraft parts—George loves the idea that if you stick a few things on and paint them silver with care and attention, they'll look great."

Take. "That smile at the end worked," Lucas says to McDiarmid. As the crew prepares another setup, he and McCallum talk about the impending Mace-Palpatine fight. "If I can get through that fight in one day, I'm home free," Lucas says.

After lunch, on Stage 7, the cameras roll, and Ian flubs his lines. During the next take, Hayden says his line, "I should kill you," but Ian responds, "Yes, you should—except for the fact that I'm standing on your cloak."

While waiting for a new setup, Lucas consults with two makeup artists, who are showing him photos of Senators for approval. "We've never really done eye shadow," he explains. "It's not part of our universe."

Going from choreography chores, to makeup and costume decisions, to camera setups, to answering a dozen rapid-fire questions, Lucas moves swiftly from subject to subject. "It's like cooking," he says, "which is like chaos. But if you're really good, you can make sure that everything comes

Left: The hallway leading to Palpatine's antechamber is the locale for the intense scene 59 between Sith and Jedi during which Anakin is tempted (insets). Above: The rigging is plainly visible above the set of Palpatine's office. Top: Technical supervisor

Michael Blanchard (standing) and assistant editor Jett Sally in the editing suite on the second floor of Stage 2.

off at exactly the same moment. When I go to film schools, sometimes I get asked, 'When you're doing a movie, I see that you're always asked a lot of different questions. How do you know what the right answer is?' And I say, 'If you don't know what the right answer is, then you're not a director.' The director has to take in what everybody else is doing, which takes training—but the way you know is in your gut."

"One of the things that can go wrong, if you don't have a strong leader," McCallum agrees, "is that you end up with a production designer making his own film, a director of photography making his own film, a costume designer making her own film—all of them making their own best interpretation of what they think the movie is. That's why I've always loved working with a writer-director. There are fewer misunderstandings."

On set, Lucas says to the actors, "You can slow it down a little bit. If we try and keep it as slow as we can, we'll be there."

Tracks are added for a dolly shot that will enable the camera to circle the actors as they circle each other. McDiarmid is now very much into character, as is Christensen. Multiple takes later, they're done. McDiarmid sits down next to Lucas in the video village. "I'm beginning to believe it!" Ian says of the scene.

Group discussion then turns to the next day. "Tomorrow's just three and one-eighth pages," Lucas says to McCallum. "And I talked to David already—he's got it lit—we're ready to roll."

"Beautiful," Rick responds.

LOCATION WRAP: 20:00   SETUPS: 31   SCRIPT SHOT TODAY: 3m 52s

SHOOT DAY 12: TUESDAY, JULY 15, 2003
LOCATION: Stage 7
SET: Int. Palpatine's office
SCENES SHOT: 89 (delegation of Senators meet Palpatine); 99pt (Palpatine cuts down Kit Fisto, Eeth Koth, Saesee Tiin, and fights Mace Windu)

The next shot begins what will be a series of scenes pitting Mace Windu against Chancellor Palpatine, first verbally—then physically. On a fairly large set, flanked by three fellow Jedi, Mace walks through the hallway to Palpatine's antechamber. "When Mace grabs his sword, you guys grab your swords, too," Lucas instructs them. But he then notices that the supporting Jedi are wearing awkward gloves made of rubber, and says, "Uh-oh. This is going to be tough."

A tentative solution is found, and they do a take. Fletcher cues McDiarmid, who is seated in a proto-Emperor chair, so he can spin around to confront the Jedi. Take. Jayne-Ann calls their attention to a dialogue error. Take. "Are you guys happy?" George asks the cameramen. "Yeah, that was good," McFarlane replies.

Above left: Anakin stands with Palpatine as Mace Windu and three Jedi arrive to inform the Chancellor of Grievous's defeat. McCallum watches the shoot (below), which can also be seen on the monitor. Right: Between setups, Lucas talks things over with Jackson (Windu), while Tux Akendoyeni (Eeth Koth) looks on.

"Okay, we're going to try the fight now while we're in position," Lucas decides rather suddenly. "I'm curious to see how this will work." Gillard walks over. "We're going to rehearse it once," Lucas tells him, "then shoot it once and see how it looks. Okay, this is it, Nick."

Gillard organizes the actors and Michael Byrne (Palaptine's fencing double) while Lucas observes from the video village. Stuntman Ben Cooke (Kit Fisto) is still having problems holding his lightsaber with his gloves. "This Kit Fisto holds it by the blade. You can tell he's not a real Jedi," Lucas jokes, watching the monitor.

"He's tough–he doesn't feel the pain," Knoll says.

Take. The spontaneous shot of the fight isn't working. "You can't win if you don't take risks," Lucas shrugs. "Well, that was interesting. I think we've exhausted that idea."

LOCATION WRAP: 20:00   SETUPS: 58
SCRIPT SHOT TODAY: 2m 52s

SHOOT DAY 13: WEDNESDAY, JULY 16, 2003
LOCATION: Stage 7
SET: Int. Palpatine's office
SCENES SHOT: 99pt
VFX [visual effects] NOTES: Sc. 99—Anakin's
lightsaber goes flying, chair is zapped out of the
way, lightsaber flies into Anakin's hand, lightsaber flies into
Palpatine's hand.

Gillard is talking logistics with Lucas and Coleman. Today is going to be one of the more difficult days of the shoot, as the Mace-Palpatine fight is one of the trickiest in terms of preparation and choreography. Fletcher asks whether the three Jedi Masters, whom Palpatine has struck down, can leave the stage. "We can lose everybody; they're all dead," Lucas responds. "We'll turn around and do Mace now."

Lucas and Gillard talk things over again. "I have to get the movie done," the director is saying. "Regardless, I have to have something on the screen that works."

"One of the first assignments for me when I got here was to spend two weeks with Nick Gillard," Coleman explains. "So Nick and I are collaborating quite a bit right now, as I try and figure out what fight elements we can achieve with animation. As fights are taken from the rehearsal room, with no set pieces, to the actual sets, sometimes the fights have to change a little bit because George will either have time constraints or set constraints, or need to change an element. And then Nick has to react right away, so I'm there as he turns around and asks, 'Can you animate that backflip? Because it would take us X amount of time–which we don't have–to do it.'"

The bell rings. "Quiet, please," third assistant director Samantha Smith says. Take. Makeup artists pat down Jackson's head for glare. He and McDiarmid are in close quarters with

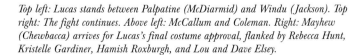

Top left: Lucas stands between Palpatine (McDiarmid) and Windu (Jackson). Top right: The fight continues. Above left: McCallum and Coleman. Right: Mayhew (Chewbacca) arrives for Lucas's final costume approval, flanked by Rebecca Hunt, Kristelle Gardiner, Hamish Roxburgh, and Lou and Dave Elsey.

their lightsabers; the Steadicam is practically on top of them, so Harding is wearing a helmet. Ian performs some lightsaber moves only just learned. Lucas asks him to keep his hands together on the saber handle.

Several takes later, Jackson and McDiarmid clash and freeze, staring into each other's eyes.

"Okay, cut!" Lucas calls out. The two almost collapse in laughter. "We're going to be here all day," the director says.

After the crew breaks for lunch and leaves the set, silhouetted against a greenscreen by the remaining lights, Lucas, McCallum, Knoll, and Coleman discuss the fight.

"I need a close-up of Ian," Lucas is saying. "We're not going to be able to do a shot like this off a digital character. We can try–and if we do it, I will applaud you tremendously. But nobody told me I couldn't shoot close-ups."

"What I think the misunderstanding is, 'cause I wasn't there–" McCallum starts.

"Nobody said anything to me till this morning," Lucas injects.

"I think there was a misunderstanding–"

Gillard arrives and suggests alterations to the fight. "There's always time," he says.

"You saw what I did. I want to see Ian's expression," Lucas says to him.

"I misunderstood. I thought it was going to be face replacement," Gillard explains.

"But I have to have some close-ups. I can't shoot the whole thing in a wide shot."

"There are places in there where they're not fighting–you could move in there," Gillard suggests, but Lucas reiterates that he doesn't want to switch too often from wide shots to close-ups, and he has doubts about digital face replacement.

"I think we can push the face replacement closer than we did last time," Knoll says.

"If the reference is really good," Coleman agrees.

"Well, that's lunch anyway," Lucas concludes.

L ater that day, Mayhew, in full costume, climbs into a station wagon– seated in the copilot's seat, of course–on his way to Stage 7 for Lucas's final approval. With staff from the creatures department in tow, he arrives on the set of Palpatine's office. George walks over and says, "Looks good. Excellent. How do you feel?"

"Great," Mayhew says from within his Wookiee mask.

"Back home," Lucas says, and then beckons to Samuel Jackson, who strolls over and says, "Oh, you're dressed today–and combed." The two actors then talk "Wookiee" together, making appropriately seal-like barking sounds and laughing.

"We walked onto the set—and I heard afterward that it was actually quite a tense time—and you could hear people suddenly gasp," Rebecca Hunt recalls. "And the noise grew, saying, 'Wow.' I was absolutely blown away. People love Artoo and they love Chewie. And he was great. When we finally took the head off, you could see Peter was just pumped up with excitement."

Between takes, Rick comes over and congratulates the creatures team. "Thank you, guys," he says.

LOCATION WRAP: 20:15   SETUPS: 62   SCRIPT SHOT TODAY: 1m 03s
TRAVEL: Jimmy Smits [Bail Organa] arrives in Sydney.

SHOOT DAY 14: THURSDAY, JULY 17, 2003

LOCATION: Stage 7
SET: Int. Palpatine's office
SCENES SHOT: 99pt (Anakin becomes Darth Vader)
VFX NOTES: Anakin cuts off Mace's hand.

Dave Elsey is putting the final touches on Ian McDiarmid as Darth Sidious, doing his face and nails. The actor then lies on the ground, blue lights flashing in his face to simulate the blue lightning coming from his fingers, which will be added in postproduction. For each take, Jackson, wearing glasses, yells his lines from off camera over the noise of a wind machine.

The next setup has Anakin in close-up as he watches Palpatine and Windu slug it out. "The thing to remember is there's a huge display of craziness going on here," Lucas reminds Christensen.

"As much as I'm watching what's going on, I think I'm really searching myself to see what I'm going to do here," Christensen says.

"Right."

"I'm listening to them but I'm also in my own head at the same time."

Lucas agrees, but adds, "We still have to get the audience into what you're thinking. When you get into these scenes, you have to be visually reacting, too."

They then shoot the moment in which Palpatine implores Anakin to help him. "At the point when Palpatine begs for Anakin's help," Jackson points out, "I'm bending those lightning bolts right back on him. I mean, that's why he's begging—because I got him. I'm like, 'Yeeeeah! Who's your daddy now?!'"

In the next scene, Anakin becomes Darth Vader. Christensen kneels before McDiarmid, rehearsing his dialogue to himself.

"Anakin's relationship with Palpatine eclipses his relationship with Obi-Wan," Christensen remarks. "But he doesn't really have a clear devotion to one or the other. Anakin as he will be played is—I don't want to say naïve, but his belief system is still open. He still isn't exactly set in his devotion to the Jedi or to Palpatine. He is looking to see how he can get more power, but his ideas of good and evil are not black and white."

"And . . . action!" Lucas calls out. After a few takes, with Hayden kneeling among a dozen crew, Anakin's transition to the dark side is complete.

LOCATION WRAP: 20:30   SETUPS: 42   SCRIPT SHOT TODAY: 4m 31s
NOTES: On wrap, it was discovered that Ian McDiarmid had suffered a considerable amount of discomfort with his contact lenses. As a result, contact lens nurse Helen Johnstone gave him an eye bath and checked for any damage.

SHOOT DAY 15: FRIDAY, JULY 18, 2003

LOCATION: Stages 7 & 4
SET: Int. Palpatine's private office; Int. Coruscant ballet
SCENES SHOT: 99 (Palpatine fights with Mace Windu), 67pt (Palpatine tells Anakin the Jedi Council wants to control the Republic)

"If we can get through this day, we'll be okay," Lucas predicts to Fletcher on the third day of shooting the Mace-Palpatine fight. The stunt crew attaches wires to Jackson so they can violently pull him backward to simulate Windu being pummeled by a particularly vicious blast of dark side lightning. Lucas describes the scene to the actor: "Your first reaction is surprise—your hand's been cut off—and then you're blasted away."

They do a rehearsal and suddenly Sam is floating above the set, pulled there by wires yanked by stuntmen jumping off a ladder to create the necessary force. "It's almost like I've practiced for this death all my life," Jackson says. "Last summer, when I was in San Francisco doing another film [*Twisted*, 2004], George and I had lunch and discussed what was going to happen in this film. And he said, 'Well you're pretty much the only important character that I can actually kill off, so it has to be a pretty spectacular death.'"

As they prepare to shoot close-ups of Anakin cutting off Mace's hand, Lucas suggests to Christensen, "It's good if it's a clean move," and then explains how the scene will go quiet afterward, with "low strings and scary music."

The next scene on the schedule is at the opera, where Palpatine continues his seduction of Anakin, recounting the story of Darth Plagueis. "A little political plotting at the ballet is just the thing after a hard day's sword-fighting," Lucas says to McDiarmid.

Makeup artists touch up Sandi Finlay (Sly Moore), David Bowers (Mas Amedda), and McDiarmid, who are seated, staring out at a performance that doesn't yet exist. "It'll take us six months to figure out what they're watching," Lucas says. Ian then recounts to Anakin the story of Plagueis

Left and insets: Lucas directs the principals as Anakin intervenes—fatally—in the Windu/Palpatine conflict. Above right: Elsey applies finishing touches to McDiarmid's Darth Sidious makeup/prosthetic. "I love the Emperor," Elsey says. "Re-creating that makeup was both a challenge and an honor."

several times in several setups, each delivery flawless and chilling.

"Scenes where Ian did most of the talking, I just had to sit there and listen," Christensen reveals. "I literally just sort of nod my head and agree with the story he's telling me—and those scenes were my favorites, because he's an amazing storyteller. I was so in awe of what he was doing in each scene, I'd find myself at times almost breaking out of character."

"I come from a tiny town called Dundee," McDiarmid remembers. "When I was four years old, I was taken by my parents to see a variety show, which completely fascinated me. It was rather scary and, at the same time, seductive. And every now and again a kind of magic seemed to happen. All those people up there doing strange things—and they wore lots of makeup in those days. Afterward, I got to meet a couple of the performers, who were charming—but they were terrifying to a small boy. Taller and in lots of makeup smiling down at me. I can still see their faces."

"That's a wrap," Lucas says. Joining McDiarmid on the set, he adds, "That was amazing, absolutely amazing. Everyone was glued to the monitors."

Just then, Anthony Daniels, in costume, arrives pushing a birthday cake on a tray for Colin Fletcher. "I'm blown over," Fletcher says.

As people break up into groups, chatting and eating cake, George says to Ian: "You've got one more fight with a little green frog, but that shouldn't be too hard."

LOCATION WRAP: 20:45   SETUPS: 40   SCRIPT SHOT TODAY: 6m 45s
NOTES: A splinter unit headed by Rick McCallum did pickup shots this morning on the "private office" set. They completed Palpatine's wire work for Sc. 99.

Top: At the opera, McDiarmid continues his performance as the insidiously proactive Palpatine. The veteran stage performer likens the Chancellor to Shakespeare's Prospero in The Tempest. *"I've played other monsters, too,"* he notes. *"Count Cenci is almost as monstrous as Palpatine. He's diabolical in every sense . . . his daughter kills him by driving nails through his eyes." Above: Lucas directs Christensen, whose fearful Anakin is no match for McDiarmid's monster.*

5 Return of the Emperor

REHEARSAL DAY: SATURDAY, JULY 19, 2003

Within a nearly empty Stage 3, Lucas is talking story with Jimmy Smits. Christensen arrives, and the two actors shake hands. Everyone is in street clothes. While leaning on the makeshift staircase leading up to the set, Lucas posits the political question *Revenge of the Sith* answers: "How do you turn over democracy to a tyrant with applause? Not with a coup, but with applause? That is the story of Caesar, Napoleon, and Hitler." He adds, "Idiocy is the controlling factor of life—particularly when you get into politics."

Bocquet, Russell, Tenggren, and dialogue coach Chris Neil are present. Portman arrives, and after they consult the visual script to learn what the scene will eventually look like, she, Smits, McGregor, and Christensen begin rehearsals on an otherwise empty set.

"Rick brought in Chris," Natalie Portman says, "who was, I would say, a rehearsal arbiter. [laughs] We did end up rehearsing a lot more, which is really, really helpful, and we had a lot of conversations. This time, Anakin and I are supposed to have been married for several years. We've supposedly been living together and made a baby together, so you have to fill in those blanks."

"One of the things we focused on in rehearsals was this sense of history between Anakin and Padmé," Neil says. "I looked out for the little touches, certain adjustments that might lighten the moment—an embrace, a line reading, or an unspoken moment that might give the audience a chance to invest emotionally in the characters.

"George's approach is to play Anakin as not consumed by the dark side from the very get-go," he adds, "but over the course of the movie. So my notes to George concerning Christensen and Natalie—Natalie especially—were to try to figure out the marker points for his progression toward the dark side."

Top: Lucas and Jimmy Smits (Bail Organa) go over the script. Above: Fletcher, Lucas, McCallum, and Matt Sloan (Plo Koon).

SHOOT DAY 16: MONDAY, JULY 21, 2003
LOCATION: Stage 4
SET: Int. Coruscant ballet
SCENES SHOT: 67

Producer Rick McCallum starts his day at 4:00 A.M. By 4:50 A.M., he's at his desk in the production office where a small mountain of faxes awaits him, accumulated during the night thanks to the time difference between Australia and the States.

Today's material—which includes ILM planning documents and animatics reports—also contains the UK payroll, so McCallum gives longtime *Star Wars* accountant Raj Patel a call in England to confirm its details. At 5:30 A.M., Rick meets with Jones and Fletcher to go over the day's work. Next is a visit to makeup and then the assistant directors' office, where 2nd AD Deborah Antoniou (known as Deb) fills him in on the actors' status. After checking out Stage 4 to make sure it's ready, McCallum joins Lucas, Jones, and Fletcher for breakfast at 7 A.M.

"The breakfasts are really big deals for us," he explains, "because George goes through the schedule for the day and we play a very crucial game. As we eat, he bounces ideas off of us—pushing us to the limit by testing out different scenarios—what happens if he finishes a certain scene at three instead of five?—which forces us to understand why we've made judgments. He's testing the assumptions of what the schedule is and conceptualizing the milestones he has to achieve in order to finish each scene—so he can guarantee we'll finish that day's work. George is one of the few directors to do that."

The rapid pace of the early morning continues as McCallum visits with Tattersall, to check on the lighting; Bocquet, to discuss the sets; Russell and Gracie, to talk over the set-building schedule; the riggers, about tonight's stage work; then back to makeup, to touch base with the actors.

By 8:50 A.M., McCallum is talking with production accountant Kevin Plummer and going through the week's budget and any possible cost overruns. The rest of the morning is filled with e-mail, return calls—and constant status reports from Deb and Colin Fletcher on anything out of the ordinary.

"Deb tells me, for example, if an actor is late," Rick says. "Colin will call and tell me that George has added another six shots. So I'll go over and talk with George about how that's going to affect the schedule. It's a wired world."

Every hour of the day, consequently, has McCallum spending ten to fifteen minutes on the set. At 11:15 A.M. today, he checks in with the construction department—a vast hangar filled with hundreds of crew. "We had a situation where we found out an outside construction company was ripping us off," Rick says. "So we got the documentary crew to tape all the arrivals of the trucks delivering the materials over a three-day period. We were ordering X feet of lumber, and they were delivering hundreds of feet less. They thought we'd be too rushed to check how much they actually sent—but we check *everything*. So I sent the tapes to the construction company and said, 'We're not going to pay your outstanding bill.' "

Meanwhile, on the set, a gum-chewing Finlay is helped into the opera box, the end of her robe carried as if she were arriving for a wedding. McDiarmid and Bowers take their seats.

"It was very interesting, the scene we did in the theater," Ian remembers. "There seemed to be lots of guests on the set that day, which could have been a distraction. On that day, it was a help. I found it was rather like playing to an audience."

Lucas explains that, following a Saturday run-through of the scene, he switched it from Palpatine's office to an opera box. "During rehearsal, I said, 'My God, this is a four-page scene—I've had five scenes in this office already—how am I going to do this?' So I put it in an opera house, watching a ballet—*Squid Lake*—which worked out great."

After the scene is finished, Lucas joins McCallum, Fletcher, and Jones for lunch. The cafeteria at Fox Studios is a temporary structure made of

wood, canvas walls, see-through plastic windows, and a corrugated metal roof. If the weather is hot, the walls can be removed. Cast and on-set crew file past two long tables stacked with main courses, which are generally very good. There is an additional table with salads, and another with desserts. Some of the crew eat outside, while others sit inside on fold-up chairs at long fold-up tables.

"Lunch is about what we accomplished," Rick says, "compared to what we thought we'd do—why didn't we get it done, what we're still trying to do, and where we can make up time."

At 2 P.M., he calls Ramos, back at the ranch, for more budget talks, particularly questions about postproduction, the groundwork for which is being laid now. "Ours is a dialogue," he notes, "that goes all the way through the filmmaking process. There's a constant juggling of assets, and Kathryn is production's alter ego—she keeps us honest. Someone once said

that it doesn't matter what it costs, if you get it right. But the truth is, it does matter how much it costs, it does matter how you do it—that's the fun part."

Today's discussion is cut short, however, as a problem is reported over the walkie-talkie. Due to a sick cast member, one scene will be pushed back and another will leap forward—so McCallum makes an emergency trip to the costume department. He and Biggar quickly go over what kind of additional staffing she might need to create the suddenly due robes. Rick then hightails it over to the art department where, with Bocquet and Gracie, he discusses what kind of overtime they'll need to finish building a set whose production just accelerated.

"It's like a miniature village," McCallum explains, "and every day there is drama."

Rick revisits the set and Lucas, and checks in with the ADs. He then meets with Fox personnel to go over what stages they might sublet from JAK. It turns out that a small independent film can shoot on a stage that is temporarily available during the weekend.

At 5:30 P.M., McCallum walks over to the second floor of Stage 2 for a review of the previous day's tape with Roger Barton, which is followed by a walk-through of all the sets and an inspection of assets that can be wrapped, shipped, or sold. Back in the production office at 6 P.M., Jacqui debriefs Rick on anything he missed, and loose ends are tied up by 7 P.M.—when it's time to meet again with Lucas and Fletcher to go over the cast-

ing of tertiary characters and tomorrow's schedule.

Production coordinator Virginia Murray then bombards McCallum with questions concerning travel, equipment, insurance, accident reports, and actor contracts. These last items will take him about two hours to read. "Film has about ten thousand separate tasks, which are highly visible and interdependent," Rick remarks, "and which have to be finished before you can deliver the movie. Each one of those has to be checked off, legal clearances have to be obtained, there are lawyers, contracts, and billing rights."

"The first real film I worked on was *101 Dalmations* [1996]," Murray says, "which included a team that were all Rick McCallum protégés from the *Young Indy* days—and that was my big break. Most of his old first and second ADs, and production coordinators, are all top-class production managers and executive producers on *Harry Potter* and goodness knows what else.

"It's the best office ever," she adds. "It *is* a bit all-or-nothing, so Rick likes everybody to have a good time."

At 10 P.M., pizza is ordered and Deb arrives to give McCallum a roundup of the cast—any problems that arose and what the general feel of the day has been. By 11 P.M., he's out the door.

LOCATION WRAP: 20:30   SETUPS: 44   SCRIPT SHOT TODAY: 1m 42s

SHOOT DAY 17: TUESDAY, JULY 22, 2003

LOCATION: Stage 3
SET: Ext. Coruscant industrial landing platform; Int. Coruscant—Jedi gunship
SCENES SHOT: 65 (Obi-Wan and Mace Windu travel with Yoda to the landing platform), 73 (Anakin waits as Palpatine emerges from his transport)

"I came in this morning and said, 'Wrong ship, guys,'" Lucas remarks to McGregor, because instead of the needed gunship, another vessel had found its way to the set. "Fortunately, we're fast on our feet here," he adds. They then stand for a few moments without speaking, Lucas sipping coffee from a Styrofoam cup.

Jackson joins them, and rehearsals begin. Yoda is, of course, invisible, so his lines are spoken by offline reader Duncan Young, a well-known Australian TV and stage actor who will voice many CG and otherwise unavailable characters during the shoot (all of whom will be overdubbed in postproduction).

This scene, in which Senators and dignitaries come to greet Palpatine following his dramatic rescue, is the first to include many extras. Among them are a few recognizable characters, such as Bail Organa and Jar Jar, as well as new faces, such as Malé-Dee (Kee Chan) and Giddean Danu (Chris Kirby). As he disembarks from his transport, the group will escort the Chancellor through a massive colonnaded area. Except for some partially built columns, this zone is mostly greenscreen, so Lucas instructs the actors and extras where to walk to avoid digital columns or ships.

Katie Lucas (Chi Eekway) and Amanda Lucas (Terr Taneel) are also among the Senators, as is Rena Owens (Nee Alavar), the voice of Taun We in *Attack of the Clones*. "Are Senators allowed to smile?" Owens asks. Lucas says yes. Smits asks if greeting the Chancellor with a nod conforms with Republic etiquette. Lucas says yes again.

After a rehearsal, Lucas walks over to the edge of the set, which is on a raised platform surrounded by many onlookers. "Do you think we should put some boxes here in case someone falls?" he asks Smith. "Some of these people can't see in their costumes." Boxes, which act as cushions, are added. Between takes, a handheld blower is used to gust air into the mouth of an overheated Mon Calamari (Paul Davies).

Director Rob Cohen (*XXX*, 2002) arrives at the video village, and Lucas explains to him that the brightness level of the plasma HD screens is tuned not so he can check the on-set lighting, but to be bright enough so he can assess the actors' performances. He also notes that he's using filters, because they're actually getting too much definition from the digital cameras. "It's a whole different way of making movies," he says. "It's painting now; it's not photography anymore."

Previous spread, top: The spontaneously created opera box, with Anakin (Christensen), Palpatine (McDiarmid), and Sly Moore (Sandi Finlay). Below: Another of John Knoll's panoramic photos shows the enormous makeshift cafeteria, which every day serves breakfast, three lunch shifts, and constant snacks—all generated by the kitchen-in-a-truck next door. Left: Lucas directs scene 73, with red guards, Mas Amedda (David Bowers) and Palpatine (McDiarmid). Top-left: Saesee Tiin (Kenji Oates) and production coordinator Virginia Murray. Above: Lucas and Jar Jar Binks (Ahmed Best). Top right: Cast and crew on the Senate landing platform.

The next shot is a close-up of C-3PO and R2-D2. The take is fine, and Daniels walks off camera—but can't see that he's heading straight toward some black knee-high borders. He continues right through the edge of the set but, luckily, not off the ledge. He goes down on his knees, then falls forward on his chest. Don Bies and others immediately run over to help him up. Lucas arrives, but Daniels appears to be okay, and shooting soon recommences.

"I walk forward—and the world changes!" Daniels exclaims, noting that he got his foot caught. "Because I'm top-heavy, I tumbled—and it made a terrible sound in the suit. I heard George call out, 'Tony, are you all right?!' because he saw my golden butt staring up."

LOCATION WRAP: 20:00   SETUPS: 56   SCRIPT SHOT TODAY: 4m 05s

SHOOT DAY 18: Wednesday, July 23, 2003
LOCATION: Stage 5
SET: Int. Senate office building—main hall
SCENES SHOT: 50 (Padmé tells Anakin she's pregnant)

While Padmé secretly meets with Anakin in the shadows, many aliens are again on stage today, and many of Trisha Biggar and her team's costumes are evident. "*Star Wars* is a fictitious environment that has to have some reality to it," Lucas says, "but it shouldn't look like it was shot in 1968 or 1980. The most important part of that are the costumes, and Trisha's been great. She's the one that has the job of taking a rough sketch and turning it into something real. She takes the fantasies and turns them into a reality that actors can actually live in, which works in the shooting environment. And that's a very hard job."

"We bought fabrics in New York, San Francisco, Los Angeles, and London," Biggar says. "I sourced a lot of fabrics through a big biannual

trade show in Paris, which features manufacturers from all over the world. So through Paris, and then through their agents in London, we bought fabrics from Japan, China, and India. I also like to use a lot of vintage fabrics, so I source them in different places: Scotland, America, France–all over the place."

Biggar grew up in Glasgow, Scotland. One summer, toward the end of her schooling, a friend of her mother's suggested she work in the theater– and Biggar wound up in that medium for more that ten years. "It was fantastic fun," she recalls. "There was a great social life. Parties all the time. It just seemed like the job you wanted to have." Years later, fellow Scot David Brown, who was *Young Indy*'s production supervisor, asked Biggar if she was interested in doing the costumes for the series' third season. She met with McCallum, who sealed the deal.

LOCATION WRAP: 20:30   SETUPS: 34   SCRIPT SHOT TODAY: 4m 40s
NOTES: Annie Leibovitz and her team did publicity stills all day.

SHOOT DAY 19: THURSDAY, JULY 24, 2003
LOCATION: Stage 7
SET: Int. Alderaan starcruiser–hallway
SCENES SHOT: 118 (Bail Organa wants to warn the Jedi),
173 (R2-D2 and C-3PO are given a new master)

One particular set on Stage 7 has been attracting visitors since the day its construction began back in early May. Today it's revealed in all its iconic glory: the hallway from *Star Wars*' Rebel blockade runner–the hallway into which Darth Vader strode twenty-six years ago.

"We get the same fan fascination ourselves," Gavin admits. "The tricky thing about building this set was that the first film wasn't really archived very well, because nobody knew it was going to be successful. So we had to rely much more on photographs; we only had a few drawings to work from."

Standing among those familiar walls of projecting rectangles, Lucas and Smits discuss how Bail Organa should deliver his line, "Have the protocol droid's mind wiped." As they attempt different readings, they both flub the line, which is somewhat of a tongue twister. "I can't even say it," Lucas jokes.

Above left: One camera is put on dolly tracks to follow the Chancellor (McDiarmid) and his soon-to-be-Sith apprentice (Christensen); although the columns are only partially built, the visual script (inset) reveals how the scene might look in post. Top right: Bocquet and Biggar. "It's nice to work for a director who's actually interested in the costumes," she says. Above: Senior cutter Anthony Phillips at work on one of those fabrics in Building 37, the costume department.

"Let's roll cameras, please," Fletcher says, and a piece of C-3PO falls off, which is somehow appropriate. The droid is hastily reassembled and they do a take. Jimmy delivers the "mindwipe" line. Take.

"This is it, the end of the movie," George says to Anthony upon completion of the scene. "Not the exact end, but the end for you for another twenty years. When you return, you're a little battered, but still charming."

LOCATION WRAP: 20:30   SETUPS: 50   SCRIPT SHOT TODAY: 2m 46s

SHOOT DAY 20: FRIDAY, JULY 25, 2003

LOCATION: Stage 7
SET: Polis Massa—medical center observation dome
SCENES SHOT: 53 (Dream: Padmé dies giving birth),
169 (the twins are delivered)

"What is truly remarkable—and this shows George's true understanding of the relationship between man and machine—is that it's done in the most callous, offhand manner," Daniels observes. "Jimmy Smits asked me, 'Should he not be upset at saying this?' And I said, 'No. I'm about as important to you as a trash can that needs emptying. You must think of me as a robot; I'm just an object.' And that's why it's very cleverly written as a throwaway line."

As droid wranglers Zeynup Selcuk and Justin Dix dress Daniels, layering his C-3PO persona over his black bodysuit, Lucas says to him, "This is almost the last dialogue in the picture: you saying, 'Oh, dear.' And you have the first dialogue in the next picture: 'Did you hear that?'"

"I know within a couple of weeks if a picture's going to work," McCallum says. "It's just a dynamic—something happens, it's magic. About three or four weeks into production, I got a sense that Episode III is going to work. But it's going to take a lot of effort to get there, because there are a lot of problems inherent in the story: It's the most adult of the six; it's the darkest—it's the most interesting."

It is perhaps this darkness—and a healthy workload—that explains the warning on the door to the props department: *Sheer Hell.* Behind this portal, however, is genial series veteran Ty Teiger (*White Hunter, Black Heart,* 1990; *Die Another Day,* 2002). "All the wall dressing, all the consoles, all the

tables, the door controls on the walls—everything apart from your hand props is built into the set," he says of his team's contribution. "Every bit of pipe, every light switch—we do all that, and that's why I end up with eighty or ninety people working for me.

"On most films, you would farm things out," Teiger continues. "But because nobody's supposed to know about what we're up to, we have to make literally everything in-house, from your molding to your engineering to carpentry to model-making to vac forming. My job is basically to get the sets ready, and then supply the hand props to my standby prop men, who

look after the set. Obviously if I'm on the floor all day long, I can't be back here orizining and making sure everything's ready and built for the next day. So you'll see me on the set the morning of a handover, and that's it. I don't like to be on the set too much—I make too much noise," he concludes with a laugh.

LOCATION WRAP: 19:45   SETUPS: 32   SCRIPT SHOT TODAY: 2m 34s

Top left: Justin Dix, Daniels in costume, Bies, and Lucas. Left: Back to the past in the Alderaan starcruiser corridor go McFarlane, Fletcher, Harding, Lucas, "B" camera clapper loader Lee Mariano, and stand-by props Robert Moxham. Above left: Property master Ty Teiger and dozens of Naboo military costume props (above right). Top: Crew prepare a camera setup for a scene in the Polis Massa medical center, which is then shot with McGregor and Portman (inset).

103

SHOOT DAY 21: MONDAY, JULY 28, 2003

LOCATION: Stages 1 & 5

SET: Int. Alderaan starcruiser—conference room; Ext. Jedi Temple—landing platform

SCENES SHOT: 171 (Bail, Yoda, and Obi-Wan make plans for the babies); 113 (Bail Organa escapes on the side of his airspeeder); 71 (Padmé tries to get Senators on her side—Bail Organa only on camera)

This morning's scene takes place in the Alderaan cruiser's meeting room. Because Yoda will be added in post, his chair has a string attached to it, which is pulled by one of the crew to simulate his movements (one of the film's more low-tech moments). Smits and McGregor rehearse with the empty chair, while Duncan Young reads Yoda's lines off camera. "Good chair acting," McCallum says after the first take.

In order to give Coleman and his team some Yoda to animate as early as possible, Lucas has asked editor Roger Barton to cut together this scene as soon as they wrap.

"I start with a few animators, five or ten, then go up to forty-five," Coleman says. "Right now, I'm expecting about eighty minutes of animation, but I don't think that I'm going to need the sixty animators I had on Episode II, because I have a more experienced team; a lot of the same animators are coming back; we know these characters a lot better than we did on Episode I; the technology has increased in terms of the speed; and I've learned a lot through my relationship with George over these last six years. When I see a piece of animation, I'm pretty clear on what his take will be."

In the cafeteria during lunch, George sits at a table with his kids. Christopher Lee, who came to Sydney straight from New Zealand where he was filming *The Return of the King* (2003), is eating and chatting with crew. In order to save him a return trip to Australia from his home in England, his scenes will be shot against bluescreen—before the general's quarters set is actually ready. He'll then be composited into the completed set later in post.

After lunch, on Stage 5, Jett Lucas plays a Jedi Padawan (Zett Jukassa) who is gunned down by clone troopers outside the Jedi Temple. Bail Organa arrives and witnesses the short and deadly battle on a raised set where everything is bluescreen except the landing platform and Bail's "Ferrari" (built on the chassis of Anakin's yellow airspeeder from Episode II). Biggar and Katie and Amanda Lucas watch from the floor. Nick speaks to Jett, who has to execute lightsaber moves and a somersault.

Take. "That was so cute. Too cute for words," Katie says.

"Very good, Jett. That was really good," his father adds.

"I said to myself, *What happened?*" Amanda remembers. "*You're not a little boy anymore!* I was very proud just to watch him do it."

After Jett and Jimmy complete the scene, production moves to Stage 5, where Smits completes pickup shots for a scene recorded earlier. Because the set was torn down weeks ago, it's all bluescreen. Having arrived a few days ago, Ahmed Best (Jar Jar Binks) watches from the video village. He asks Lucas if today has been a long day.

"Every day is a long day," Lucas replies.

LOCATION WRAP: 19:45 SETUPS: 46 SCRIPT SHOT TODAY: 3m 12s
NOTES: Hayden Christensen/burned Anakin makeup test (Stage 2). Christopher Lee (Darth Tyranus) performed some low-impact stunt rehearsals.

SHOOT DAY 22: TUESDAY, JULY 29, 2003

LOCATION: Stage 4

SET: Int. Coruscant—Senate chamber

SCENES SHOT: 137 (Palpatine announces that the Jedi rebellion has been foiled)

A painter is adding some last touches to a Senate pod that will hold Portman, Smits, and Best. With Lucas, they discuss the scene, calling Biggar into the pod for consultation. Lucas talks to the actors for a good

---

Previous spread: A Knoll panorama of the medical center. Above left: Smits (Bail Organa) prepares for a scene in the Alderaan cruiser conference room. Above: Lucas prepares his son, Jett, for his scene. Top: Crew prepare Bail's speeder on the Jedi Temple landing platform. Above right: Handmaiden Motée (Kristy Wright), Organa (Smits), and Senator Amidala (Portman) listen to the Emperor announce the end of the Republic. Right: Amanda and Katie Lucas with their father.

The second floor of Stage 2 is where ILM maintains its command post: a number of portable computers clustered together on four desks. This afternoon, it is where a departing Ahmed Best says good-bye to Rob Coleman, as two of the co-creators of the much-maligned Binks part ways.

"Whether you think Jar Jar is cool or not is completely subjective," Best observes. "There are people out there who try to justify their ideas of Jar Jar, but it's an opinion developed in the constructs of the prejudice they have in themselves. It has absolutely nothing to do with reality. By the same token, there are people who just didn't like Jar Jar as a character. And that's completely valid. But as far as Jar Jar being a negative creature, no, he wasn't."

Back on Stage 4, Ian, Sandi, and David are readied for their turn in the Senate pod. In one of those filmic sleight of hands, this scene is shot in the same pod where the others stood this morning.

"Ian, look out, all around, look up," Lucas instructs. "But at some point, look here [indicating a spot near the camera]: That's where Padmé is going to be."

Lucas tweaks the dialogue and suggests a royal wave. But McDiarmid asks, "Is everyone happy with the inside of my hands?" drawing attention to the fact that the wave will expose his palm, which hasn't been made up. The makeup team goes to work, but takes a bit long. "As soon as you can, guys, please," Fletcher urges. They depart, Emperor Palpatine's palm now white and eerie.

With each take, McDiarmid purrs the lines, "A new beginning . . ."

Between takes, Knoll points out that the Emperor has "a little shine on the end of his nose." Ian drinks water through a straw. Then, as cameras roll take after take, he never flubs a word. The scene finished, it takes a team to help the three actors down the stairs from the elevated pod, as none of them can see or walk very well in their costumes.

While waiting for the next scene to be shot, Coleman says, "In the scene tomorrow, George has decided to add a droid." Something elegant serving drinks. "You can have a year to design

ten minutes—this is an important scene, during which Palpatine dissolves the Republic and inaugurates the Empire. Smits stands outside the pod, nodding as he listens. Portman asks where she should look, where the other Senators are. Lucas tells her, adding that when she hears Palpatine's line about the Empire lasting "ten thousand years," she should look shocked and dismayed. Returning to the video village, Lucas says to "A" camera operator McFarlane, "A little lower. I need something dramatic here."

Young reads Palpatine's lines off camera, and claps when applause is called for in the script. Take. Smits paces as they set up for another angle. Portman stretches, raising her hands in the air. Jay Laga'aia watches, with a stiff leg he broke doing pickups for *The Return of the King*. Coleman is explaining to a visitor how Lucas taught him that things are either 49 or 51 percent—they either work or they don't.

Monday, July 28: Drafting begins in the art department for Darth Vader's rehabilitation chamber set.

something, or–boom–the next day it's needed." An hour later, he is showing potential designs to Lucas of sexy droid females. "I'm guessing this is the kind of stuff See-Threepio would have on his wall," Rob jokes.

Next on the schedule is a surprise: a scene for *Star Wars: Episode V The Empire Strikes Back*. "We're replacing the other actor with Ian so we have the same actor in all the films–so we have continuity," Lucas explains. The one scene featuring Darth Vader and the Emperor in that 1980 film is being reshot with McDiarmid, who took on the role in *Return of the Jedi*. The new footage will be cut into the DVD and all subsequent versions of *Empire*. The dialogue has also been altered so that it makes more sense with the continuity established in the prequel trilogy.

> DARTH VADER
> I have felt it.
>
> EMPEROR
> We have a new enemy. The young Rebel who destroyed the Death Star. I have no doubt this boy is the offspring of Anakin Skywalker.
>
> DARTH VADER
> How is that possible?
>
> EMPEROR
> Search your feelings, Lord Vader. You will know it to be true. He could destroy us.
>
> DARTH VADER
> He's just a boy. Obi-Wan can no longer help him.
>
> EMPEROR
> The Force is strong with him. The son of Skywalker must not become a Jedi.

Lucas instructs McDiarmid to "relish" the idea of turning the boy to the dark side–to take a deep breath before responding, savoring its repercussions. "Let's try it once more," he says. "Make the 'yes, yes' a little louder–and close your eyes before you say it."

Take. "Great. Cut. Now we can do a side view," Lucas says as he climbs the stairs to the pod.

"I think it's a case of tidying up," McDiarmid observes. "It was perfectly well done before, but it just makes sense. George has only slightly tweaked the words, now that we all know the history of Anakin Skywalker."

LOCATION WRAP: 20:15   SETUPS: 42   SCRIPT SHOT TODAY: 2m 45s

SHOOT DAY 23: WEDNESDAY, JULY 30, 2003
LOCATION: Stages 6 & 3
SET: Int. Bail Organa's office; Alderaan palace balcony; Bail's speeder
SCENES SHOT: 60 (Senators meet in secret), 153 (Bail rescues Yoda), 179 (Bail brings a small baby to the Queen)

Like many of the sets, Organa's office is enclosed on all four sides by blue fabric, which creates a corridor between the other side of its hanging blue "walls" and the real walls of the stage. Crew can thus circle the set through this circular corridor to reach makeup stations, sound and video technicians, food, and a tiny slit that accesses the set.

Portman, Genevieve O'Reilly (Mon Mothma), and other Senators walk

Left: Because they'll be shooting Christopher Lee against bluescreen, Lucas plots out the camera angles he'll need ahead of time on a maquette provided by Bocquet's team (above right), as inspired by earlier concept art of the general's quarters (aka "throne room"). Right: Jaeger's waitress droid concept for the scene in Bail's office.

Fed Cruiser Admiral Throne Room   Sheet 2A
Final Set Build Size

General Layout Showing Possible Moves
*Note: Very loose direction not based on latest script developments

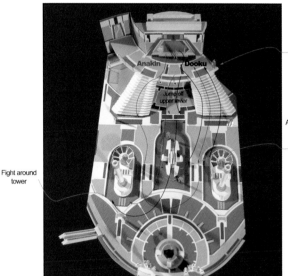

109

onto the set. Smits requests that they run the lines while their makeup is touched up. The lights cast long shadows on the set, which gives this early morning a twilight feel.

"Let's clear the eye lines, please," Fletcher asks.

"What's that noise?" Portman asks.

The origin can't be located, so Lucas decides, "This is a wide take, let's go with it."

The servant, who will eventually be replaced by an animated CG droid, walks in and out of the scene wearing a blue bodysuit.

While Lucas is on the set talking with the actors, McCallum tells a story in the video village. On location for *Young Indy*, he and Ben Burtt were out in Kenya's vast Masai Mara. Having followed the dust of their trucks for hours, a figure appeared on the horizon and very slowly approached from a great distance. As he neared, they could tell he was a local. When he finally joined the two, there was a moment of silence. Then the local asked what they were doing there. Rick explained in the simplest terms that they were making a television show. "Ah, television!" the man said, and whipped out a laminated card with location rates. "You must pay. It's $150 for TV, $500 for film."

George comes over and confides in his producer, "This is one of those terrible 'dinner' scenes, but it should be all right . . . I'm getting too old for this."

After lunch, in one of the sadder scenes of the film, Bail gives the infant Leia to his wife, the Queen of Alderaan. While prep continues, Gillard shows Lucas some test footage of the revolving set, and Bocquet shows him fab-

ric samples for approval. Lucas examines the creatures department's baby Leia while Biggar makes last-minute adjustments to the Queen's robes.

"Trisha was great," Rebecca Jackson Mendoza (the Queen of Alderaan) recalls. "The whole team was great. Just very patient. My costume actually changed: I believe it was going to be a lilac color, and then they decided to go more with the color of Alderaan, which was a nature green. My hair was almost like a crown, so I was a queen for a day."

During prep for the Bail speeder scene, Christopher Lee arrives, wearing an off-white raincoat with a red scarf, and talks with Lucas, McCallum, and Gillard. He has large hands, which he moves expressively while speaking. Lucas explains to him that the dialogue scenes will be first. "That's where I'll need your help, in terms of my reactions," Lee says. Next are the action scenes. "But I mustn't do it too fast," Lee comments.

As Smits sits down in the airspeeder, where a digital Yoda will join him, Lucas instructs, "You look up and then down as Yoda goes *plunk.*"

Behind Lucas, Lee is chatting with some visitors, discussing how films are made, telling them that the director must have a "tremendous amount of stamina—the ability to deal with endless disappointments.

"Some relatives of mine who live here came to the set," Lee says.

Top left: Bail's airspeeder on July 30—Smits's last day. "I was just getting to know everybody," he says. Left: Organa (Smits) and the Queen of Alderaan (Rebecca Jackson Mendoza). Top right: A panorama of the video village during the Lee shoot. Above left: Lucas directs Lee (Count Dooku), as Rowling and Michael Byrne (Palpatine's stunt double) look on. Above right: Fletcher and Lee, who has appeared in more than 200 films.

"They were completely bowled over. I told them that the man sitting there in front of the monitor is unique, because he decided at a certain point: no studio control. 'I will have total and complete control over my work; nobody will interfere with it; nobody will tell me what to do.' *He's* done it."

LOCATION WRAP: 20:30   SETUPS: 46   SCRIPT SHOT TODAY: 3m 27s

SHOOT DAY 24: THURSDAY, JULY 31, 2003
LOCATION: Stage 1
SET: Bluescreen; general's elevator lobby—revolve "A"
SCENES SHOT: 24pt (Count Dooku close-ups for dialogue and fight)

It's a brisk, sunny, cold morning. As technicians and craftspeople walk quickly to their various jobs, many carry Styrofoam cups with hot tea or coffee to dispel the chill. Within Stage 1, Lucas warms his hands on the portable heater by his chair, which is now quite useful.

With pulleys, the crew raises a circular bluescreen curtain, creating another enclosed area within the stage. They touch up the wooden floor with blue paint. Coleman barely slept the night before, worrying about today's shoot: It represents, potentially, an enormous amount of work for him and his department down the road. He says he won't know how it'll all work out till December, when Lucas cuts the sequence together.

The eighty-one-year-old Lee arrives on set in costume, and Lucas walks him through the shots, referring repeatedly to a miniature maquette of the future set. Christensen arrives in street clothes, as he will be off camera feeding lines to Lee. Rick confers with George. Lucas wants to be close to the actor as they shoot, so they set up a small monitor next to the "A" camera.

Soon everyone is ready to shoot Lee's dialogue for Count Dooku's violent confrontation with Obi-Wan and Anakin. Take. "We'll try one more. Excellent," Lucas says. "What we might do at the end of this one is . . . *anger!*"

For the next take, Christensen sits on a box for Lee's eye line. "Christopher, can you look to your right and left to see if there are any other Jedi?" Lucas asks.

"With my hands in my belt?" Lee asks.

"Yeah. Now you see them . . . and . . . cut! Great. That was perfect."

The day takes an optimistic turn when Lee grabs hold of a lightsaber for a shot with Christensen and McGregor, who has joined them on set. The next setup, Count Dooku's death scene, requires Lee to be on his knees for quite a long time. After the first take, Lucas instructs Lee to space out his words, and tells "B" camera operator Harding to move in.

Between takes, Lee suggests that it is out of character for Dooku to ask Palpatine for help. Lucas agrees, and Jayne-Ann cuts the word *help* from the script. For nearly twenty minutes more, the actor is still on his knees, until he is finally able to recline. "Okay. I think we got that," Lucas says.

The next scene has Dooku advancing on the Jedi. Lee walks forward, re-creating the menace of his earlier incarnations, and whips out his lightsaber.

"Not many people realize that *dooku* is Japanese for 'poison,' " Lee says. "Which is very appropriate, really, because he's lethal."

LOCATION WRAP: 20:00   SETUPS: 62   SCRIPT SHOT TODAY: 1m 35s

SHOOT DAY 25: Friday, August 1, 2003

LOCATION: Stage 1
SET: Bluescreen; Int. Trade Federation cruiser bridge
SCENES SHOT: 43pt (Obi-Wan yanks his lightsaber from the general)

"Waiting . . . waiting . . . and more waiting. "Four or five minutes," Fletcher says.

"Four or five?" Lucas asks, and Colin comes over to explain.

"The way most movies are made," Lucas would observe, "you have to have a very good ability to delay gratification. You have to be able to say, 'This will come . . . in time.'"

Gillard, with fencing doubles Michael Byrne and Kyle Rowling, rehearses a few lightsaber moves for Lee's benefit, then the actor goes through the moves himself. Riding the crest of yesterday's success, Lee is emboldened and will execute a spin. Take.

"We'll do it once more," Lucas says.

But Lee holds his head and says he's "quite dizzy." During the next take, Byrne and Rowling flank Lee, ready to catch him if he stumbles.

Andrew Lesnie, director of photography for *Lord of the Rings*, joins Lucas in the video village. Indicating the monitors showing bluescreen, Lucas says to him, "You've been shooting some of these same locations, I believe," and Lesnie laughs.

Since he knows the fight choreography intimately, Rowling tells Lee where to look during the next take, "Left, right, left, low, little turn," and gives him hand signals. Lee falters, and they leap up to grab him.

"Perfectly all right," Lee protests, pointing to the blue carpet. "It's just that I'm trying to spin on this material."

"I want to do another one," Lucas says to Lee, "with real anger in your face." Take. "That was good. I think we'll try one where you're not swinging the lightsaber as you walk." Take.

"I think we got it. You did great," Lucas says.

Lee exits the bluescreen set and pats the director on the shoulder.

Fletcher calls out, "Attention, folks. That was Christopher Lee's last shot." There is a round of applause, while McCallum and Coleman congratulate the legendary actor.

LOCATION WRAP: 19:45   SETUPS: 66   SCRIPT SHOT TODAY: 1m 10s

REHEARSAL DAY: Saturday, August 2, 2003

At 9 A.M., Lucas, McCallum, and Jett Lucas ride one of the studio's electric golf carts to the editorial suite on Stage 2 for a videoconference with Skywalker Ranch, where it is still Friday afternoon. Editor Roger Barton joins them, and, after a few attempts, a link is established with Burtt, Church, Gregoire, and other artists.

United by technology, both groups watch an animatics sequence of the film's opening space battle. Jett applauds as the *Star Wars* crawl scrolls by. McCallum taps his fingers to the music. At the end of the ten-minute sequence, cliffhanger text reads, "To be continued next week: *Jedi Death Plunge!*"

"It's starting to fill in the [visual] blanks," Gregoire says.

"But we need to clarify what's going on," Lucas notes, and, during the discussion that follows, they attempt to sort out what's missing.

"Do you want a long shot all the way into Obi-Wan's cockpit?" someone asks.

"Do you want him to try it?" McCallum seconds.

"Let's just wait till I get back," Lucas says, sounding tired. "It's a few weeks more. Seven to be exact—"

"—and three days," McCallum adds.

"We've got about a dozen Jedi getting killed," Burtt says of another sequence.

"Hopefully, in slow motion," Rick says. "With just the same Jedi getting shot over and over." Jedi death jokes follow.

The connection is severed, and Lucas says to McCallum, "When it gets down to four minutes, it'll all start making sense. We need to reboard it. The shots never show the bad guys."

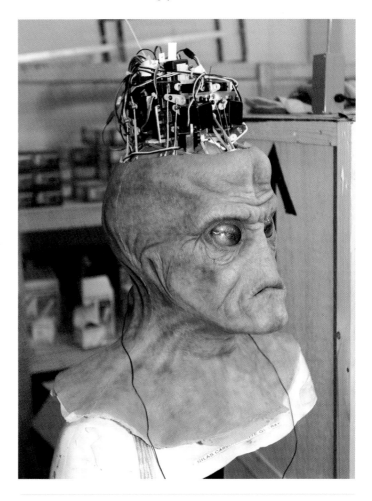

Top far left: Unidentified costume personnel, costume supervisor Nicole Young, and Coveney work on Christensen's first complete Darth Vader costume fitting. Top left: Assistant costume designer Michael Mooney checks on a Neimoidian, whose hat conceals servos and intricate mechanics (above). Left: The bridge, which took several weeks to construct, and whose lighting reference is once again a page from the visual script (top right) by Tiemens.

This Saturday morning is a key rehearsal, as Christensen, McGregor, and Portman will be running through the scene in which Anakin essentially kills Padmé by breaking her heart. In an empty, cold Stage 3, Lucas and McCallum stand on what will be a Mustafar landing platform. A maquette showing the whole of the complex Mustafar layout sits on a table, for everyone's reference. McGregor arrives, wearing black-rimmed glasses, and studies it with Lucas.

Christensen and Portman are next to climb up to the set, and the three of them run through the scene a few times, with Neil and Tenggren observing. George explains to Hayden that Anakin doesn't need to be angry when he first greets Padmé–that, in fact, he should be happy. "Everything is great for Anakin," Lucas explains, also asking Christensen to sound more like the Emperor: confident and self-assured. Continuing that thought, Lucas comes up with the idea that Christensen should leave his back turned toward McGregor: Anakin is so confident in his new powers that he doesn't need to face his former Master.

McGregor and Christensen then quickly run through part of their lightsaber battle–beautiful, quick moves–while Lucas tells Gillard that he now needs a new beginning to the fight, with Anakin jumping then flipping toward Obi-Wan from his backward position.

SHOOT DAY 26: MONDAY, AUGUST 4, 2003
LOCATION: Stage 1
SET: Int. Federation cruiser bridge
SCENES SHOT: 43pt (General Grievous escapes by smashing a window)

At dawn, Lucas, McCallum, Bocquet, Fletcher, Russell, and others meet, as they do most mornings, for a walkthrough of the sets in progress. Their quest is to identify problems, approve works in progress, and generally troubleshoot. On the Mustafar landing platform, they discuss the changes made during Saturday's rehearsal; McCallum thinks it looks "cooler" now. "It's all one scene–one shot, one take," he explains to Fletcher, who reminds them that they'll have McGregor only until 5 P.M. that day. After that, he must leave to attend the Australian premiere of his film *Down with Love* at 7:45 P.M.

Fletcher then goes down his list of shots. "We can do Padmé being thrown against the wall–"

"We can do the whole thing," Lucas says. "I'll get into the fight. And

when Ewan leaves, I'll do a little bit of Artoo and Threepio–"

"But you have to be at the premiere, too," Rick says.

"The next day, we'll finish the fight; we'll do the odds and ends–no problem," George assures.

Peter Russell, dressed in gym clothes, then goes off to inspect another set, while Ian Gracie returns to the art department to check the advance schedule. Gavin Bocquet takes off on his bicycle, as he has the most ground to cover, pedaling over to the Jedi Temple briefing room. In a gray sweatshirt and jeans, there Bocquet consults with head scenic painter Matt Connors, choosing colors for the set. As he makes each rapid-fire decision, an assistant places a piece of masking tape on the appropriate surface with the correct color code: gray 1 or 2, silver 3, etc.

Connors left school at fifteen and was looking at "a lifetime of laboring jobs," but discovered that "film was something I could get into without qualifications." He began as a set builder on *Mad Max Beyond Thunderdome* (1985) but "met the painter on that who was doing great [faux] rock faces– and it was fascinating." Sporting consistently disheveled hair and perpetually stained hands, he says that his department paints everything and can imitate any surface–metal, leather, marble–using various techniques and an arsenal of about thirteen hundred colors. He notes that a *Star Wars* film, particularly now that they're digital, demands a high level of finish.

"The sets are built primarily out of wood," Russell explains. "It's only when that last two and a half millimeters of paint goes on that it actually becomes what it is: steel, glass, stone."

At 2 P.M., on the bridge set, McGregor and Christensen are battling CG droids and a blue-suited Rowling, who duels as a physical placeholder for CG Grievous. As crew set up the next shot, Lucas and Knoll discuss

where the sun should be in relation to the bridge. The space exteriors and sun will be added later, but the lighting on set must be established now. In the next shot, McGregor and Christensen have to grab on to a banister to prevent themselves from being sucked into space as Grievous breaks a window and flees.

To cue them, Lucas calls out, "Window!" during each take. A wind machine is placed on the bridge, so Lucas's "Action!" becomes necessarily louder, electrifying them into movement as the on-set combat intensifies.

LOCATION WRAP: 20:00   SETUPS: 37   SCRIPT SHOT TODAY: 32s

Monday, August 4: After five days of drafting, prefab construction begins on Stage 4 for the Darth Vader rehabilitation chamber set.

Above left: Head scenic artist Matt Connors, Tattersall, set decorator Richard Roberts, and Bocquet make their rounds on Stage 2. On Stage 7 (above right), construction of the general's quarters as of August 6. Right: Christensen, Lucas, and McGregor study a "side" on the bridge.

SHOOT DAY 27: Tuesday, August 5, 2003

LOCATION: Stage 1
SET: Int. Bridge Federation cruiser
SCENES SHOT: 47 (Obi-Wan and Anakin cut down the droids;
Anakin pilots the cruiser to a landing platform)

"Okay, let's find us a shot," Lucas says as he arrives on set. "To me, the script is just a sketchbook," he adds, "just a list of notes, and, sometimes, I prefer the documentary feel of free flow, so I let my instincts tell me where to go. I like to create cinematically; I don't like to have a plan. I like to have a rough idea of what I'm going to do—certain themes, certain issues I'm going to deal with—and then I try to do so. At first, I shoot *around* the

side to let others pass. Because some of the technical jargon defies memorization, McGregor has taped his lines to a viewscreen.

"How manic should I be with this?" Hayden asks, indicating the vessel's controls.

"I would keep it reasonably calm and steady, as this is a pretty big ship," George replies. As the cruiser is supposed to be splitting in half, Lucas adds, "Why don't we say 'boom' or 'crash,' so everybody knows when to jerk forward."

After lunch, Jayne-Ann points out that Ewan's hair is once again out of continuity. Lucas goes over the scene's lighthearted tone with McGregor, who improvises, "Nothing to worry about, gentlemen, but we're only flying half a ship."

movie—and then [in the editing room], I figure out where the movie is in the middle of all this."

Huge lights are switched on to simulate Coruscant's sun, bathing everyone in a soothing orange glow. The actors take their places in seats aboard the bridge. While climbing the narrow staircase to the set, in costume as the Supreme Chancellor—ruler of the galaxy—Ian has to squeeze to one

More takes. "You happy with that?" Lucas asks McFarlane.
"Yeah, I'm very happy. It had a good feel."

LOCATION WRAP: 20:00   SETUPS: 44   SCRIPT SHOT TODAY: 2m 15s

Above: Lucas and Christensen. "There's this ongoing theme," the actor points out, "this undertone to the whole film concerning Anakin's suspicions of Padmé's relationship with Obi-Wan." The set was closed to all nonessential personnel while Portman and Christensen (above right) play out Anakin and Padmé's tragic end.

SHOOT DAY 28: WEDNESDAY, AUGUST 6, 2003
LOCATION: Stage 3
SET: Mustafar landing platform
SCENES SHOT: 145pt (Padmé confronts Anakin on Mustafar and
Obi-Wan arrives)

Dry ice is being used to generate jets of steam, which rise on either side of the stairs that Christensen climbs. Lucas walks back and forth, talking on a cell phone outside the stage. McCallum arrives, checks on a number of details, and exits. A cushion is given to "A" camera clapper Simon Williams, who will be astride a ladder for most of the morning. Because this scene promises to be emotional, extra care is being taken so that no

After a few takes, Lucas has a fairly long talk with Christensen, McGregor, and Portman. McCallum returns. Makeup artists walk past him on another of their endless to-and-fro journeys to touch up the actors. "What a team," he remarks. Their discussion finished, Natalie performs dance steps on stage while waiting. George watches the proceedings with his hands folded behind his head. "We'll get there—even if it breaks my heart," he says to Rick.

Multiple takes follow. "That was good," Lucas says after the most emotional one. "I think we got that—and just in time . . . for lunch."

The lunch break, however, is taken up with a design meeting in the cafeteria with Bocquet, Russell, Gracie, and others. Lucas gets up for dessert just as Knoll passes by and is sucked into the conversation. As he

one is in the actors' eye lines. Crew erect a black felt curtain to mask even the video village from their view.

"Final checks, please," Fletcher calls out. "This is a pivotal scene. No one who doesn't have to be on set should be watching."

Over the roar of the wind machines, however, it's hard to hear any of the drama without headsets. McGregor can't hear, either: "It might be a nice idea to cue me," he says, after a quick rehearsal. "I can't hear Hayden."

attempts to leave, George returns with a bowl of ice cream and deadpans, "You can't get away. You're trapped in the art department."

At 2:45, they're ready for close-ups of Hayden. Lucas discusses the tone with him. "This is Anakin's greatest moment; he's got all these new powers—everything is fine."

"Anakin's just gone and killed his family, more or less, so I've done a deed that I thought would've weighed on me," Christensen would say the

following day. "But George sees it as an outburst of almost accidental anger that Anakin then has to suffer the repercussions of for the rest of his life. Anakin thinks he's done the right thing in killing all the Jedi, so George wanted me to come to the scene with enthusiasm. Things are good. I'm the most powerful man in the universe and I'm going to be able to save Padmé."

The process continues late into the afternoon, until Lucas says to Christensen, "I think we got it."

In a matter of minutes, crew break down one setup to create another on the opposite end of the Mustafar landing platform. Lights, tables, portable screens, wires, cameras, wind machines, costumes on hangers, and more are moved quickly to the next position. Lucas leads the advance–but then stops, chin on hand for a few moments as he reflects.

During the next take, Christensen's voice cuts through the sound of the wind machine as Anakin rails about his wife's betrayal: "*Liar!* You're with *him.* You brought him here to *kill* me." He then makes a fist, choking Padmé with the dark side of the Force: "You will not take her from me!" he screams at Obi-Wan.

Between takes, Christensen stays in character, muttering his lines to himself, head bowed.

LOCATION WRAP: 20:00   SETUPS: 22   SCRIPT SHOT TODAY: 3m 30s
NOTES: Company wrapped Ewan McGregor early today to be available for the premiere of his new film *Down with Love.*

SHOOT DAY 29: THURSDAY, AUGUST 7, 2003
LOCATION: Stage 3
SET: Mustafar landing platform
SCENES SHOT: 149 (R2-D2 tries to drag Padmé back onto the skiff), 145pt (Obi-Wan walks toward Anakin and the ferocious swordfight begins)

Above: McGregor and Christensen begin their characters' climactic duel. Top right: McCaig's death-head concept for Padmé is realized on the set (below). Far right: Jun's concept for a funeral attendee. Following spread: The greed and anger of Anakin (Christensen) results in his wife's death. Key hairdresser Miles, assistant hairdresser Hellingman, set dresser Kodicek, Mooney, Biggar, and costume standby Hassan work on Portman (Padmé).

Ewan McGregor's attendance of the *Down with Love* premiere has made the morning news in Sydney. So has Lucas, who also attended the gala and whose response to a question about Episode III–"Everyone dies and the bad guys win"–has been picked up by the media Down Under.

On the quad, a golf cart drives by with a Mon Calamari head in the passenger's seat; a hairdresser runs by; a garbage truck makes its rounds. On the set, a crane lifts Anakin's starfighter into the air, the closest it will ever come to flying. Although someone could theoretically be crushed if something were to go wrong, a grip remarks that most injuries on set are due to utility knives.

The epic duel between Anakin and Obi-Wan now begins–the climax of the prequel trilogy–but their encounter starts out humorously, with nearly every take ending with Christensen and McGregor joking, fake fighting, or fake dying.

"The saber fights are like being six-year-old kids again," Christensen remarks. "Buying the best toy in the store and getting to go home and play with it for two weeks with your best friend. Nick was there every day during

rehearsals, correcting us and making sure that every single minute detail was right. Even if we were making mistakes, we had him there on the sidelines saying it was still good. It's his fight, so he deserves all the credit."

During the next few takes, Christensen and McGregor make mistakes three times in a row. "They're getting in trouble there at the end," George says to Nick, who goes over to talk with the actors. They get it right, and Hayden walks to the monitors. "That was the fastest we've ever done it," he says to Lucas.

"I'm very happy with all the fighting scenes," McGregor notes. "They're incredibly exhausting to do, and it's such an intense burst of energy, but Hayden and I have gotten them to such a pitch that they're incredibly fast. We do those fight scenes fantastically well–I think it's all right to say that–because after you've done them and you look at the playback, it looks extraordinary. I'll be very proud of them when it's all put together."

LOCATION WRAP: 20:15   SETUPS: 72   SCRIPT SHOT TODAY: 2m 49s

SHOOT DAY 30: Friday, August 8, 2003
LOCATION: Stages 2 & 4
SET: Jedi Temple briefing room; Naboo main square; Plo Koon's cockpit
SCENES SHOT: 58 (Obi-Wan tells Anakin that the Chancellor has requested his presence), 108 (clone pilots blast Plo Koon out of the sky), 175 (Padmé in coffin)

After lunch, Fay David arrives on set for a visit, after being shown around the studio by her art department counterpart Colette Birrell. "I work with this small group of artists," Fay recalls, "but to go there and see this entire network of people who take this stuff and turn it into something larger than life, in a very short period of time, was . . . overwhelming."

David is just in time for close-ups of Portman in Padmé's coffin, surrounded by bluescreen. As specified in the script, Padmé, as she lies in state, still looks pregnant and is holding the japor snippet that Anakin gave her in *The Phantom Menace*. Visitors to the set begin to multiply, as do jokes about what the gossip on Naboo might be.

"Everyone's talking about it there," Lucas says. "The tabloids say Jar Jar is the father."

Biggar arranges Portman's hair and the flowers in the coffin. Set decorator Richard Roberts (*Titanic*, 1997; *The World Is Not Enough*, 1999) and others help out, and about twenty minutes is spent at that task. More than fifty people are now on hand to watch this emotional scene. To help McFarlane gauge the speed at which he needs to pan, Lucas tells him that horse-like creatures will be pulling the coffin.

He then notices the surplus of spectators and remarks, "Oh my God, it's a real funeral."

As the setups multiply, Natalie has to remain perfectly still, both during and between takes. Biggar is asked how much she can move, just as Portman rubs her eye. "Not much," she responds, and goes to touch up the arrangement.

"I want to get the camera where I can see the snippet . . . ," Lucas is saying to McFarlane. "That's it. Perfect."

"George, you could see her breathing," Knoll observes.

"You can stop pulses, right?" Lucas asks.

After several takes from several angles, while all the assembled remain very quiet, the scene is finished.

"I think they call it the 'End Dress,' " Portman remembers, speaking of her costume. "It's really, really beautiful. I think Trisha wanted to get an ocean sense. Someone said to me that it was very 'Ophelia.' With the flowers and the hair, it does look like I'm drowning."

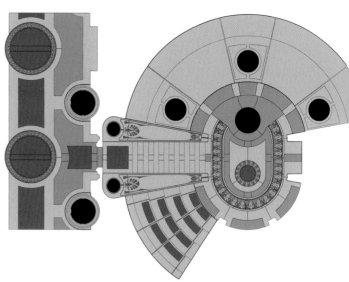

Above: The visual script illustrates the death of Plo Koon (Matt Sloan), who consults with Lucas (far right). Right: The Sydney art department's floor plan has been faithfully reproduced in the Jedi Temple briefing room, as captured by Knoll (below). While not being being used as a set, this locale serves as the site for a marriage proposal (see starwars.com for the complete story).

rinks and champagne have been announced for 6 P.M., so most of the production crew has gathered on Stage 4 to see Jedi Master Plo Koon (aka Matt Sloan, droid mechanic) meet his demise. This celebration marks the halfway point of principal photography and the completion of one thousand setups. As spectators mingle, Lucas directs Sloan, who is sitting in a starfighter cockpit: "Flying along. Look right. Look left. Okay . . . Light!"

On Lucas's cue, a mobile light representing an enemy fighter travels quickly along a steel monorail, arcing over the rear of the cockpit.

"Now!" Lucas calls out–and a special effects explosion goes off on the back of the starfighter. Sloan slumps forward and everyone applauds.

It's a wrap and the atmosphere is genial as champagne is poured, toasts are made, and people relax.

"It's midpoint," Lucas says. "We're on schedule and it looks good."

LOCATION WRAP: 19:15   SETUPS: 36   SCRIPT SHOT TODAY: 2m 18s

⑥ The Last Setup

SHOOT DAY 31: Monday, August 11, 2003

 LOCATION: Stage 4

 SET: Anakin's starfighter cockpit; Obi-Wan's starfighter cockpit

 SCENES SHOT: 2 (Obi-Wan bounces through the flak), 3 (Anakin blasts Federation droid fighters)

Following Sloan, it's Christensen's turn to sit in the cockpit of the gimbal-mounted Jedi starfighter. Indeed, there is only one, which is redressed for each occupant. A bank of red-gelled lights indicates enemy fire, and Young stands off camera to read the lines of other pilots, verbal descriptions of the action, and even R2-D2's beeps and whistles. Lucas is recording all of the aerial dialogue at one go, along with ad-libs and wild lines.

"Are we ready?" he asks.

"I don't think so," Christensen responds, noting that the lighting is still being tweaked by David Tattersall's team.

Tattersall was born just south of the Scottish border. After studying fine art for three years, he was attending the National Film School in London when MTV started up. He began moonlighting and shot more than two hundred music videos. The first bluescreen he lit was for Boy George. An admirer of Vermeer and Caravaggio, Tattersall created the paintings for a low-budget film he shot called *The Bridge* (1992), about American impressionist Philip Wilson Steer. After seeing that film, McCallum hired him as DP on *Young Indy.*

"It's not just that we're shooting on digital that makes this movie so unusual and the procedure so different," says Tattersall, who, most days, is dressed in jeans and black sneakers. "It's the colossal number of digital effects shots that will be dealt with in the course of postproduction, and the number of virtual sets, partial or total, green- or bluescreen. Really for us–for the shooting crew–we're just making a foundation that ILM will build on over the next eighteen months. To be honest, Episode III is more than fifty percent animated."

LOCATION WRAP: 20:00 SETUPS: 31 SCRIPT SHOT TODAY: 5m 30s

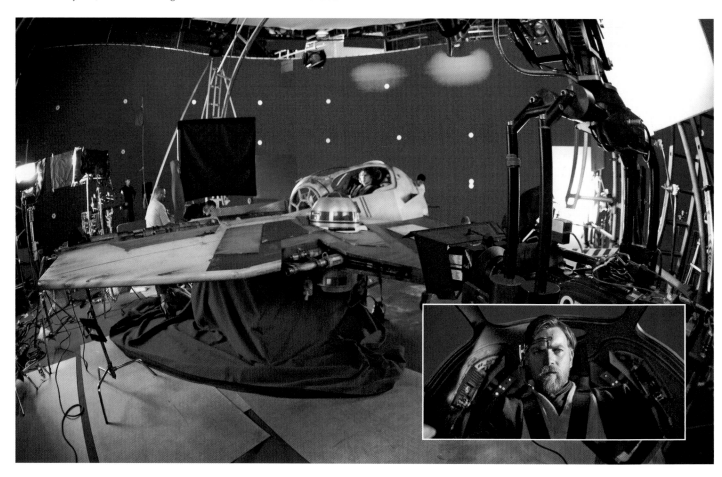

SHOOT DAY 32: TUESDAY, AUGUST 12, 2003

LOCATION: Stages 3 & 5

SET: Coruscant landing platform—Naboo skiff; hangar bay—Federation cruiser

SCENES SHOT: 143 (Padmé refuses to let Captain Typho join her, and Obi-Wan slips on board), 143A (Padmé & C-3PO pilot the Naboo skiff)

Today is the last work day for Anthony Daniels, Natalie Portman, and Jay Laga'aia. "We've accomplished all the heavy dialogue scenes, so now what we have left is all the action scenes," Jayne-Ann says.

Sitting on green crates, the three actors chat as they wait for the first setup. "Natalie's a young woman now," Laga'aia would say, "whereas before, she played a young woman, but she was really still a teenager. Every time we'd cut, she'd have her friends from school there and they'd just turn into teenagers again, which was lovely to see. But this time around, she seems to be a lot more grounded."

George approaches Natalie to tell her about a new scene aboard the Naboo skiff as it flies toward Mustafar. Padmé is distraught, he explains, because Obi-Wan has told her about Anakin's turn to the dark side. "This is you sitting there thinking about the news," Lucas says, adding that they're going to shoot the new scene two ways: with C-3PO talking to her while she's crying, and with C-3PO not talking to her as she's crying.

Ewan arrives and gives Natalie a hug. He'd like to find her before she departs, he says. Laga'aia bids farewell to Lucas, Portman, and others as he leaves the set.

Lucas then talks Daniels through the scene and lets the actor know that he can ad-lib: "You can talk about how you're not really a combat droid . . . and we'll put the dialogue in later."

"This is the climax of the movie, I can tell," Daniels says, laconically.

Seated on a box, Lucas watches the scene intently. Take. "Can we get more extreme?" he asks.

Portman asks for a cut. "We're going to do one more with a chattering Threepio, which will probably make you cry even more," Lucas jokes. Take.

"We'll do one more. Give me as much as you've got." Natalie takes a deep breath. As they're rolling, Lucas calls out instructions: "Push the autopilot button and lean back." On the monitors, a tear can be seen rolling down Portman's face.

"Folks, that was Natalie's and Anthony's last shot with us," Fletcher says shortly afterward, and there is much applause. George walks over to them. "Thank you, Tony." He hugs Natalie.

"I got a Styrofoam cup of champagne," Portman says, laughing. "The usual in the glamorous movie world."

As she leaves, Anthony autographs marker tape for crew. A few moments later, Daniels is alone. "I guess this is show business. An empty stage and already I've turned to drink," he says and takes a sip from his cup. "It's been fun. I think we can say, 'Cut.'"

LOCATION WRAP: 20:15   SETUPS: 40
SCRIPT SHOT TODAY: 2m 14s
EDITING: Anthony Daniels to do ADR [additional dialogue recording] with Jett Sally [assistant editor] on completion of sc. 143 & Naboo skiff scene.

Far left: Christensen (Anakin) and McGregor (Obi-Wan, inset) take turns in production's sole starfighter cockpit. Top left: DP Tattersall and Lucas. "George likes to shoot fast and loose," Tattersall says. "He likes to shoot with zoom lenses, and one of his phrases is, 'It's better to have more slates than takes.'" Top right: Stuntmen on the revolving set (insert), this time made up as the elevator shaft. Above: R2-D2 and Daniels.

SHOOT DAY 33: Wednesday, August 13, 2003

LOCATION: Stages 1 & 2

SET: Elevator door—revolve "B"; elevator shaft—Federation cruiser

SCENES SHOT: 22 (droids find Anakin, who flips himself up), 31pt (the elevator shaft turns; Anakin, Obi-Wan, and Palpatine hang from wires)

Ewan and Ian are sitting with George in the video village, watching the stuntmen on the revolving set. Lucas explains to the actors what's happening. Turning to McDiarmid, he says, "And then I have to place you on the spinning wall."

"I can't wait for that," Ian says, not entirely enthusiastic.

Later, Lucas does an advance inspection of the Mustafar conference room on Stage 7. Drawn up conceptually many months ago, honed and made practical by the Australia art department, the construction department actually built it. "Really, we have several different departments," construction manager Hadju explains. "Carpentry is the biggest one, followed by set finishing, the plaster department, stagehands, and riggers (who also look after lighting), then steelworkers and sculptors—three hundred forty-five crew members.

"My guys feel like they're the unsung heroes, if ya like," he adds. "I expect we'll spend around one million dollars on timber and plywood and board product. Paint, we basically run out of because the manufacturers run out. And the same with timber and plywood and MDF [medium-density fiberboard]—they pretty much run out. They don't have enough in the country to supply us. Huge amounts. Huge quantities. Just in liquid sili-

cone, which we use for taking molds, we've used nearly two tons. It's quite unlike any other show that we've ever done, or will ever get to do."

LOCATION WRAP: 19:45   SETUPS: 36   SCRIPT SHOT TODAY: 1m 11s

Top left: Preparations are made for the cruiser generator room scene. Above: Fay David visits Lucas on the set. Top right: In the video village, animatics of the scene are reviewed. Above right: McCallum and Fletcher, who, as a younger man, traveled in Europe and North America for four years, working in an English pub and on a Canadian cattle ranch. When he returned home, he got a job in television, as a studio cameraman, then a floor manager. Fletcher broke into the film business and, among many other projects, was 1st AD on Phillip Noyce's Dead Calm (1989) and with Carroll Ballard, one of Lucas's old friends, on Wind (1992).

SHOOT DAY 34: THURSDAY, AUGUST 14, 2003

LOCATION: Stage 2

SET: Underwater—generator room; underwater Utapau sinkhole/cave

SCENES SHOT: 105 & 120pt (Obi-Wan dives in, fits breathing device, swims to rock wall), 7pt (Obi-Wan in hand-to-hand combat with droid)

The permanent tub located on Stage 2 has been filled with tons of water. A protective barrier runs around it, and throughout the shoot here, the hum of generators will be heard. Of the divers in the pool, some are stuntpeople; others, camera operators.

"The stunt guys have to grab Obi-Wan just as he gets to the camera," Lucas is saying to Gillard. "It'll be fine," he adds to Fay David, "but it's going to be painful to get."

Also in the water is McGregor, who—despite swimming around in his specially-designed-for-water Jedi garb—says, "It's quite different now. When I did Episode I, I didn't really have any idea what to expect. I remember being shown around the sets by George; they were building a big submarine and I asked George whether we would be filming underwater in it. And he looked at me like I was mad, and just said that none of it's real, you know, it's not real. So nearing the end of Episode III, I'm quite well practiced in the arts of making the magic."

Between takes, actors and divers float with the aid of life preservers. "It's a good shot even if it's not a perfect shot," Lucas says to McGregor.

"I didn't really get dragged back," the actor says.

"Can you really yank him back?" Lucas asks the stuntmen, who will be

replaced by CG super battle droids intent on drowning Obi-Wan. They can, so they do one more.

"That completes that scene, folks. Moving onto the wall then," Fletcher announces, and a cave wall is lowered in to the water.

"Very good?" McCallum asks Lucas.

"Yep. There are a bunch of scenes, so it's tricky," he replies.

But by end of day, Lucas can say to Knoll, "I didn't think we were going to get this far. I thought this was going to be a total disaster, but we can do it."

LOCATION WRAP: 20:15   SETUPS: 46   SCRIPT SHOT TODAY: 1m 18s
DIVE SUPERVISOR: Rick MacClure

SHOOT DAY 35: FRIDAY, AUGUST 15, 2003

LOCATION: Stage 2

SET: Utapaun rock wall; Federation cruiser—vent shaft

SCENES SHOT: 8 (Obi-Wan and Anakin reach the hatch and get out)

Many crew are feeling the strain of constant twelve-to-sixteen hour days. On-set nurse Marguerite O'Sullivan, who used to be a Club Med nurse, sees about a hundred people per week. Neck and shoulder pain are the most common ailments, though she mostly distributes vitamins and Band-Aids. Bigger problems can include the strain of barely seeing your family for weeks or months on end.

"I explain it to my kids," McCallum says. "You don't get to go to their baseball games, their basketball games, and homecoming things. You miss out on their life and their development. But you talk every day. You keep the connection.

"And I'm not the only one. Really, you have a bunch of people who are just trying to make a living. They're all freelance, their hours are horrendous, and they, too, have to sacrifice their kids' birthdays and their wedding anniversaries. The truth is you give up an enormous amount to be in the film business."

One of the business's riskier crafts is that involving stunts. During the Mace-Palpatine fight, "Rob and I ended up doing second unit," McCallum says, "and there was a pretty complicated shot. The stuntman had rehearsed it for days and the first take was fine. But when we did a second, safety take, he hit his leg on the stairs and broke it. Rob and I were all over him, saying we were sorry, and he said, 'That's what I do.' I turned to Nick, and, without missing a beat, he said, 'Bring in the next stuntman.' That's the business they're in; those are the additional sacrifices they make."

Back at Skywalker Ranch, Ben Burtt and Dan Gregoire are in the middle of a conference call with Steven Spielberg, who is in Los Angeles. Together they're reviewing animatics of the Mustafar duel between Obi-Wan and Anakin.

Over the speakerphone, Spielberg says, "I want these guys pouring, dripping sweat. Their hair should at some point be smoking." He asks Burtt about a sequence in which Anakin seems to be hurling lava at his former Master.

"The idea is that Anakin is using the Force," Burtt explains.

"That's a great idea," Spielberg says.

In the next shot, Obi-Wan parts a wave of lava.

"The Moses effect," Spielberg comments. "I like all this because it's biblical and mythological—but it feels slow to me." So work continues.

LOCATION WRAP: 19:45   SETUPS: 60   SCRIPT SHOT TODAY: 1m 57s

SHOOT DAY 36: MONDAY, AUGUST 18, 2003

LOCATION: Stage 5

SET: Jedi Temple—hallway and alcove

SCENES SHOT: 132 (Yoda fights clone troopers), 133 (Obi-Wan and Yoda find bodies of young Jedi students)

Jayne-Ann asks Lucas if Obi-Wan should be wearing a cloak as he makes his way clandestinely through the Jedi Temple. McGregor is of the opinion that if Obi-Wan has lost it on Utapau, he should not have a new one. Lucas thinks he could've picked one up on the Alderaan cruiser.

"I wouldn't have gone to get a cloak, would I?" McGregor wonders.

"I don't think anyone's going to ask that question," Lucas predicts. "And if you're creeping around, wearing a cloak makes it feel sneakier."

Meanwhile, the Jedi younglings are in the makeup room getting prepared for their big scene. "My dad does filming on *Star Wars*," says one. "My father's a grip," says another. Among the little Padawans are Ian Gracie's son Will, and Ty Teiger's son Joel.

To the pleased looks of family and well-wishers, the younglings lie down on the set for their big scene, pretending to be Anakin's victims. After the last take, the children are all happy. "Very good, kids," Lucas says. "Nobody moved."

LOCATION WRAP: 20:30   SETUPS: 46   SCRIPT SHOT TODAY: 3m 36s

SHOOT DAY 37: TUESDAY, AUGUST 19, 2003

LOCATION: Stage 1

SET: Hallway—Federation cruiser

SCENES SHOT: 6 (Obi-Wan & Anakin meet General Grievous; Shaak Ti is killed), 42 (they are trapped in a ray shield box)

"This is Artoo's last shot," Lucas says, after discussing the blocking with droid wrangler Don Bies. "Artoo is the unsung hero of the two trilogies," he adds. "He's the only one who knows the whole story."

Following crew photo ops with R2-D2, Don Bies and Justin Dix carry away the iconic droid.

"I was in Artoo's last scene and it was quite weird," McGregor remembers. "I find myself quite choked up about it, about this robot, you know."

LOCATION WRAP: 19:45   SETUPS: 52   SCRIPT SHOT TODAY: 4m 27s

NOTES: Denise Ream & Samir Moon (ILM) arrived in Sydney.

SHOOT DAY 38: WEDNESDAY, AUGUST 20, 2003

LOCATION: Stage 1

SET: Utapau—landing platform

SCENES SHOT: 80 (Tion Medon is questioned about the visitor)

The note "SWF" on a Call Sheet next to an actor's name means it's not only his or her first day of work, but also the last, which is the case for many cast in tertiary roles. "For these sorts of characters, there's very little time to rehearse," Bruce Spense (Tion Medon) explains. "You just walk out

Above: The vent shaft under construction on July 29. One side of the wall is removable to enable the cameras to get in close and maneuver. "The camera will be 8 or 10 inches from the actor's head," assistant art director Clive Memmott explains. "So the drawings specified what every centimeter is for and assigned it a paint color and a texture." As of August 18, construction continues on the general's quarters (above right) and the Mustafar war room (right), both housed in immense Stage 7.

and do your scene on the day, so you really have to bring a lot of information to help you open up those little moments. But we did a lot of makeup tests and a lot of work on the costume, so, as we started to actually make the face move, little mannerisms, little elements, and little twitches of that character started to develop."

On a platform surrounded by greenscreen, multiple takes are quickly shot with Spense (*The Road Warrior*, 1981) and McGregor.

"Cut. Great," Lucas says. Fletcher announces that it was Bruce's last shot as the director climbs the stairs to shake the actor's hand.

LOCATION WRAP: 20:15   SETUPS: 57   SCRIPT SHOT TODAY: 2m 13s

SHOOT DAY 39: Thursday, August 21, 2003
LOCATION: Stage 1
SET: Utapau—secret landing platform
SCENES SHOT: 125 (Obi-Wan makes contact with Bail Organa)

A typical *Star Wars* set involves frequently being blinded, as cast and crew walk in and out of very intense lights. While struggling to see, it's best to stand still, rather than trip over any number of wires, cables, and electrical cords that snake endlessly along the ground. All the fiber-optic cables have one destination: the mobile "mother ship," which is the black-tented abode of high-definition supervisor Fred Meyers.

This is where the HD footage and "meta data" is vetted and monitored as it's transferred to Roger Barton and Jett Sally in the editorial suite. Here

Meyers sits day after day, never far from the set, overseeing banks of computers, electronic units with blinking lights, and keyboards glowing blue in the obscurity.

LOCATION WRAP: 20:15   SETUPS: 56   SCRIPT SHOT TODAY: 1m 36s
NOTES: Hayden Christensen had his final Darth Vader costume fitting.

SHOOT DAY 40: Friday, August 22, 2003
LOCATION: Stage 1
SET: Hangar bay on side
SCENES SHOT: 40 (Obi-Wan and Anakin struggle on pipes; Palpatine falls)

During a second day of fairly noneventful filming, Lucas is free to step back and take a look at the big picture: "You have to make sure that you're being diligent about telling the story of the movie. Because once the film gets on the screen, it's really unforgiving. Any little tangent can become boring. If you screw up five minutes, it affects the next ten or fifteen minutes. If your first half hour isn't that great, your last half hour better be really spectacular. If it isn't, then you're building up a lot of bad will."

Top: McFarlane behind the HD camera; Bruce Spense (Tion Medon), a denizen of the planet Utapau, with Lucas. Above: HD supervisor Fred Meyers in the "mother ship." Above right: Including the death of Nute Gunray, Anakin's rampage through the Mustafar conference and war rooms is portrayed for reference in the visual script.

"Over the last thirty years, the sophistication of the audience's cinema knowledge and cinema psychology has really grown. Back when I was shortcutting, it was unusual. I shortcut by not holding long shots, not doing establishing shots, and by making large leaps forward in the editing. When I was doing the first *Star Wars*, I was reasonably avant garde. Now it's completely accepted, because people's skill at reading images in motion is much better. Younger audiences can pretty much follow everything, because they see a commercial; they see MTV videos; they do it in video games. Their ability to see things and follow them is much more acute, and that's just a matter of the culture learning."

LOCATION WRAP: 19:45   SETUPS: 42   SCRIPT SHOT TODAY: 1m 49s

SHOOT DAY 41: Monday, August 25, 2003

LOCATION: Stage 2
SET: Mustafar main conference room
SCENES SHOT: 135pt (Anakin destroys the rest of the Separatists), 150pt (Obi-Wan and Anakin fight in the conference room)

"Everything was great—except obviously the door didn't open," Lucas says to Silas Carson, who plays two characters in two different death scenes. Today he is being killed as Neimoidian viceroy Nute Gunray; later he'll be blasted to death as Jedi Ki-Adi-Mundi.

In Nute's case, Anakin Skywalker does the honors. As they rehearse, Christensen walks through the set, methodically killing additional CG characters. During the first take, Fletcher calls out "droids" to cue the arrival of droidekas. Lights flash to simulate their CG blasts.

"It looked good," Lucas says to Christensen. "I'm just going to show you a picture of Wat Tambor," he adds, indicating a spot where the actor can pretend to grasp the CG Separatist—as he stabs him. "This is Shu Mai, who you kill on the table," Lucas continues, showing him another photo. "It's always nice to get to know the people you're killing."

"Final checks, please," Fletcher calls out.

As they roll cameras and Christensen moves about the room, all that can be heard are his breathing and footsteps as he cuts an imaginary swath of death. Despite some problems with cues, which create some unexpected results, Lucas remarks, "Hmm . . . That's not bad, in its own weird way."

LOCATION WRAP: 20:15   SETUPS: 33   SCRIPT SHOT TODAY: 1m 48s

SHOOT DAY 42: Tuesday, August 26, 2003

LOCATION: Stage 4
SET: Mustafar main collection plant
SCENES SHOT: 157 (Anakin and Obi-Wan fight)

"I decided to have the actors focus on their acting for the first part of the film, and then have them focus on their swordfighting," Lucas explains. "To mix those up is harder for an actor to cope with, in terms of what he has to learn. Ewan had to learn a thousand moves—and you really have to memorize them well, or you get hit in the head. It's also much more tedious shooting action scenes, because they get broken down into little

pieces. So it's difficult and dangerous, and people wear out.

"Toward the end of the movie, we have one of the longest continuous swordfights ever filmed," he adds. "Days and days and weeks and weeks of shooting, of these guys coming in at seven in the morning and fighting till seven at night, with not very much rest. It is physically exhausting for them."

As they prepare for the second half of the Obi-Wan–Anakin duel, the director goes over the schedule with Fletcher. Trisha then asks George what will be staining the Jedi robes on Mustafar: soot, dust, or lava by-product? Lucas then talks with makeup supervisor Nikki Gooley about the sweat progression for a multiday fight shot out of continuity, for the Jedi can't be dripping sweat in one scene and dry the next.

Christensen arrives on set, as does McCallum. Within a large rectangle draped in blue, McGregor and Christensen shake hands and exchange a

few warm-up parries. Lucas goes in tight and then wide: "That way, we'll save ourselves a move," he says.

Hayden then performs his own stunt, falling two yards backward onto a blue mattress. "I want to try one with more struggle," Lucas tells him. Take.

"Too much?" Hayden asks.

"No. It was good. You just have to tilt your head up." Take. "Great. That was excellent."

LOCATION WRAP: 20:00   SETUPS: 63   SCRIPT SHOT TODAY: 1m 07s

---

Wednesday, August 27: After nineteen days of prefab materials prep, construction begins on the Darth Vader rehab chamber.

Top panels: Amid a sea of green, the Jedi fight in the collection plant. The tower collection-arm battle continues on the video village monitors (above) and on the set (inset right). Above right: McGregor and Christensen stand on what will eventually be platforms floating along a lava river; director and crew look on, including "A" camera clapper loader Williams, Harding, dolly grip Brett McDowell, and Gillard.

SHOOT DAY 43: WEDNESDAY, AUGUST 27, 2003
LOCATION: Stage 3
SET: Mustafar collection tower arm, floating platforms
SCENES SHOT: 160pt (Obi-Wan and Anakin fight continues)

McGregor is standing on a small rectangular platform that's resting on springs, while Christensen is on another rectangular platform that circles Ewan's, riding on tracks.

"Ewan has always been a great swordfighter," Lucas says. "He and Ray Park [Darth Maul] were very good. Christensen is very athletic, and he's also very good at it. The difference in this particular film is they have to fight each other. As actors, there's a little bit of competitiveness about who's going to be the better swordfighter. So we got some very, very good performances."

As they approach the end of the climactic battle between Obi-Wan and Anakin, Gillard explains how he's rated the various *Star Wars* swordsmen: "On *Attack of the Clones*, I had to give them levels," he says. "Sidious is a level nine [out of ten]. On this film, Obi is eight—he's moved up—Anakin is a nine; Mace is a nine, Yoda is a nine. They're up with Sidious. Once you get to eight, you have a Pandora's box. You could go any way with it. The way not to go is the dark side. But it would tempt you, because that would jump you right past the others. So you need to arrive at level eight at the right age—not as young as Anakin. That young, the dark side is just too tempting."

LOCATION WRAP: 20:00   SETUPS: 58   SCRIPT SHOT TODAY: 1m 02s
NOTE: Hayden Christensen hurt his knee during filming today due to a lightsaber hitting him.

SHOOT DAY 44: THURSDAY, AUGUST 28, 2003
LOCATION: Stage 3
SET: Mustafar collection tower arm, floating platforms
SCENES SHOT: 158pt, 160pt

On what looks like a miniature Leaning Tower of Pisa, the battle continues—shot by the digital cameras that have performed flawlessly.

"As we do each picture, we're learning more and more how to shoot with digital technology," Lucas says. "On *Phantom Menace*, we did just a few shots, because we were really in the experimental stage. On *Attack of the Clones*, we were able to shoot the whole film digitally. But the cameras we had were the very first off the production line, so there was still a lot of experimentation going on. For the crew and myself, there was a lot of learning about how to use this new technology. On Episode III, the cameras and lenses have been improved, and we really know what we're doing.

"Digital is democratizing film," Lucas continues, "because it cuts the cost enormously—especially for lower budget films—and eventually it will cut the cost of distributing films. Ultimately, digital is the equivalent of going from frescoes to oil painting, in terms of the flexibility and the freedom it gives the artist."

"We don't believe that HD is the foundation of digital," McCallum adds. "It's just the first step. We believe there are going to be hard-disk systems where this issue of resolution will completely disappear—where the resolution will be two, three, four times that of film. That's in the future. And it's no different than what happened with color or sound or nonlinear editing. You have to go through a nascent period during which you've got people who are becoming facile with the tools. You have to learn what the

differences are, the pros and the cons. But I don't think the next generation has a single problem using digital cinematography. They're already there."

LOCATION WRAP: 20:15   SETUPS: 80   SCRIPT SHOT TODAY: 1m 43s

SHOOT DAY 45: FRIDAY, AUGUST 29, 2003
LOCATION: Stage 1
SET: Control room balcony; pipe across the lava
SCENES SHOT: 155 (Anakin is forced to tightrope walk over the lava)

A rare bit of Episode III casting news is that Keisha Castle-Hughes, whom Lucas had wanted to hire so many weeks ago, has actually been cast as the Queen of Naboo. On Friday, Biggar flies to New Zealand to take the young actress's measurements.

On the more mundane side, Nurse O'Sullivan reports that the second wave of flu is taking its toll on the crew (the first bout was back in July). With only a little more than two weeks of principal photography left, McCallum comments that this part of the shoot, for nearly all the crew, is dominated by the question: *Where is my next job coming from?*

After today's fighting wraps, in honor of the movie's two thousandth setup, production has its second champagne celebration.

LOCATION WRAP: 19:15   SETUPS: 65   SCRIPT SHOT TODAY: 0m 53s

Friday, August 29: Darth Vader rehab chamber set is dressed and rigged, after three days of construction.

SHOOT DAY 46: MONDAY, SEPTEMBER 1, 2003

LOCATION: Stages 1 & 4
SET: Mustafar volcano edge; Imperial rehab center
SCENES SHOT: 156 (Anakin and Obi-Wan fight), 174 (Darth Vader lives)

Many of the Australian crew have remarked that yesterday was the first day of spring. The second will see the rebirth of Darth Vader, the Dark Lord who has lain dormant these last twenty years.

But first, on Stage 1, production prepares to record the fall of Anakin Skywalker, just prior to his underworld renaissance. The set is a large triangle with one side placed on the floor, and the volcano cliff as the hypotenuse.

While fluorescent red is painted onto rocks to make them more lava-like, Lucas shows Biggar where Anakin is injured–"He gets cut right across the knee"–so they put blue stockings on Hayden's shins and another one on his left forearm, which will also be cut off. Anakin receives his near-fatal injury when he jumps at Obi-Wan, who, in one swipe, deprives him of his three remaining limbs. Anakin rolls down the side of the volcano, stopping perilously close to the lava.

Top right: The mask goes on, and Christensen is reborn, "more machine than man," as Darth Vader–who takes his place next to Darth Sidious (McDiarmid); the two are then recorded on the rehab center set (inset) by Harding's "B" camera with Brett McDowell astride a ladder holding the boom mike (above left). Left: Christensen (Vader) talks things over with Lucas and Tenggren.

McGregor joins Christensen on set. During the first take, McGregor stops in the middle. "Everyone in here has to be still," he says. "It's a very important moment."

After the first complete take, Lucas and McGregor discuss where he should say each line: "As you watch Anakin slide down, how about if you take one step forward," Lucas suggests. "For a moment, you think about it. Your first impulse is to save him—but then you realize you can't."

As the takes multiply and the actors find their rhythm and emotions, the scene becomes more and more powerful. Christensen yells, "I hate you!"

McGregor says, "I love you. But I will not help you." Lucas explains that what Obi-Wan's really saying to Anakin is: "*You were our only hope—and you blew it. Now we don't have any hope.*"

Take. After Anakin implores Obi-Wan to save him, George asks Ewan to say "I will not . . ." softer, almost to himself. Take. "After he bursts into flames," Lucas directs, "it's as if you're talking to a dead person. To a piece of toast." He suggests, to drive home this point, that McGregor change the words in the script to the past tense, "I *loved* you."

The actor acquiesces, but points out that his subsequent line would have to change to "But I *could* not help you." Lucas agrees, and Tenggren alters the script accordingly.

Christensen groans to get into character, and then gives an emotional delivery of the two lines, "Help me, Master," and "I hate you!"

"That was fantastic," George says.

As he leaves the set for lunch, Hayden says, "Just another day playing in the dirt." And Lucas replies, referring to the afternoon scenes, "Go become Darth Vader."

A crowd is gathering late in the afternoon on Stage 4. The set is minimal: a raised platform and a table. Christensen isn't yet in costume as he discusses the action with Lucas.

"Is it really going to be that hard to get out of the restraints?" he asks.

"No," Lucas responds, "but I need you to build up the anger in yourself."

The lights are dimmed in the middle of the rehearsal, creating a somber mood and casting long shadows. Because Christensen in his Vader costume can't walk very far, a makeshift dressing room has been constructed near the set. From behind its white curtains, laughter can be heard as Hayden

Right: Prosthetic-makeup artist Kerrin Jackson works on Christensen in his "burnt Anakin" suit. "My favorite prosthetic makeup is 'Burnt Anakin,' " Dave Elsey says, "because, in many ways I feel like I've been researching this makeup since I was a kid and first saw Return of the Jedi. *To me this was a chance to do something fresh, in every sense of the word, for* Star Wars. *Although we'd seen Vader without his helmet at the tail end of the first trilogy, I always wanted to know how he'd got so badly scarred and the reason he had to wear the Vader suit. I had read that he had fallen into volcanic lava, and had always, in my mind, been creating a prosthetic makeup that demonstrated these devastating injuries. In other words, I feel like I've been designing this since I was fifteen. And Hayden was fantastic in the makeup. He embraced it, brought it to life. He added a sense of dark evil." Left: On-set nurse Marguerite O'Sullivan cares for a crew member in the shadow of Vader. Top left: The visual script shows the moment where "burnt" Anakin is rescued by the Emperor—whose gesture echoes that of Obi-Wan touching Luke's forehead in Episode IV.*

changes. The number of spectators grows as word spreads that Darth Vader is about to appear, and those usually occupied in far-flung departments come to witness a bit of film history.

All is going according to plan when Lucas asks, "This may be a stupid question, but did anyone make ankle cuffs?" A flurry of eleventh-hour work ensues, as the answer is, plainly, no. Fortunately, it takes only twenty minutes to fabricate the cuffs from bits of a sprinkling system discovered by costume props supervisor Ivo Coveney.

Another few minutes later, Fletcher walks over to the dressing shack and asks Biggar through the curtains, "Is it working? Because there's no point in continuing if it isn't working."

"He has them on," Coveney responds. Colin then laughs to himself as he realizes that Vader doesn't need a makeup check, and so they have a bit more time than he'd thought. McDiarmid, already made up as Darth Sidious, sits on a stool waiting for his apprentice to appear.

"Okay. Cast on set, please," Fletcher announces–and the crowd applauds as Christensen, in full Darth Vader regalia, emerges. He greets McDiarmid, and they pat each other on the back.

Studio lights are turned down even lower, and the floor lights are turned up, creating a sinister ambience. Christensen inserts himself into the shackles, and the table is moved into a horizontal position to start the scene in which Vader breaks the bonds holding him to his operating table, screaming in pain.

"Action!" Lucas yells, and the table is slowly rotated to its vertical position. The leather of the Vader costume creaks as Hayden turns his head toward the Emperor, who informs him that Padmé is dead. Vader bursts his bonds and struggles forward. Upon "Cut," there is applause again.

Between takes, cool air is pumped through a ventilation system in the Vader costume. "Hayden, that was good," Lucas says, "except when you say, 'Where is Padmé? Is she all right?' Don't tilt your head back; tilt forward toward Sidious."

"I'm of the school where you don't really draw from your own experience," Christensen says. "I just try to use my imagination and what is motivating my character. I try to make that real for me as best as I can."

"The most special day of the shoot was when Hayden got into the Darth Vader suit," McCallum enthuses. "Every single person in the studio was waiting outside the stage doors–I'd told them they could get a glimpse of Hayden as Darth Vader. After he walked by, we had champagne and the party lasted for hours."

"It was thrilling," Christensen adds. "It was something I'd been looking forward to since I found out I got the part, hoping I'd get to don the dark helm. And I hope that my performance as Vader doesn't feel disjointed, that it has a linear connection, so that when people watch the original trilogy, they see my face under the mask. I hope it feels like one single character."

"Hayden is very good at doing the dark side, and always has been," Lucas says. "Having him finally make it into the suit completes the circle

---

Above: An aerial view of burnt Anakin on the operating table, with the Vader helmet suspended on a rod so it can be lowered onto Christensen's face. Above right: Immolated Anakin (Christensen) on the side of the volcano. Right: One of the hundreds of Polaroids snapped by technicians as continuity reference. The note reads "Blue screen glove; CGI dots," which refers to the computer graphics that will replace the actor's lower arm with a mechanical one.

of the movies. There was this key missing piece, which everybody's always wanted to see—and that's the return of Anakin Skywalker as Darth Vader."

Seen on the monitors in the video village, the close-ups of Vader are working, as a PA remarks that you can somehow feel his emotions through the helmet.

"Very good, Hayden," Lucas says. "Excellent."

"That's a wrap," Fletcher announces.

LOCATION WRAP: 20:30   SETUPS: 70   SCRIPT
SHOT TODAY: 1m 55s
NOTES: Company did 20 mins overtime today due to the nature of the Darth Vader costume.

SHOOT DAY 47: TUESDAY, SEPTEMBER 2, 2003
LOCATION: Stages 4 & 1
SET: Coruscant—Imperial rehab center; Mustafar—volcano edge
SCENES SHOT: 160 (Anakin slides down the embankment and bursts into flames), 164 (Darth Sidious finds Anakin still alive)

Christensen will spend nearly all of today in his burned-to-a-cinder prosthetic, or "toasty Anakin" costume. The suit is impressive, with exposed veins and pieces of charred flesh, but he describes wearing it as "being in a wet suit filled with gooey stuff." As he smokes a cigarette in his fried-flesh outfit, Hayden couldn't be more of an anti-tobacco public service announcement.

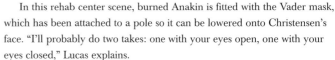

In this rehab center scene, burned Anakin is fitted with the Vader mask, which has been attached to a pole so it can be lowered onto Christensen's face. "I'll probably do two takes: one with your eyes open, one with your eyes closed," Lucas explains.

"The one with my eyes open, would you say I'm really unhappy with what's going on?" Hayden asks.

"No. You really don't know what's happening to you."

As the crew sets up, there's talk about Vader in the video village. "This puts a new perspective on Darth," McFarlane says. "He's a pathetic character, a sad character. I mean, he gets a nice new suit . . ."

"He gives up everything he loves for power," Lucas elaborates. "He makes a pact with the devil. But he kills the devil at the end, for love of his children."

Take. "Hayden," George calls up to the platform. "I'd like to try one where you keep your eyes open—and then open them real wide just as the mask comes down."

"I was thinking I could close my eyes just as the mask comes down."

"Well, the takes with your eyes open looked really good."

"Okay."

Back in the morning twilight of Stage 1, they shoot additional footage for yesterday's partially completed scene on the volcano, with

Christensen in his prosthetic. He walks over to the monitors and claps Rick's hand. "That was good," Rick says, "really moving."

The next take is just coverage, so Christensen lies on the ground, moaning for about a minute, till he cracks a smile and says he can't do anymore.

"Eyes in?" Lucas asks, and orange-yellow contacts are added to Christensen's eyes.

"Do you want me to just yell?" Hayden inquires.

"Yeah, start with your head down; look up—wait a beat—then yell, 'I hate you.' A couple of screams wouldn't hurt," Lucas answers. Take. "Great," Lucas says. "So that's lunch and then we'll do Sidious."

After lunch, Sidious's scene is quickly but poignantly completed. "There is a moment—just one moment," McDiarmid remembers. "It's just after Anakin's been almost destroyed and he's got a little life in him. Palpatine has sent for the medical team and he's waiting for them to arrive—and he just very gently touches Anakin's forehead. Sidious doesn't have any of the qualities we normally associate with humanity, except he does have a master-servant relationship with Anakin. *Anakin* means something to him."

LOCATION WRAP: 19:45   SETUPS: 62   SCRIPT SHOT TODAY: 2m 24s

SHOOT DAY 48: WEDNESDAY, SEPTEMBER 3, 2003
LOCATION: Stage 7
SET: General's quarters—Trade Federation cruiser
SCENES SHOT: 24pt (Anakin & Obi-Wan fight Count Dooku)

Ahead of schedule, the production has moved to the spectacular general's quarters. This work of art has taken more than two months to create and dress. It stretches more than fifty yards and recalls—as Lucas directed way back at the concept art stage—the Emperor's lair in *Return of the Jedi*, from its thronelike chair to its tuliped control areas.

More of the crew seem to be whistling *Star Wars* music today, perhaps because this set is so reminiscent of the first trilogy. "I remember doing *Return of the Jedi*," McDiarmid recalls. "And the Emperor was in that big set and George said, 'It's like Richard Nixon in the oval office.'

"I think it's very witty of George," he adds, "because Palpatine's first appearance in this film is in a chair that turns 'round to reveal an apparently kidnapped man strapped to it—but of course he's no less powerful than he's ever been."

What is recorded today of Kyle Rowling doubling for Dooku in his fight with Anakin will be cut together with Christopher Lee's performance, shot back in August. Wearing a T-shirt that reads MR. HORSEPOWER—given to him by his daughter Amanda in recognition of how much energy

directing requires–Lucas watches footage of Lee on a monitor and discusses with Knoll how they'll match it.

"Somehow we'll make it work," Lucas says, "and nobody will be able to tell the difference."

Moments later, he is working out the shot sequence with Fletcher, and adds, "If this goes together, it'll be a miracle."

He then goes over blocking with the principals, explaining that droids will file in as the two Jedi fight Dooku. After the first take, Lucas walks onto the set. He'd like Obi-Wan and Anakin to add a salutation to their meeting with the Chancellor: "Greetings, Chancellor," McGregor ad-libs, "today you are being rescued by Jedi Obi-Wan Kenobi and Anakin Skywalker."

McCallum arrives at that moment and Lucas says to him, "We're struggling, but we'll be okay."

But following the first rehearsal, there are more delays as lights are put in place.

"Let's just try one without dialogue before lunch or we're never going to get one in here," Lucas says, and McCallum adds, "We have to break the scene's back–if we don't, it's demoralizing for everyone."

Following lunch, during a take, someone accidentally lets a door bang close and Fletcher threatens to throw workers off the set if they can't be quiet. Rehearsals continue until Lucas says, "I say we shoot."

The drama increases, however, as Christensen's knee–injured a week ago–begins to act up, particularly when he needs to duel going upstairs.

Some of the tension dissipates after two exciting sword-slashing takes. There is some applause, too, as the crew becomes aware that Christensen is fighting through a fair amount of pain. But tension builds again as cuing problems arise, which creates more waiting. In the video village, they calculate that it's costing roughly $333 a minute to make this movie. "So if it takes three minutes to move a cable, it's one thousand dollars," Chris Neil says.

"I would've done it for twenty," McFarlane volunteers.

LOCATION WRAP: 20:00   SETUPS: 45   SCRIPT SHOT TODAY: 1m 31s

Above left: Lucas in the shirt given to him by his daughter Amanda. While (above) McCallum's daughter Mousey (Bene) poses with Nick Gillard (Cin Drallig) and Coinneach Alexander (Whie). Left and top right: McDiarmid, Christensen, and McGregor in the general's quarters. "Sometimes an actor will say, 'Gee, I feel I want to do this,' and we'll discuss it," Lucas says. "I do have to keep an open mind. So then I have to assess the change without getting led astray." Above middle: Christensen and Lucas.

SHOOT DAY 49: THURSDAY, SEPTEMBER 4, 2003
LOCATION: Stage 7
SET: General's quarters–Trade Federation cruiser
SCENES SHOT: 26pt (Anakin kills Count Dooku)

Because of his knee, Christensen is out for the first part of this morning, and his fencing double Ben Cooke fills in. "Hayden was really in pain," McCallum says. "But I was honest with him. I said we'd be in big trouble if we couldn't shoot, but that I didn't recommend cortisone because it would affect him for the rest of his life. So I said, 'Look. What I want is for you to do some physical therapy; we'll have a doctor here, and between each take we'll take a look at it'–and that helped him through the day."

In the village, Lucas discusses with Knoll a new computer program that uses "subsurface scattering" to better imitate how light reflects off different levels beneath the skin. About an hour later, Hayden arrives and takes a seat next to Knoll, putting his leg on a chair in front of him. McGregor walks over between takes. Looking at Hayden's leg, he jokes that now Obi-Wan will be the one killing Dooku. As the morning progresses, however, Christensen recuperates rapidly.

"What do you think, Hayden?" Lucas asks.

"I'm good to go."

"Okay. It's a real wide shot, so don't overdo it."

"All of this is deconstruction," Gillard says of the film's increasingly complex lightsaber battles. "They [the duelists] are always in check. If you get in check, you have to move out of it, which makes the moves much more complicated. It means that if you want to arrive at an end move, it might take you fifteen moves prior to that to get there. Just like chess. You start feinting and offering up parts of your body to try and tempt them. Anakin is offering his sword arm to Dooku, and he falls for it–and he knows as soon as Anakin draws his hand back, that it's all over. It's much more than a swordfight. The mental game that's going on is just as important as the moves. Dooku's weakness is that he's already beaten Anakin–and he's pretty sure he can do it again."

That afternoon, as they prepare to shoot Dooku's execution, Lucas says to McDiarmid and Christensen, "The thing to do is slow it down a bit. Pause before each line."

Christensen does push-ups to warm up, then they do a take.

"Try and struggle the next time on 'I shouldn't,' " Lucas suggests. Take.

"That was great," he says. "There was more struggle going on within you."

While waiting for the next setup, Ian and George talk about how

Palpatine will ultimately be disappointed with Anakin, after he's been permanently maimed by Obi-Wan: "He's less than what you bargained for," Lucas says. "By the end of the film, he's just a man in a shell. So when this young kid [Luke] comes along . . ." Lucas also explains that Darth Vader can't generate Sith lightning because he doesn't have real hands or arms.

During the next and final takes, Lucas watches a monitor on the set, with Tenggren sitting at his side. "I think that's it," he observes. "We made it."

LOCATION WRAP: 19:45   SETUPS: 63   SCRIPT SHOT TODAY: 1m 16s

SHOOT DAY 50: FRIDAY, SEPTEMBER 5, 2003

LOCATION: Stages 1 & 6
SET: Bridge—revolve; Jedi Temple—computer room
SCENES SHOT: 43 (the fight rages on as the ship rolls over), 138A (Yoda shows Obi-Wan a hologram of Anakin kneeling before Darth Sidious)

What had been scheduled for next Wednesday has been moved up to today because Christensen's knee won't permit him to do the scheduled fight scenes. As they prepare to shoot on the revolving set, McCallum arrives with questions ILM has posed about scenes to be shot next week, which will involve the lizard now known as Boga. "Originally the gimbal footage was going to be shot after the animation was done," McCallum says, "and it would've been controlled by the computer based on the animation. Rob was already back in the States when George changed his mind. I said,

'George, this is not what we discussed.' But he said, 'I want to get it over with; I don't want to be sitting six months from now on a stage with a gimbal. So let's try and make it work now.' And I said 'Okay, let's do it.' "

After reviewing ILM's inquiries, Lucas says the questions are too detailed, given the nature of what he'll be shooting. "It doesn't need to be perfect," he says to Rick. "My understanding is that I'm going to do the best I can. Anything that isn't right, we'll reshoot in March. All they have to do—all I need to know—is the lizard's gait."

After lunch, on Stage 6, Lucas goes over next week's shooting schedule with Jayne-Ann. Looking at his sides, he reads, " 'They fight . . . they fight . . . [turns page] . . . they fight.' "

LOCATION WRAP: 19:15   SETUPS: 55   SCRIPT SHOT TODAY: 4m 46s
NOTES: Governor Tarkin had an approval fitting by GWL today.

SHOOT DAY 51: MONDAY, SEPTEMBER 8, 2003

LOCATION: Stage 7
SET: Mustafar—main control room
SCENES SHOT: 130 (Anakin cuts down the rest of the Separatists)

The Mustafar control room is on the other end of Stage 7, about thirty yards from the general's quarters, which now resides in darkness. The extras playing Passel Argente, Nute Gunray, and assorted Neimoidian guards are getting into costume. The control room is another of the larger

sets. With glass vacuum tubes on control panels and copper-like fixtures, its decor is reminiscent of the golden age of horror films.

Gillard walks each of the thirteen or so Separatists through his or her death scene, as Hayden, whose knee has improved, rehearses his rampage route through the room. While waiting, Silas Carson (Nute Gunray) exercises his Neimoidian mouth, which triggers gears in his exposed animatronic head that move in sync.

"They shouldn't turn around to look at Anakin till that blast door shuts," Lucas says to Fletcher, who repeats the director's instruction to the assembled cast over the PA. After the first take, Lucas asks one Separatist to run to the blast doors. He tells another to "run back and forth, so you're basically going in circles." Colin once again clarifies through the PA: "When the hologram ends, you're all chatting; you'll hear me cue Anakin; you ignore that. The next cue you have to react to is: 'Door.' "

On "Action," Christensen goes through his choreography, with each Separatist falling as he "kills" them. As he prepares to exit the set, however, he spies a lone Neimoidian he's forgotten to kill–who gives him a cheerful wave. Hayden breaks into a large grin.

"That definitely goes on the DVD," McCallum says.

During the next take, the "A" camera goes wildly askance. Lucas asks what went wrong.

"The camera was hit by a Neimoidian," McFarlane says.

"The camera was hit by a Neimoidian?!"

"Yeah, he just ran–smack–into it."

"Those Neimoidians, always causing trouble . . ."

LOCATION WRAP: 20:00　　SETUPS: 56　　SCRIPT SHOT TODAY: 2m 34s
TRAVEL: Roger Barton (editor) and Jett Sally (assistant editor) flew SYD/LA.

Left: Obi-Wan (McGregor) watches a hologram of Vader killing Jedi, which will be added more than a year later in post. Above: Darth Vader (Christensen) cuts down two Neimoidian gunners (Dean Gould and Chris Mitchell) in the Mustafar war room. Right: A Neimoidian gets some air in the only way possible given his mask.

SHOOT DAY 52: TUESDAY, SEPTEMBER 9, 2003

    LOCATION: Stage 7

    SET: Mustafar—main control room

    SCENES SHOT: 148 (Anakin and Obi-Wan fight moves toward the control center)

One of the more intense moments of the Anakin–Obi-Wan lightsaber duel takes place toe-to-toe. "That toe-to-toe thing shows that they can't get through each other's defenses," Gillard explains, "because they know each other's moves so intimately. I think it's something like forty moves; I did the first eight and then I let them go with it."

During this action, the rhythmic *clack-clack-clack* of the steel lightsabers cracking against each other in rapid-fire succession can be heard. After one remarkable take, Christensen and McGregor repair to the village to watch the playback.

"Perfect," Lucas says, and there is applause. "That was really maybe the fastest we've ever done it," Ewan says to Hayden, and they shake hands.

"Hey, folks," Fletcher announces, "that completes the Anakin–Obi-Wan fight!"

LOCATION WRAP: 20:00   SETUPS: 51   SCRIPT SHOT TODAY: 29s
TRAVEL: Gavin Bocquet (production designer) flew Sydney-LA.

SHOOT DAY 53: WEDNESDAY, SEPTEMBER 10, 2003

    LOCATION: Stage 3

    SET: Blue elevator shaft

    SCENES SHOT: 31 (they run along elevator shaft)

With the departure of Bocquet, the editors, and many others, much of production is winding down. But for Christensen, work goes on as before.

At 6:20 A.M., after a 5:30 wake-up call and a 6:00 pick-up at his apartment on Bondi Beach, he walks, or shuffles, into the makeup room on the ground floor of Stage 2. Opera music is playing softly as hardly awake makeup artists begin their routines. Bare, uncomfortably bright lightbulbs run around the perimeters of large wood-framed mirrors clearly reflecting everyone's general fatigue. Second AD Deb sits nearby in the ADs' office. Originally from Adelaide, she fell in love with cinema watching Hitchcock classics.

Wearing a bathrobe over nondescript clothes and black sneakers, coffee in one hand, Hayden shaves himself with the other while sitting in what looks like a barber's chair. Makeup artist Shane Thomas heats up a towel in a microwave oven. Hairdresser Pip Lund and makeup artist Bliss MacGillicuddy arrive. Each actor is assigned one or more makeup people, and Shane has been assigned to Hayden. "He's making me look tan and

rested," Christensen mutters, whereas in reality he says he feels "tired and pale." Ian McDiarmid arrives at 6:30 A.M. Colin Fletcher pops in at 6:40 to verify that everyone is on schedule.

A fake scar is applied to Christensen's face with a material called Rigid Collodion, which is also used to heal cuts during boxing matches. Another scar, on his eyebrow, is real and resulted from a childhood accident on a slide. Two more scars on the left side of his chest came from a Portuguese man-of-war during a family vacation in Florida. At 7 A.M., key hairdresser Annette Miles takes over, working on Christensen's hair, and the music switches to something more contemporary.

Left: In Stage 2's hair and makeup department, makeup supervisor Nikki Gooley and makeup artist Shane Thomas prepare Christensen (Anakin) for another day on the set. "The first professional production I was in was The Member of the Wedding *by Carson McCullers," Christensen says, "I was nine or ten years old." Above and right: Weeks of training are put into action, as days and days of dueling take their toll on Christensen and McGregor.*

At 7:30 A.M., Christensen goes to his studio apartment in Stage 4, which consists of one room with a bed for naps, and another equipped with a couch, a beanbag chair, and a TV connected to a PlayStation 2 that he's never turned on. After breakfast—eggs and toast—medic Rob McMinn arrives to do what he can with Hayden's still-fragile knee, while the actor talks about a production company he's formed with his brother. Their film—*Shattered Glass*, starring Christensen and Hank Azaria—has just opened at the Toronto Film Festival.

"I definitely feel more acclimated this time around," Christensen says of his second *Star Wars* film. "Last time, I had the fish-out-of-water syndrome and was very much in awe of everything around me. It was a big change for me: I went from performing in high school plays and trying to make sure I made it on time to my tennis lessons, to playing a central role in one of the biggest films in popular culture."

"Amazed" is how he describes his reaction to seeing the finished *Attack of the Clones*. "You get to enjoy it on the same level as the public, because it's fresh and new when you see it because you haven't seen any of those sets," he says, adding, "George has amazing control, and his ability to manipulate the medium is unbelievable."

Christensen puts on his precostume clothes: two pairs of black pants, boots, and a T-shirt. By 7:50 A.M., he completes his transformation in Stage 4's changing room, which is nothing more than a closet big enough for

softened by the mats below. "Ian, are you up for another one?" Lucas asks.

"Yeah, go on," he replies.

Everyone breaks for lunch at 12:45. At two o'clock, Christensen is back in makeup for refurbishing, and, at 2:15 P.M., he's back on set. After a few more setups, Lucas happily remarks, "Well, we just do that and we're done." But Fletcher reminds him that they have an additional scene to do.

four people standing. Ian is here in the cramped quarters, too, getting dressed on the other side of a plywood wall.

"Is Palpatine here?" 2nd AD Paul Sullivan asks, poking his head in.

"Mind your own business," a voice comes from the other side.

"You see what I have to put up with?" Paul says. "Put that in your book."

By 8 A.M., Hayden is on stage. Whereas some might feel at least a twang of apprehension performing in one of the most anticipated films of all time, he feels a "rush" whenever he arrives on set—which is one of the things that attracted him to acting. Talking in a relaxed, almost subdued manner, he outlines once again how a theatrical agent spotted him when he was a kid, which led to commercials, stage acting, drama school, TV, and film.

Hayden's individual course now merges with life on the set. He and Ian must lie down on an approximately thirty-yard-long board that can be angled into the air to become a giant slide, which will in turn become an elevator shaft in postproduction. On one take, the angle is increased. Christensen grabs on to the side, but McDiarmid shoots by him, his fall

"Oh, that's right," Lucas says, less happily. "My God, why do I keep doing this to myself?"

Production moves on to the scenes pitting General Grievous against Obi-Wan, which means Christensen is done for the day. He says good-bye to Ewan and Ian. By 4:55 P.M., he's back in makeup for its removal, and Bob Marley is on the radio. McMinn comes in to go over the physical therapy plan for the next day. At 5:25 P.M., Christensen poses with McDiarmid for a public relations photo. At 5:30, Annette Miles fits him for a wig for the March reshoot (if Christensen has to change his hairstyle for any reason, they'll have an Anakin wig in reserve). At 5:40 P.M., an unusually early wrap for Christensen, he is driven the twenty minutes back to Bondi Beach.

"Doing Episode III is an immense learning experience," Hayden says in the car.

LOCATION WRAP: 20:00   SETUPS: 84   SCRIPT SHOT TODAY: 1m 11s

SHOOT DAY 54: THURSDAY, SEPTEMBER 11, 2003
LOCATION: Stages 3 & 6
SET: Utapau—Boga
SCENES SHOT: 83 (mount Boga), 87 (Obi-Wan fights General Grievous)

"What a handsome crew," communications director Lynne Hale remarks as the official on-set crew photo is snapped. Afterward, it's Obi-Wan versus Grievous and his bodyguards in another sea of green.

"Young lady, I've been doing this since before you were born," Lucas is saying to 3rd AD Samantha Smith. "I started this thirty years ago."

"Do you get time off for good behavior?" McFarlane asks.

"I got fifteen years off and raised my kids."

The fight with the bodyguards is quickly finished, and the crew applauds fencing double Michael Byrne and stuntman Dean Gould, who have finished their work on this fight.

"Is that it?" McGregor asks.

"All you have to do is fight Grievous, ride Boga, give the baby away, and you're done," Lucas says.

After lunch, McGregor continues with Rowling doubling for Grievous, who will be added later as a CG character.

"Grievous has got four arms," Gillard says of the combat. "We do a really complicated fight with two arms, but there are moves in there where Ewan is moving to the second two arms that obviously we don't have yet. We dispatch those two arms as quickly as possible. When he fights Grievous's four body-guards, it's totally different—that's quarterstaff, the same as with Darth Maul, but at another level now. If that comes off, it should be phenomenal. Ewan's done really well and is still in tip-top form."

Multiple takes and setups are quickly completed. "Very good," Lucas concludes. "I'd say we're on the wrong set."

"Guys, that completes the Obi-Grievous fight," Fletcher announces, and production moves to the next stage.

Later in the day, McGregor is astride Boga, sitting on a saddle placed on what looks like a bucking bronco machine, whose engine makes a whirring sound. A revolving six-sided mirror in the rafters reflects light onto the lizard, creating the illusion of movement. Knoll feels that the beast's motions are jerky and that it stops too suddenly. As late afternoon becomes early evening, he remarks, "Maybe it's a robot lizard."

LOCATION WRAP: 20:00   SETUPS: 64   SCRIPT SHOT TODAY: 2m 41s

SHOOT DAY 55: FRIDAY, SEPTEMBER 12, 2003
LOCATION: Stage 6
SET: Utapau—Boga
SCENES SHOT: 100 (Commander Cody returns Obi-Wan's lightsaber)

Wearing a blue bodysuit, actor Temuera Morrison is back—not as Jango Fett, whom he played in Episode II, but as Commander Cody, a Jango clone. From astride the mechanical lizard, whose move-

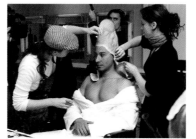

ments will be smoothed out in post, McGregor asks, "Is Grievous chasing me or am I behind him?"

"You're chasing him," Lucas replies. "So you can whip the lizard hard to catch up."

As the scenes change but the set stays the same, McGregor asks, "So I'm not chasing Grievous anymore?"

"You've killed Grievous and you're just going along."

After a few more takes and angles, they switch to Obi-Wan fighting droids while still seated on Boga. "Remember, the droids are about this high," Lucas says, indicating a level near the actor's feet. "So it's more like playing polo."

With these last few days of the shoot, crew are moving on to other projects, such as *Mask 2*, the next film scheduled at Fox Studios Australia. Today is the last day for most of the construction department. At 5:45 P.M., Lucas wraps, the earliest wrap ever for the on-set crew.

LOCATION WRAP: 20:00   SETUPS: 66   SCRIPT SHOT TODAY: 1m 15s

SHOOT DAY 56: MONDAY, SEPTEMBER 15, 2003
LOCATION: Stages 6 & 3
SET: Utapau—Boga; Tatooine
SCENES SHOT: 106 (Ki-Adi-Mundi is cut down by clone commanders), 180 (Obi-Wan hands baby to Owen Lars)

At long last, Lucas is adding to the scene he began shooting three years ago in Tunisia: Obi-Wan's gentle delivery of Luke Skywalker to the Lars family. Lucas carries the prop baby to McGregor, who, this time, will be handing Luke to Beru, not Owen. "I just felt it would be better if Luke were handed over to a woman," Lucas explains.

On "Action," McGregor gives the baby to Bonnie Maree Piesse (Aunt Beru), as followed by cameraman Harding, who pans right. Piesse then hands the baby to Owen Lars, whose part is being temporarily handled by on-set PA Hamish Roxburgh, because Joel Edgerton (young Owen) is unavailable.

Left: Holding a quarterstaff favored by Grievous and his bodyguards, Lucas demonstrates what he'd like McGregor (Obi-Wan) to do. Top: Temuera Morrison (Commander Cody), who will also play various clones, and McGregor. Middle: Silas Carson is made up as Ki-Adi-Mundi by prosthetic makeup and hair techni-

cians Katherine Brown and Sophie Fleming. Above: The "handsome" on-set production crew photo taken September 11. Sitting in the front row is McCallum, of whom art department coordinator Collette Birrell says, "He makes everyone feel they have an important role; he's generous."

Between takes, a crew member carefully cradles the prop baby to make sure the folds in its blanket remain the same for each take.

The last shot of the day belongs to Silas Carson, who is prepared for his second death scene, this time as Ki-Adi-Mundi. "You turn and look at the clones," Lucas says to him, "they pull out their guns, and—blam, blam, blam!"

LOCATION WRAP: 20:30   SETUPS: 88   SCRIPT SHOT TODAY: 1m 05s
NOTES: Ewan McGregor wrapped picture today.

SHOOT DAY 57: TUESDAY, SEPTEMBER 16, 2003
LOCATION: Stages 3 & 5
SET: Naboo main square; Chancellor's holding office
SCENES SHOT: 175pt (Padmé's funeral), 146pt (Palpatine and Yoda fight)

Taking part in Padmé's funeral procession is the Queen of Naboo, as played by Keisha Castle-Hughes. Resplendently mournful in her costume and headdress, she is followed by hooded dignitaries, blue guards, and about two dozen others. Leading them is Padmé's coffin (sans Portman) on a metal table with wheels. "There's one girl who's not following the way she should," Lucas remarks. The group walks in circles, and the only audible effect is the sound of their footsteps.

Ivo Coveney works on thirteen-year-old Keisha's headdress between takes. "It was about a month ago they first said something about *Star Wars*," she says. "I discussed it with my agent and my mom, then we decid-

ed like only a week and a half ago that I would come over and play the part. It was pretty tight; we came to Australia in the day before filming. I only just met George today, and I was really excited."

In keeping with *Star Wars* crowd-scene tradition, many of the crew have been cast in background parts, among them assistant publicist Lisa Shaunessy (a female Senator) and Jacqui Louez (Senator Jacquito)—George Lucas's and Rick McCallum's assistant.

"I officially have the best job on the film," Louez says, "which is to protect them and to make their lives easier."

LOCATION WRAP: 20:15   SETUPS: 58   SCRIPT SHOT TODAY: 3m 05s

SHOOT DAY 58–END OF PRINCIPAL PHOTOGRAPHY: WEDNESDAY, SEPTEMBER 17, 2003
LOCATION: Stages 4 & 2
SET: Imperial Star Destroyer
SCENES SHOT: 177 (the Emperor, Tarkin, and Darth Vader watch the construction of the Death Star)

Star Wars has returned to the bridge of a Star Destroyer. Imperial uniforms like those seen in *A New Hope* are making their first prequel trilogy appearance, worn by "pit" officers. The tension and joy are palpable among the crew and the crowd who have come to witness the end of the shoot. "The last day was very moving," McCallum says "It was a special, wacky day, because we shot on seven different sets—we were running constantly."

Lucas stands on the ramparts above the pit, giving directions to McDiarmid, Christensen, and Wayne Pygram (Tarkin): "It's your average Star Destroyer. Tarkin and the Emperor look at each other. Then Anakin steps up; Tarkin turns, looks at Anakin, and leaves. Then Anakin and the Emperor both turn and look out the window to contemplate the Death Star."

"Final checks, please," Fletcher calls out. Coveney puts Vader's helmet on Christensen.

"I hope he can see," Lucas says, as once again the actors are perched fairly high above the ground.

"And . . . action!" he calls out.

Left: Michael Byrne (Darth Sidious double) leaps from a Senate pod during the Sith's battle with Yoda. Above left: Keisha Castle-Hughes (Queen of Naboo) is touched up between takes, and then takes part in the funeral flanked by handmaidens and a Sio Bibble picture double. Right: Crew prepare the "pit" of the Star Destroyer. Above right: An aerial view of set; McCallum handles the slate for the last shot of the film (above, far right).

Darth Vader strides forward, taking his place next to the Emperor. Looks are exchanged. Tarkin exits, and the two Sith turn to look out into space.

"And . . . cut!" Lucas says.

He sets up another angle. "We need to do one more with highlights," the director says, referring to the lighting. During the next take, he instructs, "And you look at each other and . . . you look back. A little more to the right . . . okay, cut. I have to do one more."

As he did the first, McCallum prepares the last slate. "You got speed?" he asks. "V 177 G, Take One."

"And . . . action!" Lucas calls out–for the last time.

Vader crosses his arms.

"Take a half step forward, Ian . . . right there!" George says, and Ian stops.

"Cut. That's it. Done. Finished. All done!" Lucas announces–and many people applaud, as Rick hugs Hayden and everyone celebrates.

"You were fantastic," Lucas says to the two actors.

"Thank you for the opportunity," Christensen says.

"I can't wait to put it all together," Lucas says. "I think we have some great stuff." He then finds David Tattersall and informs him excitedly, "A hundred setups we did today! You can put *that* on a T-shirt."

"A hundred setups?!" Tattersall asks, genuinely surprised.

"A hundred. That's why I did that last one again."

"Just don't let the word out, or everyone will want to do it," McFarlane chimes in.

"Get those drinks going," Rick says.

Gillard and Lucas shake hands. Lucas then locates Knoll and says, "I've been working on it for eighteen months and I have exactly eighteen months to go."

"I feel like my vacation just ended," Knoll remarks, for, as of this moment, the burden of production has shifted to ILM.

As drinks are poured and tremendous relief is felt, bystanders and crew form a long semicircle facing McCallum, who, with mike in one hand and drink in another, says to the assembled: "This is a very emotional moment for me. But I do want to tell you, you have been the most fantastic group of people to work with. And definitely the nicest, the most fun–you've made it such an easy thing for us–I can't thank you all enough . . . and here's George."

Taking the mike offered by McCallum, Lucas says, "What Rick says goes for me, too. I must say this is actually the most fun film I've ever worked on. It's been really easy, and it's been very swift. And at the same time, everyone's worked in harmony, and that's extremely important. And there hasn't been a lot of crazy politics and ego and all the other things one finds on movie sets. This has definitely been the best crew I've ever worked with. I really enjoyed being with all of you. And I think we've made a great movie. I'm really looking forward to going in and cutting it and seeing what happens. Thank you–thank you very much–to all of you."

They all drink a toast. Someone from the back yells, "Thank you, George!" Everyone then watches a highlight reel of the shoot, which finishes with Fletcher saying, "And that's a wrap, everybody."

LOCATION WRAP: 21:00   SETUPS: 100   SCRIPT SHOT TODAY: 1m 57s
NOTES: End of principal photography–production wrapped five days ahead of schedule.

TOTALS:
PAGES SHOT TO DATE: 121 [OUT OF 130]
TOTAL SETUPS: 2883
TOTAL SCENES: 144
TOTAL SCENES TO COMPLETE: 41
TOTAL HOURS WORKED (FROM FIRST SHOT TO CAMERA WRAP): 709 hours 25 minutes
TOTAL SCRIPT TIMING SHOT: 144 minutes 46 seconds
[APPROXIMATE TIME SPENT PER SCRIPT-MINUTE FILMED: 4.9 hours]

NOTE ON LAST CALL SHEET:

To Everyone on the Crew,
Just a short note to tell you how truly fantastic you have been to work with–your professionalism, energy, humor, and lightning speed have allowed you to be unemployed 5 days earlier than originally scheduled!!! Seriously, though, it has been an honor and a truly great experience for us, and I hope you know how much both George and I appreciate all the hard work you have done. We are very grateful and indebted to all of you. You have made it so easy!

Australia Rules!!!

All Love, Rick.

EPILOGUE

On Day One, Trisha remembers Gavin saying to her, "Isn't it sad? This is our last start day for a *Star Wars* film."

About twenty-five hundred people attend the wrap party a few days after the end of principal photography. Many promise to work together again, but the atmosphere is slightly melancholy. Additional shooting for *Revenge* is scheduled, but no one knows for certain if they'll be involved. The greatest of their creative efforts is over, and an epoch has come to an end.

"I was happy; I was relieved," Jayne-Ann says. "It was a great shoot. It was fast and intense, and it was a lot of work, but it was civilized."

"It's amazing how it all comes together," Ty Teiger notes. "Because at the beginning, you get the script and think, *How are we going to get through it?* The trilogy has been a long part of my life. Both of my children have been born while I've been on these films. It's not often in your lifetime, as a film technician, that you can have the joy of working on such an amazing thing."

"It's always devastating to end a shoot," McCallum admits, "because you've really connected with people–no matter how many films you've done. But you've got to shut it off; you can't carry it with you. And then I get excited about postproduction."

"You're all friends, you know each other," Lucas says. "But I have a tendency to not let my private life and my professional life mix–and once the movie finishes, everybody goes their own way. When you're together, you're together, and when you're not, you're not."

Far left: Darth Vader (Christensen) arrives on the Star Destroyer bridge and gazes at the construction of the Death Star (inset, visual script). Left: Stills photographer Keith Hamshere and Lynne Hale; Murray and Birrell. Above: Lucas, McCallum, and Jacqui Louez with Christensen.

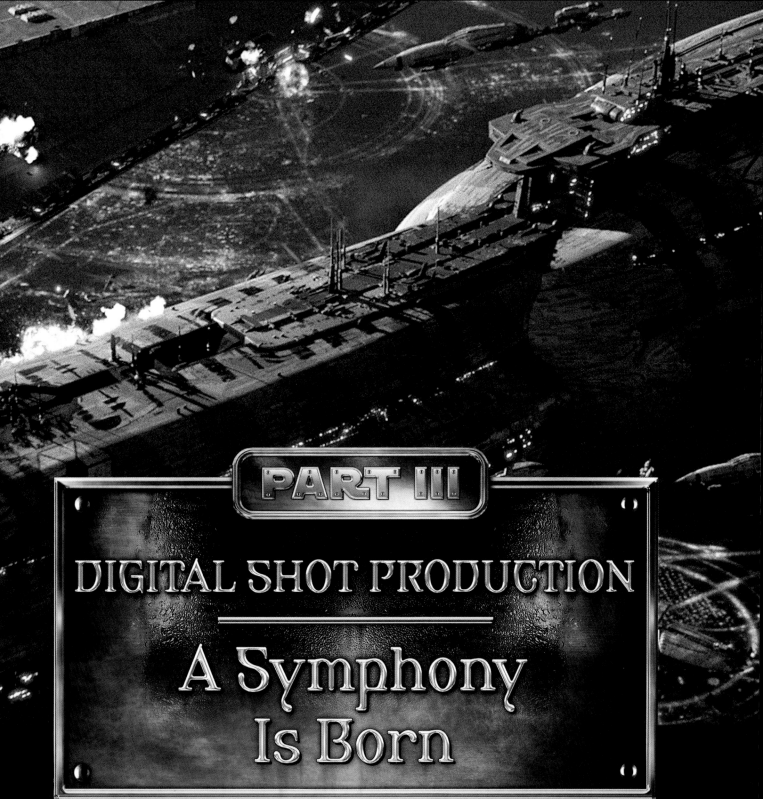

PART III

DIGITAL SHOT PRODUCTION

A Symphony Is Born

PROLOGUE: Editing

Previous spread: Like huge naval vessels, a Jedi cruiser and a Separatist flag ship exchange withering blaster-cannon exchanges in this final frame. Above: Lucas works with editor Roger Barton on the Avid. Right: McCallum, Tattersall, and Lucas. Below: In Sydney, dressed as stormtroopers and a Jedi are: assistant editor Jett Sally, Barton, apprentice editor John Briggs, and assistant editor Jason Ballantine.

"The auteur theory is very abstract and intellectual until you get to know filmmakers," Lucas says. "But when you know them personally and you know how they make their decisions, then you realize these people *are* their movies. Marty [Scorcese] *is* Marty's movies; Francis [Ford Coppola] *is* Francis's movies; Steven [Spielberg] *is* Steven's movies. You can actually see their sensibilities in their films.

"I come out of abstract filmmaking. I like the idea of cutting together contrasting images and ideas so they flow one after the other. If you watch a silent movie, you can see how a story is told; if you watch abstract films, you can see that by juxtaposing images, you also tell stories, and, in doing so, the issue of cutting on one frame rather than on another becomes very important.

"On the editorial level, which is the cinematic level, movies are a mass of objects moving across a large surface. You're watching these little details, which are the ones that make the cut work, as they move through the back of the frame. You're orchestrating how these things flow, by deciding how you cut from one shot to another. The subtlety of the medium demands that a star break the frame at the right moment, because what reaction you get has a lot to do with spatial relationships: where things are in the frame, what color things are, where the bright objects are--and where your eye is going to be.

"When the movie cuts to a different shot, if your eye has to move a great distance to follow an object, it becomes a rough cut; if your eye stays in the same place, then it's a smooth cut. If your eye has to move too much, you're usually lost for two frames on a cut. You don't understand what you're seeing because you can't register it that fast. If you're just cutting dialogue, it doesn't matter; it's just talking heads and the emphasis is *all* on the dialogue. But in my films, the dialogue is not where the movie is. My films are basically in the graphics. The emotional impact comes from the music—and from juxtaposing one image with the next.

"Cinema is about moving images. But it's moving from one image to the next that creates the emotional impact."

7 Directing on Three Fronts

Following the completion of principal photography, for most of the Australian crew, work on the film is over. As of October 2003, however, Lucas, Ben Burtt, and Roger Barton have begun editing in earnest. Because more than 50 percent of the movie–the digital percent–has yet to be created, Lucas says, "What I'm doing, in essence, is cutting the movie without seeing it. So I guess and I theorize that the editing might be right."

"We're in a weird, scary place right now," McCallum says, "which is normal at this stage. You know, we don't really have a movie yet. We've shot everything that was scheduled, but the digital elements are still to come. What's happening now is that George works with Ben from about 9 A.M. until 1 P.M., primarily on the action sequences. From 1 P.M. until about 2:30, he has lunch upstairs in the animatics department while working on visual effects shots to use as placeholders, so we can actually see the film just before Christmas 'complete.' It'll be very crude, but it will at least give us an indication of where everything is going.

"At about 3 P.M., George works for about three to four hours with Roger, primarily on the dramatic sequences. Together, George, Ben, and Roger are just going straight through the movie, assembling the picture and creating the first rough cut."

Of the three fronts Lucas is attacking, editorial and animatics are two. The third front, of course, is ILM. At this still-early stage, the visual effects juggernaut is continuing, primarily, to transform concepts into digital creatures, sets, and vehicles. ILM's workload will increase dramatically as soon as Lucas begins to turn

over edited sequences–a combination of principal photography, animatics, and concept art. At that point, ILM will start to meld the digital components to the images–characters, digi-matte paintings and so on–eventually showing them to Lucas as "finals": shots deemed complete, which Lucas reviews during "dailies." He may agree that a shot is "final," or send it back for additional work. If it's finalized, the shot is dropped into the cut, where Lucas has to approve it again. Even after this point, shots may change or be omitted as the film evolves.

Each step toward finals is closely monitored by ILM visual effects executive producer Denise Ream and producers Janet Lewin and Jill Brooks. Working hand in hand with visual effects supervisor John Knoll, animation director Rob Coleman, and a growing roster of department heads, they budget and analyze every sequence that ILM receives from editorial and every digital asset they have to create. They then strategize with McCallum and Kathryn Ramos to fine-tune their methodologies.

"Denise's job is to coordinate all the supervisors and make sure ILM has their working spaces, their environments, and everything else that they need to actually start to work," McCallum explains. Lewin deals with the "front end"–modeling, layout, animation, and digital simulation work–while Brooks is producing the technical directors, compositors, and stage work, or the "back end."

"So now I have this brief period up until Christmas, during which my job is to set up ILM," McCallum says. "If you arrive on a set that has a hundred fifty people, and you're not shooting, you still pay those hundred fifty people. In the same way, if you don't make up your mind about a visual effects shot, then you have about three hundred fifty people getting paid to do nothing. A film used to have maybe ten to fifty effects shots; we have at least two thousand. Where you once had a million dollars in effects shots, now you have forty or fifty million dollars' worth. On *Revenge*, the production crew worked for nine months, the shooting crew for three months—but the visual effects crew will work for eighteen months. And even as big as our sets were, we only spent about four and a half million dollars on all of them combined. We'll spend ten million dollars on our digital sets.

"One of the problems with these big visual effects films is that there's always been a distance between the filmmaking community and the effects community. But this has been a happy experience so far because we got ILM involved at the very beginning. They're such an integral part of the crew—the largest part of the crew—and they're doing the most awesome, mind-blowing work. They're all incredibly conscious of what it is that we need, the schedule we're up against, the amount of money we have to spend.

"So it's also a challenge for George," McCallum concludes. "He has to finish the first twenty-five minutes of the film by December 19. Then we have to be ready to move and shake by January 5."

FRIDAY, OCTOBER 31, 2003

ILM: As promised on the set, Lucas has cut together and turned over seven brief Yoda scenes, which amount to ninety-eight shots, for Coleman and his animation team to get started on.

"I'm in a very good place right now," Coleman says. In fact, his department has nearly finished replacing the Episode I Yoda puppet with digital Yoda—an exercise that Lucas and Coleman agreed would serve as a good warm-up—so the animation department is now primed and ready for Yoda's Episode III performance.

Friday, October 31: The following scenes have been turned over to ILM:
Sc. 56: CYQ (Coruscant Yoda's quarters)
Sc. 61, 62, 70: CJC 1 & 2 (Coruscant Jedi Council)
Sc. 171, 172, 173: SAC 2 & 3 (Alderaan space cruiser)
Note: The three-letter acronyms that follow scene numbers are used to designate scene locales; subsequent single digits indicate whether it's the first, second, or third scene to take place in that locale.

TUESDAY, NOVEMBER 4, 2003

ILM: Every day, various departments—layout, digi-matte painting, view paint, CG model making, compositing—meet to discuss works in progress. "We're in ILM mode," Fay David says, explaining that even much of what the Skywalker Ranch art department does is now geared toward helping ILM build assets in the spirit of the original concept art. While still creating conceptual designs when called for by Lucas and the animatics depart-

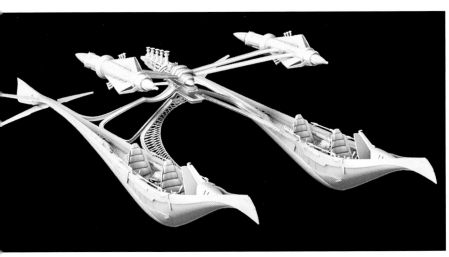

ment, Tiemens is acting as consultant to ILM's digi-matte painting department, while Church works with ILMers creating CG vehicles. Because the projects are so numerous, ILM also has two of its own art directors: former concept artist Alex Jaeger and Aaron McBride (*Minority Report*, 2002; *Pirates of the Caribbean*, 2003), who both work hand in hand with Church and Tiemens while art directing the CG model shop and CG creatures, respectively.

Today's ILM art department meeting has Church, Tiemens, Jaeger, McBride, and Knoll—who carries a coffee mug saying I KNOW MORE THAN YOU DO—touring the computer graphics department, reviewing digital reconstructions of sets on terminals. The work spaces are informal: One has three aquariums, another has a giant leftover *Star Trek* hull (NCC-1701-A) affixed to the wall; Japanese screens divide some cubicles, while one area has a large sculpture of a soft-drink can hanging over the door.

Talk with the CG modelers reveals that some are wrestling with the ambiguities inherent in the creation of digital versions of real sets. Knoll instructs them to duplicate the inconsistencies of the real-life sets, not to correct them. Throughout the next eighteen months, because he was the only one at ILM to be on set throughout the shoot, Knoll will be a valuable source of reference. "Whenever someone asks me why we didn't do X or Y on the set, which would've made their job easier," Knoll says, "I just say, 'You have no idea what it's like, how intense sets are.' "

McCallum is also quick to note Knoll's importance: "I've been blessed to work with John Knoll over the last ten years."

Although pinned to his office door is a rejection letter from ILM dated January 25, 1985, Knoll's rise here has been rapid. "I always enjoyed movies," he says of his childhood. "And when I'd see things that had to have been manufactured, I thought it was fascinating and I wondered, *How did they do that?* By nine or ten, I was model making. When I was in high school, my dad got an Apple II as part of his university research, and he encouraged my brother and me to use it. I'd get home from school and it was just sitting there. There wasn't

Left: McCallum and Wookiee #5 (Axel Dench); #7 (David Stiff); #2 (Steven Foy); #1 (James Rowland); #6 (Julian Khazzouh); #4 (Robert Cope); #3 "Tarfful" (Michael Kingma). Above left: Wookiee catamaran by CG hard-surface modeler Howie Weed, supervised by Pam Choy. Above right: Concept sketches (Jun) and sculpt (Murnane) of a Wookiee ripping apart a droid. Right: Wookiee by CG creature supervisor Aaron Ferguson. "Wookiees are all about hair," viewpaint supervisor Susan Ross says. "Many maps are made to create fur, for color (tip and root), length, density, jitter, and tufting."

157

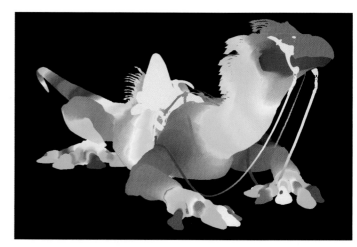

any software for it, but there was a built-in basic interpreter, so I learned how to program it [Knoll and his brother Thomas would go on to create Photoshop].

"I had a life-changing experience in May of 1978," Knoll remembers. "My dad had a Society of Nuclear Medicine conference in Anaheim, so he brought my brothers and me out to California. At this point ILM was still down in Van Nuys, and I'd been reading all these magazines about how *Star Wars* was done. On a lark, I picked up the phone book and found a listing for Industrial Light & Magic. I called up and said, 'I'm a model maker and I'm interested in doing this work for a living'; and they said, 'Why don't you come on down.' So my dad dropped me off and I hung out at ILM for a whole day—and boy, that was an awesome experience. I got there in the morning and saw dailies and how the optical department put the elements together; I saw models under construction. It was really cool, and the experience also made it real to me. I thought, *I could be one of these guys!*

"Later, at USC film school, I think I was the only one in the program who hadn't decided they were going to be a writer-director. I was interested in the technical aspects of filmmaking. In the end, I'm a craftsman at heart."

November 5-20, 2003: On the (Virtual) Cutting Room Floor I
While the following scenes have been turned over to ILM . . .
Sc. 131-132: CJE (Coruscant Jedi entry)
Sc. 138-138A: CTC (Coruscant Jedi Temple control center)
Sc. 167: PMM-1 (Polis Massa Medical Center)

. . . these scenes have been cut:
Sc. 68-69: CPA-2 (Obi-Wan tells Padmé of his worries about Anakin and that he knows they're in love)
Sc. 71: CPA-3 (Bail Organa and other Senators discourage Padmé from talking to Obi-Wan about their plan to present Palpatine with a petition protesting his handling of the war)
Sc. 73: CCT (Palpatine arrives at the Senate, and Anakin informs him that Obi-Wan "will soon have Grievous's head")
Sc. 74: CSH-2 (Jar Jar greets Anakin inside the Senate, and Palpatine insinuates to Anakin that Obi-Wan's mind has been clouded "by the influence of a certain female Senator")
Sc. 75: CPA-4 (Anakin confronts Padmé, but says he's not the Jedi he once thought he was)
Sc. 76-77: SRC (a Republic cruiser comes out of hyperspace near Utapau)
Sc. 86: KHA (Mace Windu talks with Yoda on Kashyyyk via hologram, telling him of his plans to arrest Palpatine)

During his last semester, Knoll built a motion-control camera for his advanced animation class. As a result, about six months after he graduated, in 1986, one of his professors from USC called and said ILM was looking for a motion-control cameraman. This time, Knoll was hired.

"*Star Wars Special Edition* was the first time I got to work with George," he notes. "I'd put together these animation tests of individual shots and show them to George for his feedback. And George is not a real outgoing, gregarious guy, at least at first. If he hasn't gotten to know you, he doesn't joke around. But as we would continue to work together [on Episodes I

and II], and we got to know each other better, he would be a little more jovial, and humor would start getting injected into the situations."

FRIDAY, NOVEMBER 21, 2003
SKYWALKER RANCH (SR): The animatics department is a long room equipped with a tan couch and comfy white chair, a dozen work spaces with several dozen computers, and black ceiling lamps that extend downward from an arched fifteen-foot-high wood-beamed ceiling. According to

---

Top left: Male lizard modeled by Sunny Wei, technical directed by Kevin Reuter; and painted by viewpaint supervisor Susan Ross (middle right; viewpaint supervisor Elbert Yen is middle left), who explains. "We made separate maps for the front and the back of the feathers. Splines were placed by the modeler and hair was grown along the lines to mimic feathers." Top right: Female lizard by Aaron Ferguson.

pre-visualization supervisor Dan Gregoire, his department is now "under the gun." Lucas's afternoon visits are multiplying and being extended. The intention is to finish sequences and then give them to ILM and say, "Make it real." Using a software program called iViz, the animatics artists are continuing to create low-res digital scenes that ILM will eventually re-create, enhance, and make photo-real. "You load in your models," McCallum explains, "and you have a virtual camera you can actually move around. It helps George plan out a shot in real time."

Above left and right: Two shots from the deleted scene 71, in which Senators discourage Padmé from talking to the Jedi of their petition; (left) Chi Eekway (Katie Lucas), Padmé (Portman), Mon Mothma (Genevieve O'Reilly); (right) C-3PO (Daniels), Giddean Danu (Chris Kirby), Bana Breemu (Bai Ling), Fang Zar (Warren Owens). Top right: The animatics department.

Dan Gregoire was born in Winelander, Wisconsin, and grew up in Minnesota. Throughout his schooling, he benefited from an interest in art that was well served by good art programs and teachers. Like Church, Gregoire was consumed by planes and flying them. The real sea change occurred when his college girlfriend ended their relationship. "If she hadn't broken up with me and left me just completely stranded mentally," Gregoire says, "I'd have never dropped aviation and dedicated the amount of time I did to the computer."

The head of his college's technology education department was William (Bill) H. Brown. Gregoire became close with Brown and, after learning many of the newer software programs of the early 1990s (Illustrator, Photoshop, and others), began instructing Brown's summer classes. "Teaching taught me that I really don't know anything until I try and teach it to somebody else. That made me really learn what I was doing." It also made him the ideal supervisor. Not long afterward, Gregoire worked with David Dozoretz on *Titan A.E.* (2000). Dozoretz had worked on Episode I; when he needed help on Episode II, he called in Gregoire, who had recently finished work on *Moulin Rouge* at Fox Studios, Australia.

In many ways, a visit to the animatics department is like a visit to a virtual set–actually, several virtual sets, as each of the artists is working on a different locale. Although there are specialists within the group, "at this point," Gregoire says, "everybody's expected to do some modeling, texturing, and setup, as well as actually animating and compositing their own shots"–while he keeps busy doing everything from working on a veranda shot and updating the shot-tracking database to "playing IT support for broken or crashing desktops." A quick partial survey reveals who is working on what . . .

Chris Edwards has already completed six thousand frames of animation. "Recently, George's been coming upstairs and for the first time has been hands-on with us," Edwards says. "He sits next to me at my desk so he can stage scenes with Artoo in the Federation cruiser hangar. George has me animate all the characters, placing the cameras as he gets ideas, and then we shoot coverage as you would live action from different angles. He's been experimenting quite a bit. He called up [Francis Ford] Coppola and said, 'I'm shooting my film digitally in the computer—and it goes really fast!' "

Greg Rizzi is working on the opening space battle (or "OSB"). Joshua Wassung is adding Coruscant to the background of one scene, filling in empty spots that are sometimes created in editorial when shots are rotated or minimized. Eric Carney is establishing tracking—essential for the digital cameras—while Nathan Frigard is creating computer models, with complex skeletal rigs designed to work easily with minimal computer memory.

Before getting a job here by responding to a blind listing on the Internet, senior animatics artist Brad Alexander was in the air force for four years loading armaments onto military attack aircraft. When he had the opportunity to show his demo reel to Lucasfilm prior to Episode II, "I ended up staying awake for around five days straight and drank a good ten gallons of coffee, preparing my portfolio and demo reel." In addition to working on the OSB, Alexander is touching up a scene in which Yoda and Obi-Wan watch a hologram, adding animations to computer screens.

Senior animatics artist Euisung Lee (*Titan A.E.; Moulin Rouge*) has also

been concentrating for about six months on the OSB. According to Lee, Lucas has now designated the opening shot as being one minute long, during which he wants Anakin and Obi-Wan to fly in perfect harmony to express their friendship.

To help the department create the OSB's flying sequences, and those throughout the film, Scott Benza has been giving the animatics department flying lessons. ILM's lead animator for *Pearl Harbor* (2001) and responsible for much of that film's aerial action, Benza's presence here is in part the solution to a recent problem.

"There were things George was waiting for that he wasn't getting, and he didn't understand why," Gregoire explains. "I think that perhaps my communication with George wasn't as clear as it could've been in terms of the amount of work he was asking us to do, which meant pulling people off of things to do other things that he wanted immediately. Meanwhile, Rick was going to be paying for a ton of ILM artists who were being specifically hired to do the space battle at the beginning of the year. But if we weren't done with the space battle, George wasn't going to turn it over. We were scheduled to finish it by the end of the year, but it wasn't going to happen.

"So I got on the phone one day with Rick, and he said, 'You've got to get the space battle done by the time we go on vacation or we're in real trouble. George doesn't understand—he's not seeing the shots—what is going on?!' "

"Afterward, I went downstairs to editorial to talk to George and said, 'I just got off the phone with Rick and I need to know what the frustration level is down here. Because he's telling me I have to get the space battle done by the end of the year, which means I can't get to all this other stuff—I just can't do it.' So then we talked about it. George talked. Ben talked. And they said okay; they understood. Shortly after that, things started rolling. He started seeing more stuff. I was going to editorial more often—communication improved. That's also when George started coming up on a daily basis,

Top, from left: Senior animatic artist Brad Alexander, and animatic artists Dorian Bustamante, Nick Markel, Hiroshi Mori, Greg Rizzi, Joshua Wassung. Above: Lucas and Knoll, and Dan Gregoire and Lucas.

which helped tremendously. He started heading off problems at the pass, and saw we were working. He said, 'I want to teach you how to fly.' "

THURSDAY, DECEMBER 4, 2003

ILM: Because ILM is still ramping up, dailies take place in a small viewing room within the UJ Building, whose acronym stems from its former existence as a factory where Unknown Jerome's Cookies were made. Following its conversion to an ILM facility, the space became a stage known as Turbo Bay, where parts of *Star Trek II: The Wrath of Khan* (1982), *Congo* (1995), and *Men in Black,* among many other films, were shot.

The assembled–Lucas, McCallum, Knoll, Coleman, Church, Tiemens, David, lead animators, and a few others–are not here to watch footage of what was shot on the set–or what used to be called dailies. Instead, every Tuesday and Thursday morning at eight thirty, they're here to review visual effects work, which could be anything from finals and animation to

digital doubles and cloth sims. On an approximately four-by-six-foot screen, a CG model turnaround of a Jedi starfighter, with burnished-steel parts, is examined. "I like that," Lucas says.

Knoll has a question about digital statues: they could make one and use it twice in different locations. But Lucas would prefer to have them custom-made.

"Nice try," McCallum says.

"Well, I'm trying to save you money," Knoll explains.

"But this is art," Lucas says in mock shock. "Art!"

"The idea for Episode II was to make it for ten percent less than Episode I," McCallum says. "And we did. The next challenge was to shoot Episode III for exactly what we shot Episode I for, and we did–even though, between Episode I and Episode III, there was virtually twenty-four percent inflation. So we're happy with our achievement in Sydney. Everybody worked hard and nobody got greedy. Ultimately, it cost $59

million to shoot, and it will cost $55 to $60 million for the effects, so around $115 million total."

Following Episode III dailies, Lucas, McCallum, and postproduction supervisor Mike Blanchard walk across the parking lot from UJ to C Theatre, where, for the next few months, Lucas's first feature film *THX 1138* (1971) and his *Star Wars Trilogy* will be reviewed pending their release on DVD. Lucas needs to sign off on their restoration processes and enhancements, which he can do only while watching them on C Theatre's large screen.

The lights go down and scenes from the 1977 *Star Wars* are projected. In the detention block shootout aboard the Death Star, a corridor has been elongated and the color corrected. "I've always seen it as this way," Lucas says.

Return of the Jedi's celebration scene on Coruscant has also been extended so that the rebuilt Jedi Temple is now visible in the background. Lucas requests more and brighter lights on the buildings. For the shot in which

Top right: Animatics of the OSB by Alexander. Top left: FGQ.050 (General's quarters, October 13), Alexander combines animatics with plates shot in Sydney. Above: R2-D2 in the Separatist cruiser (visual script); a Jaeger illustration of hangar bay details and refueling crane (middle left, October 23); Eric Carney's animatics for FHR.046 (middle, November 17), ILM's finishing touches (middle right).

Luke Skywalker sees his father appear as a spirit in the company of Yoda and Obi-Wan, Hayden Christensen has been inserted in place of Sebastian Shaw. Following a brief discussion, Lucas confirms that he does not want to age Christensen, explaining that Anakin has reverted to who he was before he went over to the dark side.

After a pause, Lucas jokes, "What if, behind Yoda, we add . . . Qui-Gon!"

"Oh my God," says Rick.

In order to check color timing, the first two reels of *THX 1138* are then projected. Lucas is happy with the results, and occasionally remarks on his 1971 work: "I loved working with Bobby [Robert Duvall] . . . The cameramen were documentary guys who had never done a feature before . . . Look at these grays!" He mentions how the film was shot almost entirely on location for less than a million dollars with a twenty-five-person crew, and adds, "People have forgotten where I came from."

MONDAY, DECEMBER 8, 2003

SR: Lucas walks upstairs to the animatics department with his usual lunch—a soft drink and a sandwich in a brown to-go box from the kitchen downstairs—which he'll eat while working.

After meeting with Edwards and Wassung, he talks with Gregoire and Alexander about the symmetry involved in the opening space battle. "They're two sets of shots," the director explains, "with the second shot introducing another ship flying in the opposite direction, which the camera follows."

Through a window in the attic, sunlit trees can be seen on a hill, over which turkey vultures circle. Inside, the steady hum of hard drives permeates the long room. Lucas returns to Edwards (*Dinosaur*, 2000; *Treasure Planet*, 2002), whose three-minute film about vegetables battling among themselves for control of a refrigerator first garnered attention from Disney. Like most of the animartists, he has a two-computer setup. Lucas asks him to add a door to the cruiser hangar, so Edwards calls up menus and submenus, rapidly clicking through dozens of virtual windows.

"I have so much respect for Dan and all the animatic crew," McCallum says. "They work under such enormous pressure because they have to make real what George dreams up every day. And often we're talking about forty or fifty shots a day, which means two hundred or two hundred fifty shots a

week, of which only about ten or fifteen will actually be used. But they have to make the shots in order for him to be able to pick them. So they're working ninety- to one-hundred-hour weeks for the whole three years. Often they spend nights. They've brought up their own tents to sleep in. They have alarm clocks so they can be woken up at three o'clock in the morning, after a shot's been rendered by the computer, so they can start rendering another shot. They are true filmmakers, in the virtual sense."

Left: ILM art director Aaron McBride's illustration of the Grievous bodyguards' cloak fastener (November 12). Insets: Hard-surface modeling by Simon Cheung (top), while Moon Kang built their cloaks (middle). Viewpaint by Elbert Yen (bottom). Top left: Gregoire in the animatics department, along with (top right) Carney, Edwards, and Lucas, who would regularly spend two to three hours nearly every afternoon directing the animartists. Right, top: the animatics group, and (below) examples of their animatics. Far right: Wassung and Edwards.

THURSDAY, DECEMBER 11, 2003

ILM: At UJ's dailies, a shot of Obi-Wan sitting, in which the set has been extended over a small bit of bluescreen, is the first visual effects shot final to be finalized by Lucas–and there's small but enthusiastic applause. Only about 1,999 to go.

Lucas and a few of the others are here despite low-grade winter colds. As he occasionally coughs, George makes many adjustments to a shot in which a gunship carries Yoda, Mace, and Obi-Wan through Coruscant airspace. "This lane needs more traffic; the gunship should be coming out of one lane, then merging with another." He pans up, zooms out, and requests other changes. He mentions that he'll soon be ready to hand over more scenes.

"Anything you're ready to turn over, turn over," Coleman says.

On the way to C Theatre for more *Star Wars* and *THX 1138* work, the group passes a flyer announcing a screening of *Howard the Duck* (1986) at ILM, and Lucas comments, "That's how wacky *they* are!"

The Rain People. The two have of course gone on to work together on several projects, including the founding of American Zoetrope, *THX 1138, American Graffiti, Captain EO* (1986), and *Tucker: The Man and His Dream* (1988).

Today the two sit down with Euisung Lee so the former USC student can show the former UCLA student his virtual directing techniques: "I describe a picture," Lucas starts, "the art department draws it; animatics builds a three-D world . . ."

"So [Lee] translates it," Coppola says, putting his hand on Lucas's shoulder.

"I shoot it like a movie," George says, "then I send it to ILM."

"Do you have to have a hefty computer?"

"Just a desktop PC," Gregoire answers.

"Are you changing the script much, or is it holding up pretty well?" Coppola asks.

"It's holding up."

TUESDAY, DECEMBER 16, 2003

SR: When Lucas arrives in the animatics department, he is accompanied by Francis Ford Coppola. Dressed in a gray suit, Lucas's old friend, former mentor, and fêted director has come over to see how George is directing the film in the computer.

Lucas and Coppola first met at Warner Bros., where Coppola was working on *Finian's Rainbow* (1968). They recognized a kindred spirit in each other, and, shortly afterward, Lucas became Coppola's assistant on

Friday, December 19: The following scenes have been turned over to ILM: Sc. 1-5: OSB (opening space battle)

Top left: On December 11, Obi-Wan (McGregor) sitting in the Jedi Council chamber is the first Episode III shot finalized. Above left: In ILM's C Theatre, Lucas reviews early animatics of Kashyyyk. After Yoda is attacked (top right) and then tracked by clone troopers (above right), Euisung Lee creates a shot in which a Wookiee emerges from the water à la Martin Sheen in Apocalypse Now *(top middle). Scene 56 from the visual script (right) in which Yoda, Mace, and Obi-Wan discuss Anakin will be cut from the film as of early March 2004.*

Episode III

000065 kvl055 - v01 12-16-03 Artist: Euisung Lee

Episode III

0259 kib030 - v01 Artist: Eric Carney

"I've never been up here before, in this attic," Coppola notes, looking around. "You're doing what you like to do most–having fun."

"I'm making movies," Lucas says. "Some people do storyboards and intellectualize it–I prefer to do it this way." He adds that Robert Rodriguez is doing something similar, and that Spielberg worked in like manner on *A.I.* "You set up your camera, your actors, the action, and then you shoot coverage. Think of it as a disposable camera–you only get one shot. Then I go in with the editor and we cut it together like a regular movie."

When Lucas has to leave the room for a moment, Coppola jokes about kidnapping the entire department so he can use them on his film *Megalopolis.* Lucas returns and, sitting down, says, "I just want to tell a story and make it work."

As they talk, Lucas is also developing a Kashyyyk sequence in which Wookiees ambush clone troopers. "This can be our *Apocalypse Now* shot," he decides suddenly. "Put the camera down on the water."

After a few adjustments, Lee has a Wookiee emerging from the water as Martin Sheen does in Coppola's 1979 film.

"Will you accept this as an homage?" George asks, and Francis seems pleased.

"Are you pretty much on schedule?"

"Well, we're running a little bit behind."

As they go downstairs to view material in editorial, Coppola jokes about the word *pre-visualization.*

"How can it be *pre*?" he asks. "What came before?"

TUESDAY, JANUARY 6, 2004

SR: Tiemens shows Lucas an impressive cyclorama of Padmé's funeral on Naboo. George requests more people, saying it should look like "the Kennedy funeral."

He then goes down the hall to the animatics department, where he sits with Barry Howell, who made his career choice after seeing *Jurassic Park* (1993). "I decided right then and there to focus my attention on CG." He's working on a sequence where Obi-Wan sneaks onto Padmé's ship. The way the shot has been locked down, the engine of the ship is preventing the camera from seeing Obi-Wan. So Lucas asks Howell to move the engine forward and cut off as necessary till the shot works. "When in doubt, cut it out," he says. "You can redesign the ship for the shot–that's the great thing about digital."

Talk turns toward the Mars polar landing, so Lucas and the artists gather round a monitor to look at the first color panoramic photograph of the red planet.

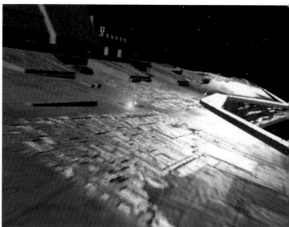

THURSDAY, JANUARY 8, 2004

ILM: Episode III dailies have moved from UJ to C Theatre. While waiting for Lucas's arrival, everyone is quiet, whispering, seated in plush red chairs beneath a scalloped ceiling. The change in venues is due both to the importance of seeing the film as it will eventually appear in movie houses and to the increase in the number of attendees, which from now till the end of production will number in the dozens. Today is also the official turnover of the OSB.

When Lucas arrives, he sits next to Knoll in the second row, with Coleman on his other side. McCallum sits in the first row with Kathryn Ramos and Denise Ream.

"Our first C Theatre screening," Lucas says.

Editors Burtt (who became a grandfather yesterday) and Barton are also here, exceptionally, as are regular attendees David, Church, Tiemens, and Gregoire. Lucas seems excited: "This is the first thing I've actually seen on the big screen!" he says. "I'm turning over fifty-two scenes to animatics."

"Good. Never let them rest," Knoll says.

"Well, as they go, so go you," Lucas cautions. "We're starting to kick this stuff out."

Thursday, January 8: The following sequences have been turned over to ILM:
Sc. 59: CCO-1 (Coruscant Chancellor's office)
Sc. 64-65: CJG (Coruscant Jedi gunship)
Sc. 70: CJC2 (Coruscant Jedi Council)

Above: The "waterfall" animatics of Euisung Lee, as directed by Lucas. Top right: a comic by Episode II concept artist Jay Shuster humorously describes the "history" of animatics. Middle right: Frank Oz first performed the puppetry of Yoda on Monday, August 6, 1979, Shoot Day 108 of The Empire Strikes Back. *A quarter of a century later, he continues to voice the venerable Jedi. Right: "Space battle laser scale and look chart" by Alex Jaeger and OSB painting by Tiemens (inset).*

The lights go down, and, as the familiar music begins with the opening crawl, the energy level in the cinema increases. Images fly by, all CG except for Christensen and McGregor in their cockpits. Many of the shots have new dialogue, with placeholder performances recorded by Burtt. The fourth draft's opening line, "Flying is for droids," has been moved to a minute or more into the action, as much of the script has been reorganized and rewritten. A new theme illustrates how Anakin relies heavily on droids and computers to target the enemy (the opposite of his son, who will use the Force).

After they watch the sequence once, which ends with Obi-Wan crash-landing into the cruiser hangar, the assembled do a second run-through, with explanations, questions, and repeated viewings of particular shots. This routine will become the norm for each turnover from editorial to ILM.

"Our biggest challenge here is readability," Lucas says as they re-view the opening sequence, which feature a potentially confusing array of craft and action. "It may be that some of these shots are a little fast."

In one, he feels a Jedi starfighter is spewing too much blue exhaust, which could prevent people from seeing the other craft. As the starfighters fly between two enormous capital ships, Knoll suggests that it might be nice if they were firing on each other, but Lucas says, "Well, that's okay, except they're on the same side," and laughs. "We just have to make sure the triangles [Republic ships] are attacking the circles [Separatist ships]."

When the missiles carrying the buzz droids arrive on screen, Knoll notes, "We never see where those missiles come from. Is that okay?"

"Yeah, we cut that out. We decided we don't need to know."

When Anakin's starfighter crushes one of the buzz droids against the windscreen of Obi-Wan's cockpit, Lucas says, "The idea is: dead mosquito on window."

"Looking in with a sort of forlorn expression," Knoll adds.

SATURDAY, JANUARY 10–SUNDAY, JANUARY 11, 2004
Although the March pickups have been delayed, animation forges ahead–helped by the fact that Lucas and Frank Oz are able to sync up their schedules so that Lucas is able to tape the latter as Yoda.

"When we got into this little hovel of a recording place," Coleman remembers, "Frank slid right into Yoda, no problem. They would record it ten times with different intonations, and George would say, 'I like that one and I like that one.' Matt [Wood, sound supervisor] would take a minute, and then you could watch the movie with the lines cut right in. So George was able to make sure the reading worked for the length of the shot and for any body or hand actions.

"I was afraid Frank wouldn't be able to sustain his voice hour after hour after hour. He must have drunk two gallons of water, but he kept going for five hours."

MONDAY, JANUARY 12, 2004

SR: Lucas arrives in the animatics department with his lunch, prepared to spend his usual three or more hours. At Wassung's station, he watches an early version of the death of Jedi Aayla Secura. Like fellow animatics artist Nick Markel, Joshua Wassung first met Gregoire at SIGGRAPH, the annual computer graphics industry conference. "Before I left, I was able to give Dan a copy of my work," he recalls, "One week later I got a letter asking me to fly out for an interview. Next thing I knew I was moving cross-country two days after graduating. It was pretty surreal."

After watching Secura in silence, Lucas thinks for a few moments and then decides to reorganize her scene. "We need to start with her and the clones walking through Felucia," he says.

"Staggered column?" asks Gregoire, who's been watching.

"Well, Vietnam," Lucas responds. "She'll send the clones into the bush . . ."

Wassung does so.

"Let them walk for about three seconds, then she stops—"

"And they fan?" he asks.

"All but these three guys," Lucas specifies. "That's when one of the clones gets the call from Sidious." The new footage then merges with the early version: Secura is shot in the back and the camera pulls back as the clones continually fire upon her corpse.

March will be the time when we'll examine what works, what doesn't work, and what we could do better. Of course, we do this soul searching throughout production—right up through 2005—but this is probably the biggest hit we'll take, and it will likely result in our most complicated pickups."

TUESDAY, JANUARY 20, 2004

SR: More visitors have been touring the animatics department. The director of *Akira* (1988), Katsuhiro Otomo, who's finishing up the sound mix of his latest film at Skywalker Sound, came to visit, as did Lucas's old friend and filmmaker Matthew Robbins.

This afternoon, after spending some time with animatics artist Carney, Lucas takes a seat next to Euisung Lee and asks him to slow down Obi-Wan's action as he swings from one pipe to another: "You have to show what's going to happen to him before it happens, otherwise people are confused—and they stop following the action for fifteen seconds—and that can be deadly."

He then reorganizes the layout of the Mustafar landing platform. "The most important thing is to make the landings look good. Then once we get down there, the geography just has to be mostly right," Lucas says, adding, "Continuity is for wimps."

This phrase will be heard often during the next sixteen months, and is born from the fact that *Revenge* will ultimately be able to show only about two dozen landscapes—which need to be as striking as possible.

"You just don't get the camera way back very often," George points out. "Everything else is talking heads against backgrounds. So every wide shot is a signature shot."

TUESDAY, JANUARY 27, 2004

ILM: In C Theatre, as Knoll takes a seat, he receives congratulations for his Oscar nomination (see page 171), as does Jill Brooks, who was the visual effects producer. "It's nice to wake up to that," Knoll says.

The rest of dailies are marked by the delicate balance between the need to get things done quickly and the need to make things work. After Lucas and McCallum take a seat, a CG model of the Imperial shuttle is shown. "Is this a final?" Lucas asks, with some hesitation. "It looks like a final . . ."

THURSDAY, JANUARY 15, 2004

ILM: While Hayden Christensen and Nick Gillard are being motion-captured on ILM's Windward Stage, just across the road in C Theatre, Lucas is saying, "I'm happy to announce that I've cut out one of the completed shots."

This announcement is met by laughter, as nearly everyone here is well acquainted with Lucas's working techniques. They know that, until the film is in theaters, he can and will change it. Nevertheless, the first rough cut is 75 percent complete.

"The end of January is when we'll really start tweaking things and thinking about new scenes to add," McCallum explains. "February and early

January 15: ILM receives 13 nominations from the Visual Effects Society for the 2003 Visual Effects Awards, for its work on: *Pirates of the Caribbean: The Curse of the Black Pearl; The Hulk; Master and Commander: The Far Side of the World; Peter Pan;* and *Terminator 3: Rise of the Machines.* Lucas will receive a Lifetime Achievement Award at the show, which will be held at the Hollywood Palladium on February 18.

January 15–22: The following sequences have been turned over to ILM:
Sc. 6: FCS (FedCruiser Shaak Ti)
Sc. 15: FEH (FedCruiser Elevator Hallway)
Sc. 72: CCL (Coruscant clone landing platform)
Sc. 94: CCS (Coruscant Chancellor's office Sith)
Sc. 121: KVL (Kashyyyk village lake)
Sc. 122: KYE (Kashyyyk Yoda escape pod)

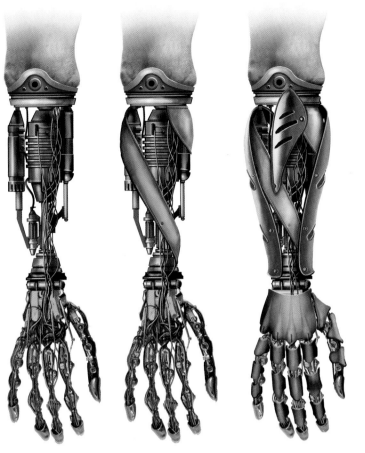

"Move on to the next one," McCallum urges, but too late. A conversation begins about how the shuttle door opens.

In the shot of Anakin waking up after his nightmare, Lucas asks that his mechanical hand catch the sunlight filtering into the room and reflect it. He also decides to change the position of the sun in the background. "Oh no . . . ," McCallum moans.

The producer's reactions come on the heels of a slew of changes made last week, which included new costume designs for Neimoidians; the combining of the planets Cato Neimoidia and Saleucami (bridge world); and the reinstatement of the lemur creatures, who now live on Mygeeto.

Of course, McCallum is well aware of the positive side of Lucas's creativity. "It's the thing about him that has always fascinated me," he explains. "We basically take the same road back and forth to work. I drive home at the end of a hard day, and he drives home. And he comes back to work and I come back—but the stuff that happens to him from the time he leaves and returns is just incredible. In the morning, he'll start off a conversation, 'What if we did this?' Every day, there's a new idea coming in. And it's just a fantastic way to work. It's mind-boggling."

THURSDAY, JANUARY 29, 2004

ILM: Lucas takes a look at CG clone troopers and changes their backpack gear so it's more individualized and jerry-rigged. "The other thing is, the armor on their butts should be scraped," he says.

"If you need any reference, just tell me," McCallum offers.

Following the turnover of the OSB, it's up to the newly formed layout

Wednesday, January 28: *The Art of Star Wars*, a new major museum exhibition featuring props, costumes, models, and artwork from Episodes I and II, as well as artifacts from Episodes IV through VI, debuts in Kyoto. The exhibit will travel through Japan until September.

January 30–February 9: The following sequences have been turned over to ILM:
Sc. 7-37: Miscellaneous FedCruiser
Sc. 66: CPV-1 (Coruscant Padmé veranda)
Sc. 67: CGO (Coruscant Galaxies Opera House)

department to block out the shots based on the animatics. Headed by Brian Cantwell, this group is the result of a postmortem on Episode II, whose attendees recommended better preparation for the CG work so that questions about choreography and geography could be worked out sooner in the process, saving time and money.

Naturally, the layout department has started with the first shot of the OSB, which features an enormous Republic assault ship. The two Jedi starfighters fly its length and then plunge off its edge, as if it were a waterfall—hence the name of this sequence, "the waterfall shot"—then, as the camera follows them over the edge, the rest of the gigantic battle is revealed far below. After he makes a few adjustments, Lucas approves the layout, and work on the next stages can begin.

Afterward, more of the *Star Wars Trilogy* is examined for the upcoming DVD release. "I can't cope with this," Lucas jokes. "I have too many movies. It's my whole life flashing before me."

THURSDAY, FEBRUARY 5, 2004

ILM: Lucas is about 85 percent done with the rough cut. Outside C Theatre, he remarks to Coleman, "You realize this is an animated movie." Coleman replies that he's already calculated that eighty to eighty-five minutes of *Revenge of the Sith* will be animated, which is the average length of a Disney feature. Inside C Theatre, Lucas finals the first Yoda shot. He then reviews the opera scenes that have just been turned over.

"I think this part of the city should be slightly more Las Vegas–like," he says. For a shot of people walking up the opera house steps, he asks that evening wear be designed. Vehicles will be pulling up, so he requests that space-age limos be created. This expanded scene, he adds, will be part of the pickups.

The interior of the opera, as Lucas describes it, is a big ball of liquid in which there are aliens swimming around with "something" attached to them.

"The Mon Calamari Dancers," McCallum says.

"That's it!" Lucas says, "that's what we'll call them." He also suggests adding "some ETs in the opera seats, throwing popcorn."

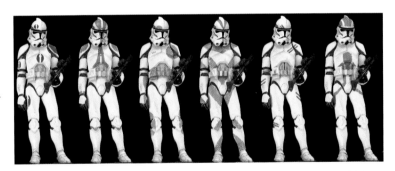

January 30–February 9: The following sequences have been turned over to ILM:
Sc. 7-37: Miscellaneous FedCruiser
Sc. 66: CPV-1 (Coruscant Padmé veranda)
Sc. 67: CGO (Coruscant Galaxies Opera House)

Top left: Animatics by Joshua Wassung depict Jedi Master Aayla Secura on Felucia just before she is shot down by her former soldiers. Above left, strip: Lucas directs Euisung Lee's animatics, while Fay David, J.W. Rinzler, and Erik Tiemens look on. Top right: The "inner mechanical layers" of Anakin's arm by Aaron McBride (November 3, 2003). Above: Clone commander variations designed for different theaters of war by Alex Jaeger.

Sang Jun Lee
SW3 2, 24, 04
opera female Costume #9

TUESDAY, FEBRUARY 10, 2004

ILM: Looking at the animatic of Count Dooku jumping from a balcony to confront the Jedi, Lucas asks for "a more elegant flip. This one's not very Jedi."

The two battle droids accompanying the Count fire, miss and are cut down by Obi-Wan. "You really want these guys?" Coleman asks. "They can't hit the side of a barn!"

"That's what's so funny about them," Lucas says, but then concedes, "We can make them anything you guys like. We'll make them the big droids."

More animatics reveal some changes to the Dooku-Jedi fight: Now the Count levitates Obi-Wan into the air, strangling him with the Force; he then kicks Anakin and flings Obi-Wan across the room. These shots, and some of the old, are marked with an R for "reshoot" (although in most cases it's a "new" shoot or a pickup).

In the last shot, Anakin beheads Dooku, and the latter's head rolls away. "Now, talk to me about this head," McCallum turns to Lucas.

"What kind of rating are we going for?" Coleman asks.

"This is the boys upstairs [in the animatics department] enjoying themselves," Lucas says. "We're somewhere between an extremely hard PG and a PG-13."

"How about a PG-18?" Rick suggests.

"Wait till you get to the end," George counters. "This is nothing."

THURSDAY, FEBRUARY 12, 2004

ILM: As of today, a whiteboard in the UJ building ticks off the numbers:

EPISODE III SHOT STATUS

Total # of shots: 2,000

Finals: 46

Final omits: 1

Shots turned over: 1,031

Shots left to go: 1,954

Finals needed per week: 32

Weeks to go: 59

The "Total #" refers to the number of shots with visual effects in them, which is nearly every shot in the film. "Finals" are those shots deemed complete by Lucas, after reviewing them at dailies. "Final omits" refers to finals that have been dropped because of the film being recut. "Shots turned over" refers to those sent from editorial to ILM.

"This is the fun part," Lucas says. "Though I'm struggling to get through the final drama of making the film work, twice a week, I get in ten to twenty shots—which I've been waiting years for. So that's exciting; that's fun. It's like getting stuff in the mail when you were a kid—'Oh, look! I got the Master Spy Ring.' I'm getting these little gifts. Sometimes they're disappointing and you have to send them back to be redone—and sometimes they're fantastic. Then I cut the shots in, so I get two hits: one is when I see it on the big screen, and two is when I actually see it work and see a scene fall together."

TUESDAY, FEBRUARY 17, 2004

SR: Back in the art department, concept artist Sang Jun Lee has returned to work on Episode III, designing costumes for the grandiose opera staircase scene. In his critique of Jun's first sketches, Lucas asks for "an array of things, so they look like they're from different cultures . . . sexier, formal, more glamorous."

During his tour of duty in animatics, he sits with Euisung Lee. It's pouring rain outside. Tiemens sketches while observing. Church and Gregoire keep watch, also sketching, as Lucas directs while eating lunch. All three are here in case Lucas needs them, and to keep track of changes made to the movie. "It's Kamino weather today," Tiemens remarks.

Lucas consecrates about forty-five minutes of his time to a complicated shot. A flying tank must be seen to descend into an Utapau sinkhole and turn toward the camera as it fires two shots, which the camera quickly follows into the hangar, where one gun is destroyed; the camera then drops down to pick up more choreographed combat action.

"Try to make it a nice, consistent, smooth pan," he tells Lee.

On a pop-up screen, Lee complies by plotting the camera's trajectory.

"That'll be cool," Tiemens remarks.

Gregoire mentions that tomorrow Lucas will receive the Lifetime Achievement Award from the Visual Effects Society, which will be handed to him by James Cameron.

Tuesday, February 10: Lucasfilm and Twentieth Century Fox announce a September release for the *Star Wars Trilogy* on DVD.

Left: Opera costume illustrations and sketches by concept artist Sang Jun Lee for Lucas's new staircase scene. Above: One of the intricately choreographed animatic frames of UTC.730 (Utapau Tenth-Level control center) by Bustamante.

SBT.790

000107

sbt790 - v02
11-24-03

Artist: Dorian Bustamante

Direction of falling / rolling peices

WEDNESDAY, FEBRUARY 18, 2004

ILM: In C Theatre, Lucas explains that a deceptively simple shot of Padmé sleeping is a combination: blowup, zoom, and rotate. "The art of editing is also how you manipulate images to get the best performances out of the actors," he says. "And what we've done is move that to another level, where we can actually move the characters around within the frame and change what's going on, rather than just cutting from one frame to another."

"George told me that he likes to do what he calls three-dimensional editing," editor Barton explains. "Whereas editors are used to working in a linear mind-set, he'll want to work not only in terms of piecing one shot next to another—but within each frame, he'll be editing it, resizing things, and moving the camera around within the frame. That's something new to me. That's something I'll have to wrap my head around."

Roger Barton grew up in southern California and Oregon. "My dad told me that you have to fight and struggle to get what you want out of life," he notes. After attending Long Beach State, he broke into editing on a documentary called *The Wild West*, which was being cut on a brand-new Avid. The night before his interview, Barton bought a book about nonlinear editing and learned just enough to convince the producer to hire him. "Later, I worked on what was a very difficult film about a sinking ship you may have heard about," Barton jokes.

"We interviewed about sixty-five editors over a period of four months," McCallum says. "Jamie [Forester, postproduction supervisor] and I flew to Los Angeles six times. I made it very clear to every editor. I said, 'Look. You're going to get your own cut while we're shooting the movie. The rest of the time, you're going to be working for George.' "

"I do believe that what comes around goes around," Barton says, "and karma definitely has something to do with why I'm here. Maybe it was also because George felt like he could control me maybe more than a more established, well-known editor. I'd like to think that it was just a natural fit. I consider myself, now that I'm on the movie, to be the luckiest person alive."

TUESDAY, FEBRUARY 24, 2004

ILM: Outside C Theatre is a courtyard where stands "Java the Hutt": a sheet-metal construct where coffee and pastries can be purchased. Before dailies, people congregate outside this venerable institution, milling about or sitting at the one picnic table. Large potted trees dot the asphalt area, most of which are left over from ILM's work on *Jurassic Park III* (2001). An artificial tree, with blue-green leaves and thick fake vines, is from *Planet of the Apes* (2001). Usually McCallum is the first to arrive, followed a few minutes later by Ramos, Brooks, Lewin, Ream, and others.

ILM executive producer Denise Ream began her visual effects career after being hit by a car while jogging. Temporarily unable to do the more physical work of an on-set production supervisor, she eventually found a niche as the optical coordinator at Boss Film Studios, something that made her grandfather—Linwood Dunn, the inventor of the first mass-produced 16mm optical printer (in 1944: the Acme-Dunn Optical Printer for the U.S. Navy's Central Photographic Laboratory)—quite happy. Hired by ILM in 1993, Ream is responsible, among other things, for working with McCallum to build a team that works together well. "I don't think you can underestimate the chemistry involved," she says.

"I wanted working with ILM to be a happy experience," Rick adds. "And I wanted to have somebody I could totally trust, who would be hands-on and really take care of the people who were working for us. The first minute that both Kathryn and I met Denise, we immediately fell in love with her. She was honest; she was straight; she was smart. And she had no problem whatsoever during the next few weeks telling me when I was wrong."

Lucas arrives, gets his coffee, and everyone moves inside, where others are already seated. First up is the layout stage of the Republic embarkation center. Per a Star Destroyer taking off, he says, "I think you can slow it down even more."

"Good. I was hoping you'd say that," Knoll says, pointing out that these ships are more than a mile long and would take a while to go past camera.

February 23-27: The following sequences have been turned over to ILM:
Sc. 70: CJC-2 (Coruscant Jedi Council—this is not the first turnover of CJC-2; some sequences have been reworked and resubmitted)
Sc. 115-116: CPV-2 (Coruscant Padmé's veranda)
Sc. 144: CHO-1 & 2 (Coruscant Chancellor's holding office)

Left: For SBT.790 (space battle tri-droids), Editor McBride shows the damage to the Federation core ship (January 15). Top: Editor Roger Barton and Lucas at work cutting the movie. Middle: Standing in front of Javva the Hutt are: Tiemens, Coleman, David, ILM producer Jill Brooks, ILM president Chrissie England, Kathryn Ramos, (below) Knoll, Lucas, Brooks, Janet Lewin, and ILM VFX executive producer Denise Ream.

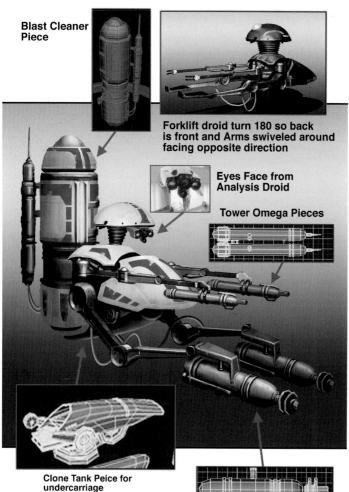

Blast Cleaner Piece

Forklift droid turn 180 so back is front and Arms swiveled around facing opposite direction

Eyes Face from Analysis Droid

Tower Omega Pieces

Clone Tank Peice for undercarriage

Tower Omega Pieces

SR: George studies Jun's additional opera costumes. He inserts a slit in a skirt, makes a bust metal, changes one dress to black, and adds silver and diamond beads to a skirt–in general, he makes the garbs sexier. "Tell Trisha," he turns to David, "if none of this works, she can do what she wants, but I think we can keep trying. We really need some designs for aliens. We do have a Greedo and a Greedess."

Tiemens suggests a Mon Calamari creature and Lucas agrees. "Yeah, the family of the entertainers."

"We could put Jar Jar in there with a female Jar Jar," Tiemens adds.

"How about if Jar Jar is with a Kaminoan?" Church suggests.

"That could be a good one. I'll think about that," Lucas says and pauses. "Okay. Jar Jar and a Kaminon. As he's been cut out of the rest of the film"–a comment that leads him to comment on the rough cut in general. He plans on watching it twice: once with the temp music, once without.

"Music is a really powerful source, and, unless it's really right, it can throw everything else off," Lucas notes. "It can get to be confusing as to why something isn't working: Is it the music or is it the way it's cut?"

March 1-11, 2003: On the (Virtual) Cutting Room Floor II
While the following scenes have been turned over to ILM . . .
Sc. 4: CEL (Coruscant emergency landing platform)
Sc. 57-58: CJB (Coruscant Jedi briefing room)
Sc. 42: FRH (FedCruiser ray shield hallway)

. . . these other scenes have been cut:
Sc. 48: CEL (Mace Windu greets Palpatine and the Jedi right after the crash-landing)
Sc. 56: CYQ (Yoda, Obi-Wan, and Mace discuss the dark side in Yoda's quarters)
Sc. 60: CBO (Bail Organa and fellow Senators speak about the Senate)
Sc. 83: UDC (Obi-Wan chooses his lizard-mount, Boga)
Sc. 121: KVL ("crazy" Yoda and Chewbacca ambush an AT-ST)

Above: McBride's droid illustrations. Top left: Scene 48 of Mace Windu at the site of the crash-landing (visual script) would be cut and reworked to take place at "Senate office parking entry" as illustrated by Church. Right page: Digi-matte paintings (top) Kashyyyk beachhead by Max Dennison. Middle, from left: Utapau from space by Simon Wicker; rehab center by Jeremy Cook; view from Padmé's apartment by Christian Haley; ILM digital matte supervisor Jonathan Harb. Right: Senate establishing shot by Yusei Uesugi.

After the film has been shortened, inevitably, certain information will have been deleted, so he'll then decide how to reinsert key plot points. Though the pickups have been pushed back to August, because the rough cut is taking longer than expected, Lucas is telling the editorial group to "keep up the faith."

TUESDAY, MARCH 2, 2004

ILM: As soon as Lucas takes a seat, the lights goes down, a shot of Anakin with the Jedi Council is projected, and the subject of the sky is discussed.

"We're just going through a whole thing with the backgrounds," he observes.

"I've heard about these machinations," Knoll says.

"Well, this is the same day as the storm," Lucas continues, pointing out that scenes taking place on the same day on the same planet will be related: A storm that occurs in a later scene can be prefigured in an earlier one. (The result is a lengthy time and weather chart that now stretches around two walls of the art department.)

Next up is the partially complete opening waterfall shot. "It'd be nice if, when the starfighters go into the darkness, we could see the interior lights of their cockpits," George says. He also asks that the speed of the ships in relation to the rotation of the planet be worked out, so that it's clear to the audience how fast things are moving.

"It's going to be an amazing shot," Coleman notes.

TUESDAY, MARCH 9, 2004

ILM: A final is projected of Bail Organa in his office. But the first thing Lucas says is: "As of yesterday, this is a DVD shot [that is, it's been cut]. Right now, it's an everything-must-go sale," he adds, explaining that the rough cut—or what is now being referred to as more of a rough "assembly"—is done, and he's now into two to three weeks of reorganizing.

"The first script I wrote had stories for everybody," Lucas notes per the reorg, "and I cut it down and we had a script. But when we cut it together, there were still problems. Finally, I said, 'Okay, let's be even more hard-nosed here and take out every scene that doesn't

have anything to do with Anakin.' But that causes you to juxtapose certain scenes that you were never contemplating juxtaposing before. And these scenes take on different qualities than before, because the scenes were never meant to be next to each other.

"In one case, there was supposed to be a scene with Padmé and Bail Organa between two Anakin scenes, because we were following her story along with his. And when most of those scenes were cut out, suddenly all sorts of weird things started to happen that weren't intended in the script—but in some cases it actually worked much better.

"What happens then is that some of the themes grab hold of each other and really strengthen themselves in ways that are fascinating. You pull things together and suddenly a theme is drawn out because it's in three consecutive scenes instead of just one. Suddenly one theme is infinitely stronger than it was before, so we'll strengthen that theme because it seems poetic."

Above: Anakin (Christensen) in the Jedi Council recorded in Sydney and the reverse-angle final frame (top). The storm clouds behind Anakin are foreshadowed in earlier scenes and evolve in later ones, thanks to the flexibility of digital cinema.

A Diamond in the Rough

FRIDAY, MARCH 12, 2004

ILM: Work here is advancing on multiple fronts. On ILM's Windward Stage, crew are wrapping up the Jedi starfighter (which had been shipped over from Sydney) shoot, providing OSB insert shots. Technical directors, layout artists, CG model makers, and others now have their hands full.

In UJ, Coleman is conducting animation dailies with his lead animators. He tells them that the lemurs are probably out again and that Lucas has said, half seriously, that Jar Jar might be sent to Alderaan (which is blown to bits in *A New Hope*). As the animators file out of the room, John Knoll comes by, excited. "You wanna see an explosion?! Come with me."

Animators and others rush into another viewing station to watch a spectacular fireball created with new technology by R&D technical troubleshooter Willi Geiger, who, according to Knoll, has made a "valve volume fluid sim that they're feeding particles through."

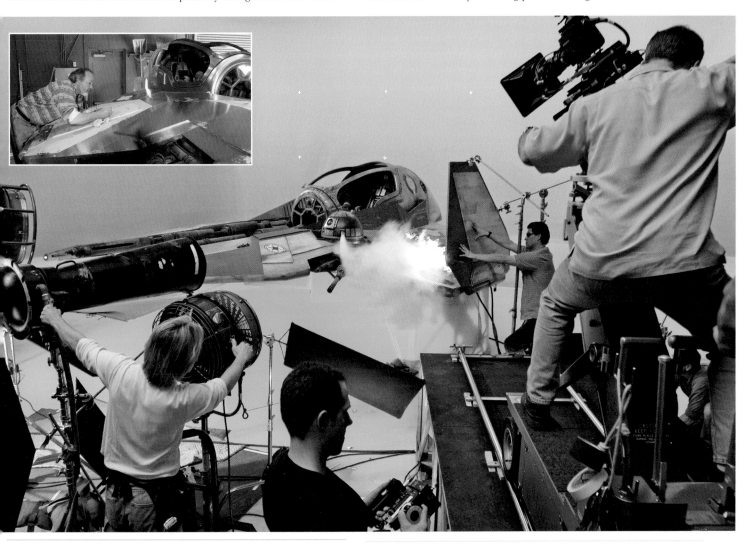

March 29–April 2: The following sequences have been turned over to ILM:
Sc. 94: CCS (Coruscant Chancellor's office Sith—recut with new time of day)
Sc. 78-82: UJA (Utapau Jedi arrival)
Sc. 82A: KJB (Kashyyyk Jedi battle)
Sc. 90A: CJW (Coruscant Jedi war room)
Sc. 153-154: CYE (Coruscant Yoda escape)

Shooting Obi-Wan's starfighter during pickups at ILM are: DP Carl Miller, stage crew Mike Olague and Mark Walas. Knoll supervised these insert shots of boots, cockpit interiors, hands, astromech droids, etc. Inset: To change Obi-Wan's starfighter into Anakin's, model-maker Charlie Bailey helps paint it yellow.

March 15-22, 2004: On the (Virtual) Cutting Room Floor III

While the following scenes have been turned over to ILM...

Sc. 49: CSL-1 (Coruscant Senate landing platform)

Sc. 139-140: CLP (Coruscant landing platform Padmé)

Sc. 109: FJB (Felucia Jedi battle)

...these scenes are now cut:

Sc. 88-89: CCO-2 (Padmé presents to Palpatine the Senators' petition)

Sc. 6, 7, 8-14, 25, 28, 30, 32, 37-41 (various FedCruiser scenes—Grievous killing Shaak Ti; Anakin and Obi-Wan using their lightsabers to escape Grievous; their underwater swim through the generator rooms, with droids in pursuit; their climb through the vent shaft; many of the R2-D2 hangar gags; and, following the death of Dooku, many of the Jedi-Palpatine cliffhangers have been cut)

Left: Burtt's editing work is backed up in a nearby room that is Michael Blanchard's responsibility. "We have four terabytes of storage, because George wants all dailies available from the last two films [principal photography and successive cuts]," Blanchard says. "Avid said it would be impossible to do that, but we did it—and every file is mirrored. George always forces us to come up with a better way of doing things." In addition to his editing duties, Burtt is the sound designer. "I've done something different than ever before," he notes. "I've built a portable sound setup that fits in a suitcase, which enables me to connect to the 5,700 sounds that I've made in the past for Star Wars, *which normally reside in the Tech Building library. So far, I've probably made about 150 new sounds, about a tenth of what I'll need, which I test on George. Usually the director of a film doesn't hear these until the last moment, but George hears them as they're created. The final mix will therefore be a performance of sounds that have already been rehearsed."*

Above left and right: Sequences cut from the film: FCS.070—The death of Shaak Ti aboard the FedCruiser, as originally scripted and shot in Sydney on August 19, 2003; animatics by Gregory Rizzi, January 15, 2004. FCS.200—Following the murder of Shaak Ti, the Jedi ignite their lightsabers in Sydney; CG droids are added by Nathan Frigard in the animatics department on January 12, 2004. FCS.300—Seeing they're outnumbered, the Jedi use their lightsabers to cut a hole in the floor, and drop to the generator room below; animatics by Euisung Lee, January 9, 2004. FCG.020—The Jedi will extinguish their sabers when they realize they've fallen into a room leaking fuel; animatics by Dorian Bustamante, January 26, 2004. FCG.530—As fuel floods the room, Obi-Wan swims to escape, only to be dragged down by a pursuing super battle droid. McGregor was shot in Sydney on August 14, 2003; animatics by Eric Carney, January 23, 2004.

Right: Responding to Lucas's new scene in the Jedi Temple, Church creates a war room concept on February 9, 2004.

SR: "We cut out another ten minutes of the opening sequence," Lucas says, while visiting the animatics department. "We're trying to get it down to twenty minutes, if we can, from forty minutes."

Other major changes consist of new scenes. After Palpatine reveals to Anakin that he is a Sith, the Jedi now takes this information to Mace Windu. The latter decides to arrest the Chancellor–but leaves Anakin behind. Alone in the Jedi Council chamber, Anakin thinks about Padmé and how the Sith can prevent death. He decides to intervene, hopping in an airspeeder and arriving just as the Windu-Palpatine fight reaches its climax.

"What I like about what George has done is that he's taken this new scene and injected into it more distrust between Mace and Anakin," Barton says. "George will sometimes come up with an idea and quickly write some lines while sitting in the editing room. Then we'll steal frames from

000862   fcg020 - v01   Artist: **DORIAN BUSTAMANTE**
01-26-04

ILM: In C Theatre, Lucas watches reels five and six of *The Empire Strikes Back*, the images flickering across the glasses of the man who made them twenty-four years ago. Though satisfied with the color timing, he mentions that a shot on Bespin will need to be reworked for a future re-release.

SR: In the office next to Barton's, Burtt is editing side by side with Lucas. The setup includes two monitors–one is the Avid, one displays the files–and an HD screen with a 5.1 surround sound system. On the walls are a poster for *El Capitan Blood*, with Errol Flynn and Olivia de Havilland, and Fellini's *La Douceur de Vivre* (*La Dolce Vita*), along with images from reels one through seven. As Ben prepares a sequence for his review, George reads the paper.

"As we've made this trio of films, this process of making things up as we go along has increased," Burtt says. "I think it's satisfying for George to take the characters and the tools, and experiment with them, because he's

0136   fcg530 - v02   Artist: Eric Carney
01/23/04

different images in the movie and record the dialogue, just so he can get a sense of it.

"I have to admit that sometimes it takes me a couple minutes to understand where George is going with something. He'll have me join pieces of completely different scenes together–but once he's in that zone, I don't want to interrupt. He just wants to put together those images and see if they'll work. Of all the movies I've worked on–and some have been big visual effects movies–they just don't come close to the amount of reinvention that goes on in postproduction here."

developed it all, over many, many years. The way George works–where he shoots and then reshoots–is a real luxury. Historically, only Charlie Chaplin has had this kind of control.

"So I come in every day to help George figure out what he wants. Quite often we're in here for long stretches making things up, quite literally going along until we get stuck–and then saying, 'Now what could happen?' It's like a series of brainstorming sessions. Sometimes it's like having a bored teenager in the back of the car, and we're changing things just because it's stimulating for him. But George certainly doesn't hold on to material because it's sacred. He's very able to look at something and say, 'It's gotta go,' or, 'Let's try something completely different today.'

"His approach is also very close to how someone would do an animated movie. I call it recomposing the movie. You're free to split apart the visual elements within a shot–the people, the objects, the setting–and rearrange them. We put in a shoulder, raise an arm, take out a blink. This is the process we do every day. There isn't a shot or a scene or a moment that isn't deeply affected by this process, and there isn't a day in the editing room where we don't discover something interesting through that process."

FINALS: 91   SHOTS LEFT: 1,914   WEEKS TO GO: 52 (ONE YEAR LEFT!)

THURSDAY, APRIL 1, 2004
ILM: Yoda crawls through a service tube filled with wires, after his defeat at the hands of the Emperor. In his airspeeder, Bail pulls up far below the tube's opening to rescue the Jedi Master, and Knoll asks, "Why does Bail stop two hundred meters under that opening and make Yoda jump?"

Lucas reflects a moment. "Good point," he says, and changes the shot so Yoda has less distance to drop.

SR: Lucas stops by the animatics department to briefly check on things before leaving on a ten-day vacation. He advises Gregoire to have his team work on the establishing shots. He also predicts that they'll have a first rough cut by May. Gregoire wonders if some shots are taking too long to finish.

"Everything is taking too long," Lucas says, only half jokingly. "From this point on, it's a permanent 911."

TUESDAY, APRIL 13, 2004
SR: In the art department, Knoll, Church, Tiemens, Gregoire, and David prepare for a Mustafar meeting. They need to hear from Lucas exactly what he wants and doesn't want logistically, so that work can begin in earnest on assets both in the animatics department and at ILM. Knoll is particularly concerned because *Revenge of the Sith* has many sequences that require lengthy builds for only a few shots.

"It's a house of cards," Tiemens says, "everything is connected."

"Yeah, I know," Gregoire agrees. "I had to redo an entire sequence last night."

Lucas arrives and Knoll says, "Our goal is to get a working map."

"That's why these entry shots are critical," the director responds. "You have to get all the pictures together or you're going to paint yourself into a corner. The theories don't count anymore."

He then points out that there's a problem with the Mustafar environment, because Anakin and Obi-Wan end up on the wrong side of the lava river at the end of the fight. "We have to figure out where in relation to that river they're standing at all times."

"The time to do that is now," Knoll concurs, noting that they have a year to go, which is not a long time.

"I don't think it's a long time," Lucas says. "Not at all."

"You wouldn't consider a 2006 release, would you?" Knoll asks, almost rhetorically. When Lucas replies in the negative, he adds, "Then we'll have to throw a lot of bodies at it."

"The sooner, the better," Lucas says.

Monday, April 5: Lucasfilm announces that Episode III will be released domestically on Thursday, May 19, 2005, with a "near-simultaneous release around the world."

TUESDAY, APRIL 27, 2004
ILM: With forty-eight weeks to go, and 1,973 visual effects shots to finish, people congregate once again in C Theatre. ILM has started what will be months of shooting miniature models (some of which are actually several yards long or tall), including a Kashyyyk tree, Utapau sinkhole, and the Jedi embarkation center. The majority of these miniatures will be scanned using a process called Zenviro, which creates digital environments out of the models, which in turn enables Lucas to place his camera wherever he wants (for locked-down shots, digi-matte paintings will be used).

Later in the day, Lucas, McCallum, Burtt, and Barton watch the second version of Lucas's rough assembly.

April 12–16:
The following sequences have been turned over to ILM:
Sc. 177: SIS (Space Imperial Star Destroyer)
Sc. 178–79: ACB (Alderaan castle balcony)
Sc. 102: CCC (Coruscant Chancellor clones attack)
Note: The present cut is running, without end credits, at 2 hours 11 minutes 23 seconds.

Top: During a miniature shoot of the opera box at ILM are: Jason Snell, DP Carl Miller, model shop supervisor Brian Gernand (behind Miller), Knoll, and match-mover Josh Livingston. Below at work on the Polis Massa crater miniature is veteran model-maker Lorne Peterson. Right: Carl Miller (center), camera assistant Dennis Rodgers (top in white), grip Mike Olague (front at left) and key grip Tom Cloutier (right) on the ILM Utapau miniature sinkhole set.

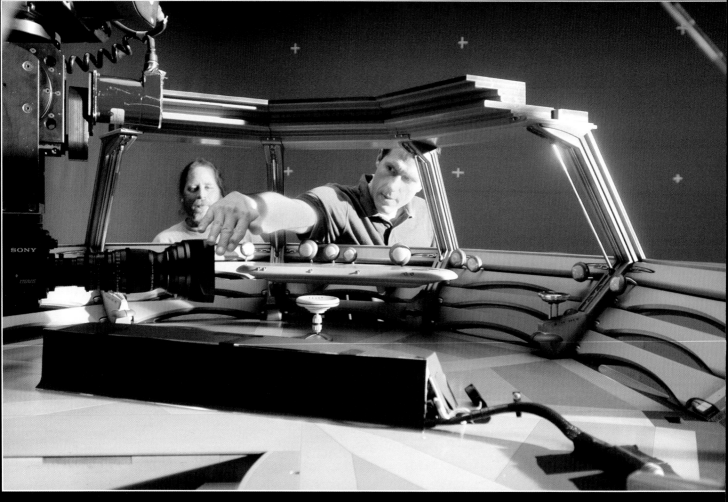

WEDNESDAY, APRIL 28, 2004

SR: In a follow-up to the April 13 meeting, today's gathering is designed to forever pin down Mustafar geography. Euisung Lee, Tiemens, and digi-matte artist Yanick Dusseault have collaborated for the last two weeks, with the latter two painting on top of animatics derived from concept paintings to create what they hope are the most cohesive and fantastic landscapes possible. If Lucas finds fault with their shot-by-shot breakdown, however, it's back to the drawing board.

After he arrives and examines the angles and backgrounds, it's clear that George likes the presentation.

"Do we have a plan?" Knoll asks.

"We have a plan," Lucas says.

As they walk down the hall to the animatics department, Lucas informs Gregoire that it's Anakin who now kills Shaak Ti in the Jedi Temple while she's meditating.

"I want Anakin walking in there," he says. "Anakin walks around, he kneels down, and then he stabs her."

TOTAL # OF SHOTS: 2,100   FINALS: 135   FINAL OMITS: 35

SHOTS TURNED OVER: 1,255   SHOTS LEFT TO GO: 1,961

FINALS NEEDED PER WEEK: 40   WEEKS TO GO: 48

TUESDAY, MAY 4, 2004

ILM: In the still chilly morning, people clutch hot coffees in front of Javva the Hutt. Fay David arrives and McCallum suddenly motions everyone to be quiet as the public-address system says, "Congratulations to Fay David on her engagement." She receives many smiles and congratulations, and Lucas gives her a hug.

During dailies, Lucas tells Knoll that some birdlike creatures have been cut out of the Felucia sequence. Because that particular creature build is already 60 percent done, John asks if the CG model department can finish it for inclusion in other shots.

"See if you have more time in June next year," McCallum suggests.

"Rick's the boss," Lucas says. "I'm just the poor director."

Clockwise from top left: model-maker Jon Foreman and Rogers work on the ILM Polis Massa observation dome miniature. Wagner works with Jaeger on the Felucia miniature. Model-maker Grant Imahara adjusts the cruiser hangar bay set. Model-maker Carol Bauman works on the Federation battleship gun. Model-makers Fon Davis and Pierre Maurer piece together the hangar bay wall. Above: Evidence of the Mustafar rethink—Tiemens's view of the landing platform and an aerial view—along with a page from the visual script (top right). Right: Wagner and costume archivist Gillian Libbert prepare Amy Allen (Aayla Secura) for her scenes.

THURSDAY, MAY 6, 2004

Crew are preparing for today's pickup shoot featuring the death of Jedi Aayla Secura (Amy Allen). Not surprisingly, the set is nothing but a floor and three walls of green, which will eventually become the exotic landscape of Felucia. There are about a dozen crew, including DP Carl Miller. Concept model maker Danny Wagner, who is also a makeup artist, has just finished transforming Allen into an alien. He says it was a three-hour job; he used Real Creation body inks to turn her skin green.

Lucas arrives with McCallum. While the former studies the camera setup, the latter surveys the general situation while leaning on a ladder. As they prepare a complex shot, Lucas reminisces about making *Raiders of the Lost Ark* (1981), in particular the now famous scene in which Indy dispatches his fancy scimitar-wielding foe. There were "huge crowd control problems," he recalls.

They try the shot, and when Allen fails to show up on camera, Lucas remarks, "We certainly learned something, didn't we?" They simplify and do another take. He asks Allen to change her walk to more of a stalk. Take. Lucas adds a "stop-and-look" to her prowling.

He then explains to Allen her character's death scene (she's shot in the back by clone troopers). Take. She falls. "I like how her feet came back up into camera," Knoll says. Take. Lucas asks her to scream next time. After nine more setups, Lucas concludes, "I know we have great stuff in there somewhere"—and these pickups are a wrap.

FOX STUDIOS, AUSTRALIA
LOCATION: Stage 2
SETS: Bluescreen—Kashyyyk and Cockpit
SCHEDULED SCENES SHOT: Lead Wookiee climbs up on barricade and roars; crane down as Wookiees run away from camera; lead Wookiee rips droid apart; Wookiees run away as tank explodes; front on shot of clone's face through visor—burned makeup
TOTAL SETUPS: 98

McCallum has spent the last week in Australia preparing for this two-day shoot, which Coleman is directing. "The week before the Wookiee shoot," Coleman says, "I met with George and we went over the Wookiee hero shots. In Sydney, I went to Fox Studios on Friday, which was a prep day, and met with Rick in Building 28. It was surreal. Everyone was sitting in the same spot: Virginia [Murray, production coordinator] and Stephen [Jones, production supervisor] were at the same desks, and Rick was in the same office.

"Monday, we shot everyone but Chewbacca and Tarfful. We shot the preparation for the battle and the battle itself, and then I was asked to pick up some clone pilot shots with Temuera Morrison. I was working on adrenaline and nerves."

"George and I gave Rob the shot to direct," McCallum points out. "I know that he wants to direct and I think he would make a great director, because performance is all he's concerned about. But he'd never had the experience of actually dealing with live action; he'd always directed within

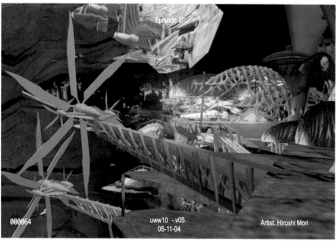

the computer. But I knew I could trust him, and he did a great job."

Though Coleman had use of only one camera, he was aided by the fact that many of the Australian crew returned for these two days–he had the same focus pullers and crane crew, Simon Harding operated the camera, and Colin Fletcher was back as first assistant director. "He was fantastic," Coleman says. "I couldn't have done it without him."

Animation director Rob Coleman grew up in Toronto, Canada, and has been interested in art since "before I can remember." He loved the Warner Bros. cartoons–particularly the Chuck Jones classics *Duck! Rabbit! Duck!* (1953) and *Duck Amuck* (1953). His parents used to project 16mm films, and Coleman recalls watching *Dumbo* (1941) on a screen in their living room. "You could see these little pictures on the film," he notes, "so it made sense to me that you could create these drawings that would become movies."

After a false start studying journalism, Coleman enrolled in Concordia University, where, because he'd been self-taught up till then, he was inundated by new cinematic experiences. "I remember immersing myself in the Canadian Film Board shorts." He would also spend hours using the school's 16mm analyzing projector to dissect animated films, such as Ryan Larkin's *En Marchant* (*Walking*, 1969) and Zdenko Gasparovic's *Satiemania* (1978).

After graduating, Coleman worked on *Captain Power and the Soldiers of the Future* (1987), which was the first TV show to combine live action with computer animation. One of his mentors, Zlatko Grgic, who was on his deathbed at the time, recommended Rob to Derek Lamb, an Oscar-winning film board director. With Lamb, Coleman worked on *Karate Kids*, a documentary designed to educate street children around the world about the dangers of AIDS.

Years later, after seeing *Jurassic Park*, whose computer animation changed the lives of so many modern animators, Coleman immediately applied to ILM. At SIGGRAPH, Coleman recalls, "I'll never forget: I checked into the hotel and there was a message from ILM saying they wanted to interview me–I was so happy I went up to my room and jumped on the bed!"

ILM had used six animators for *Jurassic Park*, and though they were looking to expand, Coleman went through a lengthy interview process. When he was finally hired in October 1993, he became ILM's ninth animator. Following his work on *Men in Black*, Coleman was flown out to the set of Episode I, at McCallum's request, to spend some time with Lucas and "see if the chemistry was right."

"I had seen some early work from *Men in Black*," Rick notes, "and I was so bowled over by not only the imagination, but the realization of all the animation. I said, 'We've got to have him. Because this guy is an awesome piece of talent.' Little did I know what an awesome person he is, which means he's also a brilliant manager of his crew."

Friday, May 14: The following scenes have been turned over to ILM:
Sc. 151-152: CSC-3 (Coruscant Senate chamber)
Sc. 168: CRL (Coruscant rehabilitation center landing platform)
The following scenes have been cut:
Sc. 93-93A: UWW 1-2 (Utapau windmill scenes)

Monday, May 17: The Academy of Science Fiction, Fantasy and Horror Films gives its Saturn Award for the Best DVD Collection of the Year to *The Adventures of Indiana Jones DVD Collection*. At this year's ceremony, composer John Williams, who has written and conducted all of the soundtracks for the *Star Wars* and *Indiana Jones* films, receives a Lifetime Achievement Award.

Monday, May 24: Lucasfilm announces that *THX 1138: The George Lucas Director's Cut* will be released on DVD on September 14.

Lucas was looking for an animation director, so, as Rob tells the story, "I spent the next ten days sitting with George trying to be myself." A conversation about the Canadian Film Board indicated a shared love of animation, so, at the end of Coleman's time there, "Rick put his arm around me and said, 'You're the guy.' "

FRIDAY, MAY 28, 2004

ILM: During Friday's animation dailies—which are not part of Lucas's weekly schedule—Coleman announces that the first rough cut was finished as of May 18. And, after watching it, Lucas said that he felt that the character of General Grievous needed further development. If he was a bounty hunter slaughtering Jedi for their lightsabers, Lucas asked, why does he have bodyguards? This week, the director has decided that Grievous should be more cunning than fearsome, a villain who makes others fight for him—unless cornered.

"He's mentioned vampires and spiders," Coleman says. "He's mentioned Nosferatu specifically."

Consequently, as they review some early Grievous animation, Rob asks his animators to make his head more "birdlike," and says that Grievous's fight scenes will skip the animatics department and come straight to the animation department, as time is running out.

THURSDAY, JUNE 3, 2004

ILM, C Theatre: While Knoll and Miller shoot pickups of dignitaries and Senators on the Windward Stage, Lucas reviews a shot of the slaughtered younglings. Coleman, McCallum, and Lucas then discuss Frank Oz's visit tomorrow to record Yoda dialogue for a marketing initiative. Rob and Rick would like to take advantage of his presence to tape the lines for a new

Although they had gone from concept paintings (above left, by Church) and animatics (below left, by Hiroshi Mori), scenes 93 and 93A of the Utapau windmills are cut. Above: Back in Sydney, the Wookiees are caught on tape by Coleman (left). The live-action actors for the two-day shoot are James Rowland, Steven Foy, Robert Cope, Axel Dench, Julian Khazzouh, and David Stiff. Right: Tarfful (Michael Kingma) grabs Dave Elsey on September 16, 2003.

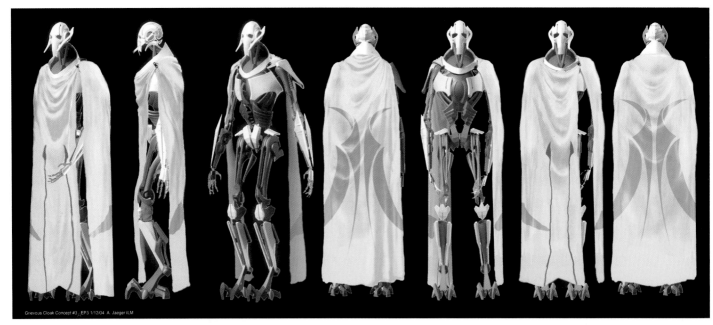

Grievous Cloak Concept #3 EP3 1/12/04 A. Jaeger ILM

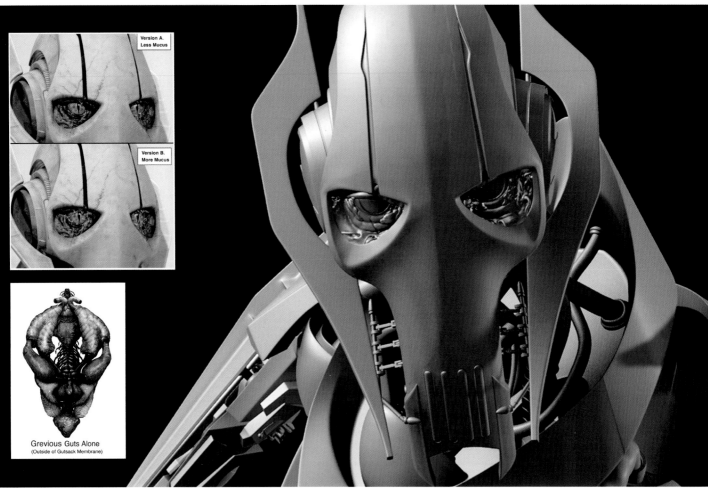

Version A. Less Mucus

Version B. More Mucus

Grevious Guts Alone
(Outside of Gutsack Membrane)

Yoda-Anakin scene. "I'd have to write the dialogue," Lucas agrees. "I'd have to write it this afternoon, but I can do that . . . I hope."

UJ: During animation dailies, which always follow C Theatre dailies, Lucas has been directing the movie within the movie—aka the animated parts of *Revenge of the Sith*—since late 2003. These meetings are new to the prequel trilogy process, and are specifically designed to give Lucas more one-on-one

Two CG characters are worked out at ILM. Grievous's cloak concepts are by Jaeger (top left), his eye-mucus and guts are by McBride (insets), and his hard-surface modeling is supervised by Pam Choy (above). Yoda's "facial expressions" are crafted by lead animator Jamy Wheless (middle right), while Coleman (top right) and lead animator Tim Harrington (right) create his physical performance—during the Jedi Master's Senate duel with Sidious—by first recording their own motions and then animating them.

time with the lead animators. Thus, in addition to Coleman, McCallum, and the ILM producers, Jamy Wheless, Scott Benza, Glen McIntosh, and Paul Kavanaugh are present. Tim Harrington (*Eraser*, 1996; *Men in Black*), who supervised the Yoda-Dooku duel in *Attack of the Clones*, is here for the first time, as preliminary animation has begun on the Yoda-Palpatine fight.

After going over animation for that confrontation, Lucas reviews a Yoda shot in his new scene with Anakin. "Yoda doesn't look like he's thinking," he notes.

"I haven't found the emotional tone yet–it's not working," Coleman says, so Lucas explains what's going through Yoda's mind: "*My feelings are correct*, Yoda's thinking. *The kid's going to be a problem.* It's not: listen, think, concern–it's immediate concern."

Speaking of Grievous, Lucas says to the group, "We've got a little hissing now . . . We're making him more and more slimy. He's a manipulative coward. He's Dracula Droid." Looking at animation of a Grievous bodyguard on Utapau, he remarks, "This part is all different now; we've changed it around in editorial."

In the back of the room, McCallum leans forward in his seat and takes his head in his hands.

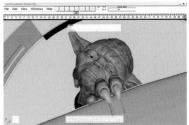

SR: On a wall in the animatics department are the architectural blueprints with the exact Lars homestead set measurements, which were made for Episode II's location shoot in Tunisia. Euisung Lee is using these numbers for animatics of the movie's last shot, which he's preparing as reference for impending pickups. During his short visit, Lucas quickly approves the animatic and leaves.

"So, no new huge changes," Tiemens says, and Lee looks relieved.

TOTAL # OF SHOTS: 2,203   FINALS: 196   FINAL OMITS: 63
SHOTS TURNED OVER: 1,430   SHOTS LEFT TO GO: 2,007   WEEKS TO GO: 44

FRIDAY, JUNE 4, 2004

With Coleman directing, Frank Oz is about to record some lines as Yoda for an international publicity program. In a small, cold room, a microphone is set up for the actor-director. After going over his lines, Oz emphasizes how Yoda has to be himself. "He's not a stand-up comic."

A cell phone rings. It's Lucas, who asks Oz whether he'd mind doing guideline voice-overs for Episode III after he's wrapped the marketing material. Oz says it's "not a problem at all." After audio levels are taken, he puts his head down a moment and comes up speaking as Yoda. Take. "Not good," Oz says, "I'm just getting into it, guys . . ." During the next take, it seems like Yoda has entered the room.

The previous afternoon, Lucas completed writing scene 56:

```
                        YODA
        Premonitions . . . premonitions . . . Hmmmm . . .
                  these visions you have . . .

                       ANAKIN
            They are of pain, suffering, death . . .

                        YODA
          Yourself you speak of, or someone you know?

                       ANAKIN
                   Someone . . .

                        YODA
                . . . close to you?

                       ANAKIN
                     Yes.

                        YODA
       Careful you must be when sensing the future, Anakin. The
            fear of loss is a path to the dark side.

                       ANAKIN
           I won't let my visions come true, Master Yoda.

                        YODA
       Rejoice for those around you who transform into the Force.
       Mourn them, do not. Miss them, do not. Attachment leads to
                jealousy. The shadow of greed, that is.

                       ANAKIN
                What must I do, Master?

                        YODA
          Train yourself to let go of everything you
                    fear to lose.
```

Yoda Facial Expressions

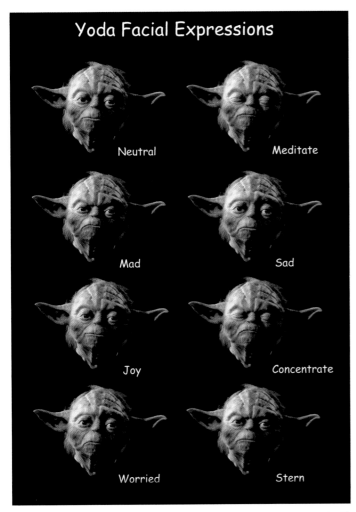

Neutral   Meditate

Mad   Sad

Joy   Concentrate

Worried   Stern

FGQ290—Tk5—FNEP3-08140   05-20-04

FGQ.290

18

SATURDAY, JUNE 19, 2004

Earlier this week, after showing the first rough cut to a select group from ILM, Lucas decided to show it to Steven Spielberg and Jeff Nathanson, the screenwriter of the former's latest film, *The Terminal* (2004). "Steven saw the rough cut," Lucas says, sitting at home at a table in his kitchen. "I felt I needed to show it to Steven to figure out what the reality was, because we'd earlier had a rough-cut screening for ILM to test the film, and some of the people had strong opinions about things that were contrary to the way I was going. Some people were having a hard time with the reason that Anakin goes bad. Somebody asked whether somebody could kill Anakin's best friend, so that he really gets angry. They wanted a real betrayal, such as, 'You tried to kill me so now I'm going to try and kill you.' They didn't understand the fact that Anakin is simply greedy. There is no revenge. The revenge of the Sith is Palpatine. It doesn't have much to do with Darth Vader; he's a pawn in the whole scheme.

"But then there were larger issues. So I had to ask myself, *What was I trying to say and didn't I say it? Did it just get missed or is it not there?* I had to look at it very hard. I had to ask myself, *Is this how the audience is going to react?* Fortunately, Steven confirmed that most of everything was working. So, I may lose a certain demographic—maybe, maybe not. But I had to make a decision, and I decided that I'm not going to alter the film to make it more commercial or marketable. I have to be true to my vision, which is thirty years old, but I have to be true to it."

THURSDAY, JUNE 24, 2004

ILM, C THEATRE: "Here it is," Knoll says to Lucas—and without any more ado, the hall goes dark and the *final* of the first OSB sequence unrolls.

June 4–18: The following scenes have been turned over to ILM:
Sc. 92–95: UMP (Utapau main city plaza)
Sc. 97–99: CCM (Coruscant Chancellor-Mace fight)
Sc. 124–125: SOS (Space Obi-Wan starfighter)
Sc. 176: DPS (Dagobah pod swamp)
Note: The film at present, without credits, has a running time of 2 hours, 17 minutes, 59 seconds.

From where the opening crawl will be, the camera pans down, traversing a dense field of stars till a blinding sun is seen rising over Coruscant. Two Jedi starfighters zoom over camera, which then follows them as they accelerate across the beautifully detailed surface of a massively long Republic assault ship, finally plummeting over its side in the waterfall shot. Though sound effects will be added months from now, the sequence continues to dazzle with spectacular imagery and the fantastic maneuvers of the Jedi starfighters as they blast through explosions and debris. It's all over in about forty-five seconds—when there is spontaneous applause.

"I'm dizzy now," Lucas says. "Excellent! I'm sold."

Moments later, as they file out, Denise Ream says to the crew, "Thanks to everyone who worked on that shot."

ILM, UJ: Harrington calls up one shot from a server listing of hundreds. Looking at a moment from the Yoda-Sidious fight, Lucas adds twenty-four frames, or one second, so the audience will understand that Yoda has stopped, in midair, a Senate pod that the Emperor has thrown at him. To accommodate new dialogue, another fourteen frames are "slid" into the sequence where Yoda jumps into Bail's conveniently closer airspeeder.

Reviewing a complex shot that travels from an extreme wide shot into a close-up of the bridge interior of the Federation cruiser as it crash-lands, Lucas says, per composer John Williams, "I know Johnny will make it work.

"Johnny will come up in July and I'll show him the movie," he adds, "And I'll say, *This is what you're up against.* Then he'll come back in September and we'll spot the music. I'll say, *This is what I want here and this is what I want there*, and we'll take notes. Then he'll start composing the music."

TOTAL # OF SHOTS: 2278   FINALS: 293   SHOTS LEFT TO GO: 1985
FINALS NEEDED PER WEEK: 49   WEEKS TO GO: 40

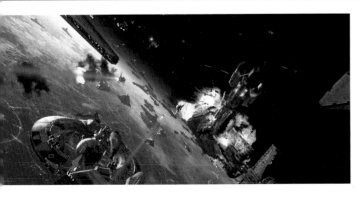

Top left: Animators use a big blue ball to help them animate and simulate Dooku's use of the Force on Obi-Wan. Far left: Animatics by Bustamante of Cato Neimoidia and by Wassung of Jedi Quinlan Vos—the antihero created by Dark Horse comics—on Kashyyyk; early versions of the script had him getting killed in the purge, but the sequence was never filmed. Left, above, and following spread: After years of preparation, the first final frames of the OSB—by Knoll, Coleman, 3-D supervisor David Meny, compositing supervisors Eddie Pasquarello and Pat Tubach, 3-D sequence supervisor Neil Herzinger, lead animators Scott Benza and Glen McIntosh, view-paint supervisors Pam Choy and Elbert Yen, lead 3-D artists David Weitzberg, Willi Geiger, and Jean-Paul Beaulieu, digi-matte painter Joshua Ong, and many others—all led by Lucas.

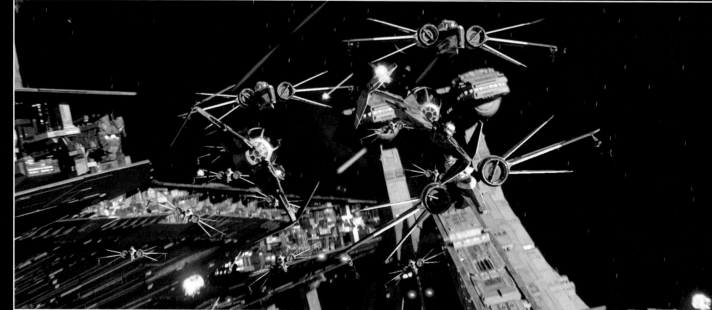

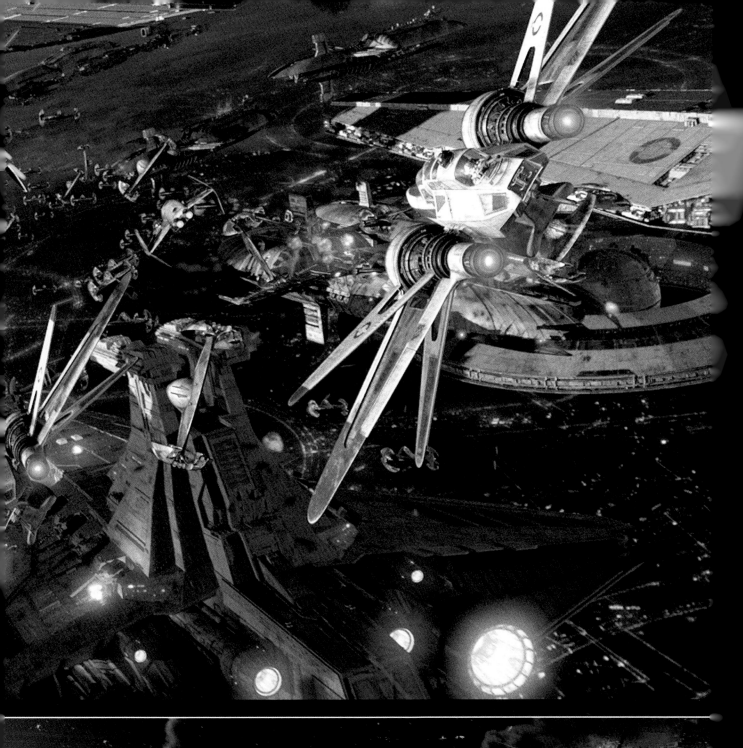

Additional photography—eleven days of shooting—has now been scheduled from August 23 to September 4 at Shepperton Studios, about an hour's drive from London, England.

"It will be primarily blue- and greenscreen shooting," says McCallum, who will leave soon for six weeks of prep. "There won't be any full sets, but there may be large set pieces. We have four or five hundred shots to

Above and far right: Final frames for FBC.640, with a digi-matte painting by Johan Thorngren and the animatics by Alexander that preceded them (right).

do in two weeks. It's almost like shooting another movie. Pretty much all the principal actors are coming."

"The scheduling of this particular two weeks is very intense," Lucas says. "Trying to get all those people from all over the world back at a particular moment, away from other movies, creates a lot of restrictions on what we shoot. We have three or four dramatic scenes we're going to be adding—that's a lot of shooting—and the rest are pickups."

In order to help ILM finish on time, as of August 3, Roger Guyett (*Saving Private Ryan*, 1998; *Harry Potter and the Prisoner of Azkaban*, 2004) will be joining John Knoll as the second visual effects supervisor (his team will be produced by Janet Lewin, while Jill Brooks will now produce Knoll's team). "In Episodes I and II, we had three supervisors from the very start.

This time we're bringing them in over time, though, right from day one, we had planned on Roger coming on," says McCallum. "Roger will have huge sequences–Kashyyyk and Mustafar–to start with. He's been a godsend."

choices for the opera costumes. Among them are samples for Lucas's costume–he'll be making a cameo on the opera house stairs as Baron Papanoida–as well as those for Amanda Lucas's and her friend Jason Hallikainen's. David explains, diplomatically, that Biggar has pointed out that these fabrics are leftovers from Sydney.

"In other words," Lucas smiles, "approve them–or else!"

TOTAL # OF SHOTS: 2278   FINALS: 466   SHOTS LEFT TO GO: 1812
FINALS NEEDED PER WEEK: 49   WEEKS TO GO: 35

TUESDAY, JULY 13, 2004

ILM, C THEATRE: "How's the cut coming?" Knoll asks.

"We're now adjusting it," Lucas says, of the second rough cut, which he finished on July 9.

"What areas are the most fluid?"

"Reels four and five. They've settled down."

In UJ, the new scene with Yoda and Anakin is reviewed. Frank Oz can already be heard saying, "Fear of loss is a path to the dark side."

"Everything leads to the dark side!" Lucas jokes.

"Even carbohydrates," Knoll agrees.

A shot of Padmé in her coffin reveals that ILM has succeeded in taking away Natalie Portman's pulse, as Lucas predicted they could back on the set.

TUESDAY, JULY 27, 2004

ILM, C THEATRE: "Soon the space battle is going to be over," Knoll says.

"Good," responds Lucas. "Rick is pushing for some reels to be finished by January."

After dailies, Lucas is on the phone to Rick, who's in England paving the way for the pickups. "I'm having Anne type up the script today."

SR: This afternoon in the art department, David shows Lucas fabric

WEDNESDAY, JULY 28, 2004

Peter Mayhew is on hand to reprise his role as Chewbacca. Michael Kingma (as the Wookiee general Tarfful) is also here. At 8:30 A.M., a small crew and Lucas are on a greenscreen set. Inside a black tent nearby are three transplants from Australia–Dave and Lou Elsey, and Rebecca Hunt, who have set up a small creatures department.

When called, Mayhew and Kingma walk onto the set–towering over the crew–in their complete Wookiee regalia. "They're incredible," Denise Ream says. "It was an awesome moment," McCallum adds. "Everybody stopped in their tracks. I thought it was beautiful–and Chewbacca gave me a kiss."

Lucas shows Mayhew and Kingma animatics of the scene–a hologram moment on Kashyyyk–the two then return to the tent for final hair adjustments. When they're not before the cameras, tubes running from ice chests into their suits keep the actors cool. While waiting for Miller and his crew to ready the first setup, Lucas talks about multi-element shots in *Return of the Jedi* as compared with today's work.

Top left: Visual effects supervisor Roger Guyett will supervise scenes on Mustafar (digi-matte painting by Brett Northcutt, above) and on Tatooine (visual script painting by Tiemens, top right), among others. Right, middle: The Millennium Falcon *makes a cameo in CSL.005 (Coruscant Senate landing platform), animatics by Bustamante (May 17), courtesy of Lucas. On August 10, Jaeger reverse-engineers the craft, eliminating its rust-colored panels and blast marks (far right)–after all, it's twenty years younger.*

Saturday, July 24: At the San Diego International Comic Convention, the title of Episode III–Revenge of the Sith–is announced to the public and picked up on CNN that night.

"Dailies used to take a lot longer—and it was almost exclusively discussions about matte lines," he recalls, and then jokes: "I survived the optical compositing era."

"I helped kill it, too," Knoll chimes in, referring to the work he's done to advance computer graphics.

"Wookiees coming out! Everybody in position, please," the 1st assistant director calls out.

The Wookiees climb up on small green boxes, which will eventually be replaced by a lush Kashyyyk environment and a raging Clone War in the background. "You're standing there looking like a bodyguard," Lucas says to Kingma. "There's a lot of commotion, so you can look out at the tanks."

During the take itself, Lucas calls out instructions, "Peter, you can fold your arms . . . tilt your head—great!"

FRIDAY, JULY 29, 2004

"Okay, we're done," Lucas says the next morning after the remaining setups are quickly shot.

"Thank you, Wookiees," the 1st AD says.

The Wookiees bow. Kingma is on his way from Australia to Denmark, where he's trying out for its national basketball team. Mayhew says he feels "fabulous" finally completing his scenes. "It's been a long time. It's great to be doing something I helped start so long ago."

"Uncle Owen will be here in about twelve minutes," Miller announces. And twelve minutes later, Joel Edgerton walks onto the set.

"It's Uncle Owen, looking great," Lucas says. "This is the end of the movie—the very last shot."

After reviewing the animatics with Roxburgh cut in from principal photography, Edgerton walks over to the green ramp that will be the ridge of the crater on Tatooine. "Bring your back foot down a little on the ramp, so it's a little more John Wayne–like," Lucas calls out.

1

2

3

The crew, lights, and cameras are ready, and Lucas directs what will be the final shot of the film—the traditional "iris" shot that ends each *Star Wars* episode.

"Okay, we'll try one more," he says, "and . . . Action!"

Thursday, August 5, 2004

ILM: In C Theatre, the first Mustafar final is reviewed—a simple shot of Anakin strangling Obi-Wan—and approved.

In UJ, it's the last meeting before Lucas leaves for England. Animation has begun on Yoda's departure from Kashyyyk and his good-bye to Chewbacca, so Coleman asks what's going through Yoda's head at that point.

"I think he's determined," Lucas says, after a moment's thought. "He suspects that things are bad, but he's thinking about where he's going and what's going to happen."

"By working so closely with Frank Oz and George," McCallum observes, "Rob has totally transformed the performance of Yoda. Everything we ever dreamed Yoda could do, Rob has been able to pull off."

Turning from one CG character to another, Lucas examines a shot that has Jar Jar in the background. "There was a time," he jokes, "when I was going to have Jar Jar walk through every scene, like Hitchcock."

An ILM breakdown composited by Mike Conte, of Anakin strangling Obi-Wan in the Mustafar war room: 1. Principal photography; 2. Bluescreen extraction; 3. Digimatte painting element added; 4. Steam element shot on stage added; 5. Bluescreen over background; 6. Digital rear-wall element added; 7. Window composite and color correction effected; 8. Lightsaber matte added; 9. Final frame.

Monday, August 2: The establishment of Lucasfilm Animation Singapore is announced.

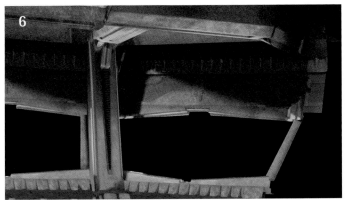

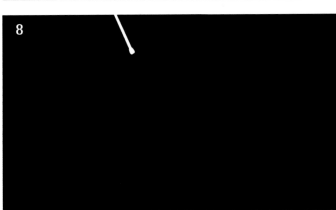

In the Mustafar control room during Anakin's rampage, Lucas adds a droid getting hit in one shot and falling apart in the next. "It gives the audience a little bit of geography to hang on to," he explains.

SR: Later that afternoon, Lucas is in the animatics department working on the Jedi hangar scene, in which Anakin tells Mace Windu that Palpatine is a Sith Lord. He adds a low sun outside the hangar, so that, in this crucial scene, a sense of light and darkness is evident.

"Anakin should be standing in the light on the edge of the shadow," Lucas says to Alexander. "Anakin is in the sun, but behind him everything is dark."

He adds new scenes like the one in the Jedi hangar as well:

                        ANAKIN
          He won't give up his power. I have learned a
        terrible truth. I think Chancellor Palpatine is a Sith Lord
        [. . .] The one we have been looking for [. . .]
          He knows the ways of the Force. He has been trained
                  to use the Dark Side.

                      MACE WINDU
                 Are you sure about this?

                        ANAKIN
          Absolutely [. . .] Master, the Chancellor is very
          powerful. You will need my help if you are going
                     to arrest him.

                      MACE WINDU
        For your own good, you stay out of this conflict. I sense
        much confusion in you, young Skywalker. You carry a great
              deal of fear that clouds your judgment.

                        ANAKIN
                 That's not true, Master.

                      MACE WINDU
        We'll see. If what you say about the Chancellor is true,
                 you will have earned my trust.

Some of the script has names in place but dialogue listed "to be written," while a key Padmé scene is "to be rewritten."

TOTAL # OF SHOTS: 2,300   FINALS: 540   SHOTS LEFT TO GO: 1,760
FINALS NEEDED PER WEEK: 53   WEEKS TO GO: 33

FRIDAY, AUGUST 6, 2004

SR: Anne Merrifield finishes typing up the "Reshoot Script," which bears today's date. In addition to continuity pickups, Lucas has included miscellaneous dialogue additions—such as this exchange after Anakin kills Dooku:

                        ANAKIN
                It's not the Jedi way.

                      PALPATINE
        It is only natural. He cut off your arm, and you wanted
                 revenge. It wasn't the first time.

NOTE: On August 19-20, for the Kashyyyk battle sequences, ILM will shoot the following elements: water planes, tank droid wakes, churning water, and other beach and water assets, some of which will be recorded at the Berkeley Aquatic Park.

Above: Final frames of Count Dooku's death at the hands of Anakin. The Jedi's fall i
further illustrated by Lucas's new scene in the Jedi hangar (left, by Tiemens; August 6
in which Skywalker stands on the threshold between sunlight and darkness.

Revenge Rashomon-Style

ADDITIONAL PHOTOGRAPHY DAY 1: MONDAY, AUGUST 23, 2004

LOCATION: Shepperton Studios, England—R Stage

CREW CALL: 7:30 A.M.

SET: Chancellor's office/hallway; opera house

SCHEDULED SCENES SHOT: Palpatine reveals he is a Sith; Anakin runs up opera house stairs [NOTE: *Not all scenes shot are listed.*]

Lucas and McCallum sit by side as preparations are made for shooting the enhancements to the scene in which Palpatine seduces Anakin. In addition to the English crew, many of whom have worked on Episodes I or II, some of the Episode III crew are back: supervising art director Peter Russell, "A" camera operator Calum McFarlane, stunt coordinator–sword master Nick Gillard, first assistant director Colin Fletcher, costume designer Trisha Biggar, and others. Though Lucas is using a small on-set crew of forty-four, it's going to be a short, intense two weeks.

Shepperton is a large, sprawling studio where many English TV productions have their home and where many of cinema's legends have worked—Alfred Hitchcock, Stanley Kubrick, Orson Welles, David Lean, and many more—including Lucas, who shot part of *Star Wars* here back in 1976. *Batman Begins* (2005) has just wrapped, and other films are just starting up. Though older, Shepperton is like Fox Studios, Sydney—even more

Top left: Lucas, "A" camera operator Calum McFarlane, and Hayden Christensen; Knoll and McCallum. Above: The giant opera staircase featured the only crowd scene of the pickups and squished the video village into a corner of Stage R. Barry Howell's animatics of CGO.020 (inset, June 23), using a concept painting by Church, show Lucas in Jun's early costume design concept for his character Baron Papanoida. Next to him is his daughter Katie (Chi Eekway).

so–in its fragile constructions. Its layout seems to obey the laws of urban sprawl, while some structures have the distinct look of abandoned World War II aerodromes. The JAK production office is a tiny room, with cheaply made desks cluttered together and a pervasive smell of tobacco.

The first set is crowded. Actors and crew are wedged into one side of the already smallish R Stage, thanks to the enormous staircase built for the opera scene, which occupies the other half of the stage. Because it's the first day of pickups, the first shot takes some time to prepare. "Close?" McCallum asks Fletcher. "Is Ian here?"

Not long afterward, Hayden Christensen and Ian McDiarmid arrive in their dressing gowns. Lucas shows them on a video monitor the scene as it presently appears–an editorial collage consisting of shots taken from other scenes, dialogue voiced by Burtt, and animatics, which combine into something a little bewildering for the actors.

"You'll keep us right," McDiarmid says to Lucas.

"Yeah, it's difficult, but don't get thrown off by all that," the director reassures. "By the time you guys get dressed, we'll have the set ready."

The video village is the usual setup, but this time Giles Nuttgens is DP, Victoria Pike is script supervisor, and Duncan Blackman is matchmove supervisor. Many of the newer faces actually go way back with either Lucas or McCallum. Nuttgens originally met the latter while focus pulling on *Blackeyes*, and later worked on *Young Indy* as DP.

By 8:30 A.M., Christensen and McDiarmid are in costume and on the set.

"Stand by for rehearsal," Fletcher says.

Though a year has passed, everyone, new and old, knows the routine. Lucas explains to the actors that although Anakin is delivering big news– Obi-Wan has found General Grievous–the Chancellor's reaction is personal, not political, and designed to seduce Anakin. "He doesn't talk about whether the war should continue or not–he responds to *you*," George emphasizes to Hayden.

PALPATINE
It is upsetting to me to see that the Council doesn't
seem to fully appreciate your talents. Don't you
wonder why they wouldn't make you a Jedi Master?

Wearing her usual long black coat, Biggar arrives and asks Lucas if he had a nice weekend. "I had to write part of the script, *because* . . . ," he deadpans, "there were some people who were anxious about what they were going to say."

Unlike the intentionally simple first day of principal photography, today's opera scene involves an ambitious use of costumes and extras, so he indicates the stairs and adds, "This wasn't my idea."

"I was told it was Rick's idea," Biggar says laughing.

As the morning continues, the importance of hairdresser Pip Lund and makeup artist Shane Thomas–both of whom traveled here from Sydney– becomes obvious as questions of continuity arise. "The real question is how much the hair matches–that's always the big issue," Lucas says. Indeed, he and Knoll will consult throughout the next two weeks, verifying that what is about to be shot will match a preexisting plate, or what came before, or what comes after. Continuity problems can be anything from lighting, scale, and angle to choreography, eye lines, makeup, and wardrobe.

Following lunch in the Orangery–a choice of chicken, pasta, or salad– is the afternoon's big opera scene. Creature heads on sticks adorn long tables. Gillard is supervising safety to ensure that no one falls off the roughly ten-yard-high stairs. People who can see in their costumes are placed near the edges. Those who can't see are led to their marks by hand. Opera attendees include everything from enormous "hippo" creatures to scantily clad humanoids. Hidden among them is Anthony Daniels, who, as "Captain" Faytonni, is reprising his brief "human" appearance in *Attack of the Clones*.

"I'm just reminding everyone not to go too close to the edges," Fletcher says. "No closer than you were at rehearsal."

On "Action," they all elegantly ascend the stairs. On Fletcher's cue, Christensen disembarks from a blue placeholder vehicle and races up the steps, maneuvering among the extras. "One more!" Lucas calls out, and a PA immediately yells, "Resetting!"

Though this shot is quickly recorded, its sixty costumes took more than two months to make–requiring the skills of Biggar, her key collaborators, four cutters, and a milliner–while the creatures took two weeks of prep and the services of the Elseys, Rebecca Hunt, prosthetics makeup artist Colin Ware, and their small team.

"George, we're ready for first rehearsal," a PA says, while Lucas and Christensen talk about key scenes to come.

"As for what's written on the page?" Hayden asks.

Above: Day 2 sees Lucas adding to the visual script's illustration of Padmé watching the Jedi Temple burning, intuiting that her husband is somehow responsible. Right: Meanwhile, back at ILM, technicians and crew begin their six-month Mustafar miniature shoot (bottom right, lead model-maker Nick D'Abo).

"I'm open to alternatives," Lucas says. "It's not set in stone." Per the climactic duel, he adds, "I haven't quite figured out how to attack it. I need to come up with something that fits, but the dialogue would have to be short and powerful. You'll have it the day we shoot."

As the last shot is prepped, a PA asks McCallum if it's been a good first day.

"I would've been happier if it we'd finished twenty-five minutes earlier," he replies, "but, considering the extras, it's a good start."

After Fletcher makes it a wrap, a surprise birthday cake is wheeled out for Rick, who lights a cigarette with the candles and then blows them out.

LOCATION WRAP: 19:15   SETUPS: 33

ADDITIONAL PHOTOGRAPHY DAY 2: TUESDAY, AUGUST 24, 2004
LOCATION: B Stage
SET: Padmé's apt; clone & Senate landing platform; Mustafar control center
SCENES SHOT: Obi-Wan tells Anakin that he's a hero; Anakin surveys the slaughter on Mustafar

Having been picked up at 4:15 A.M. and in makeup by 5:15–an hour earlier than anyone else–Natalie Portman is now on the set: a green bench and two arcs, which is all the shot needs of her apartment.

"Okay, here we go–shooting. Bell up!" Fletcher says. "Roll cameras, please."

For this nondialogue scene in which Padmé senses something is wrong, Lucas calls out, "When you decide to get up and go to the window, don't do it as if you heard something. You can actually see the Jedi Temple on fire."

"Okay," Portman says. "Got it."

Looking at the actress on the HD monitor, which appears next to what was shot a year ago on the video monitor, Lucas says, "In the last twelve months, she's really grown up." He walks over to the set and mentions that.

"Thank you," Portman says.

"So I've decided to go back and reshoot the whole movie," Lucas jokes.

Back in the video village, which is, unusually, lodged in a set (the work-in-progress Naboo Skiff), Lucas goes over mentally which Padmé scenes come before and after this one, and talks over the problem with Knoll. He also shows McCallum the difference.

Between setups, Portman sits on a stool reading the latest edition of *The New Yorker* while Lucas sits writing dialogue for the Obi-Wan/Anakin duel, having been inspired during his drive from London this morning.

                    OBI-WAN
   Much of what I've taught you, you're using against me.

                    ANAKIN
   I should have known the Jedi were plotting to take over.

                    OBI-WAN
   From the Sith!!! Anakin, the Chancellor is evil.

                    ANAKIN
   From the Jedi point of view. From my point of view, the
                  Jedi are evil.

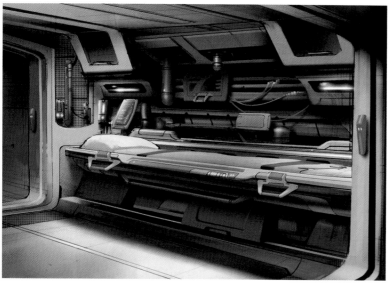

"Hot off the presses," Lucas says to Knoll, as he hands the sheets to a PA, who will get them typed up. "Written by hand! None of this digital nonsense for me."

"You! Of all people," Knoll replies.

They finish Portman's scene, and McGregor arrives with Christensen for the next one.

Spotting Ewan, Lucas says, "I couldn't sleep for months!" referring to McGregor's recent around-the-world motorcycle trip.

"I did get bit by a mosquito," McGregor admits, "which the Russian papers picked up."

"How many miles?" McCallum asks.

"Eighteen and a half thousand."

As the actors rehearse the scene, McCallum informs Lucas that he's reserved a week at the end of January 2005 at Shepperton for the next pickups, which will precede the recording sessions with John Williams in early February. "Well, obviously, the more I can do [looping, reshooting, music] at once, the better," Lucas says.

"The better for all of us," McCallum agrees.

A PA hands Lucas the typed-up dialogue on one page of pink paper.

ANAKIN
Your combat skills have always been poor,
Master. You're called "the negotiator" because you
can't fight . . .

OBI-WAN
It's over Anakin. I have the high ground. Don't
try it.

ANAKIN
You underestimate the power of the dark side.

After lunch, Portman and Christensen stand with miniature motorized fans in hand as makeup prepares them for their close-ups. "In the classic Hollywood tradition," Lucas tells his DP, "light her so she's beautiful."

He then talks with Christensen, noting that he needs a "nice, vicious, crazed close-up" for when Anakin surveys the carnage he's created on Mustafar. He also tells him how, in the editing room, he changed things around so that "all the subplots now relate to Anakin. It's all knitted much more tightly together."

"Sounds good," Christensen says.

Moments later, after cutting out a few shots he realized weren't necessary, Lucas tells McCallum, "I'm following in the footsteps of John Ford—I'm ripping everything out of the script!" referring to that director's legendary method of dealing with producers who felt he was going too slowly.

Anthony Daniels arrives, ready to resume his role under armor as C-3PO, who is resplendent—so much so that Knoll is afraid that the camera will catch reflections of cameras and equipment in his metal.

"I remember having a fit about this in Sydney," he says. "There's too many people on the set. I can see every one of them reflected in his head."

"Well, go have a fit," Lucas says.

Knoll leaves the video village to find a remedy, and Lucas and McCallum both call out, "Giles!"

When the DP comes over, Lucas says to him, "John wants to have a fit."

The upshot is, they tone down the golden droid's reflection factor.

CAMERA WRAP: 18:44   SETUPS: 31

ADDITIONAL PHOTOGAPHY DAY 3: WEDNESDAY, AUGUST 25, 2004
LOCATION: B Stage
SET: Mustafar landing platform, locker room, secret landing platform
SCENES SHOT: Anakin chokes Padmé; Obi-Wan dispatches Grievous

For the moment just before Anakin assassinates the Separatist leaders, Christensen is having trouble putting on his hood.

"It's the hood's fault," Lucas calls out from the village.

Though a seemingly minor gesture, the donning of the cowl must look seamless and menacing. After another flubbed take, Lucas walks over to help layer the pleats correctly. The next shot, in which Vader espies

Top right: Church's concept art of July 19, 2004, depicts the Naboo skiff's "medbed." Peter Russell's art department built the set based on the drawings, and the new scene was filmed on August 25, 2004, with McGregor, Daniels, and Portman—who wears a costume designed by McCaig in December 2002. Above right: Obi-Wan (McGregor) slips into the locker/closet aboard the Naboo skiff in another new scene. Right: Fletcher, DP Giles Nutggens, Lucas, Daniels, and McCallum.

Padmé's ship, has Anakin taking *off* his hood, which goes without a hitch.

The following setups are for one of the new scenes, and take place in an actual set of the Naboo skiff interior. Although relatively small, the skiff set has one thing that almost none of the sets had in Sydney: a ceiling.

In the first shot, Obi-Wan must hide in a utility closet—and jokes abound.

"R2-D2 walks by and hears someone banging on the door who can't get out," Lucas says, "but moves on."

"Or," McGregor offers, "I disappear into this small cupboard where they keep the mops. Light-years later, I emerge as Alec Guinness!"

As the jokes continue, they inadvertently reveal that the closet is mysteriously and unrealistically empty of objects, so Lucas, Peter Russell, and art director David Lee quickly come up with something to make it more lived-in. A few minutes later, the closet contains some air-conditioner hose and a few plastic containers.

"I'd like to try that little Jedi thing with my hand when I'm inside," McGregor says, "to close the door." Lucas agrees, and the shots are quickly recorded.

Wearing the costume that concept artist Iain McCaig drew up nearly two years ago, Portman lies on the skiff's bunk for a scene in which Obi-Wan checks on her condition after Anakin has attacked her. While they set up, unit photographer Keith Hamshere snaps some stills. In 1975, when Lucas was still in search of a location for his desert planet, Hamshere showed him and *Star Wars* production designer John Barry photographs of a recce he'd done in Algeria for Stanley Donen's *The Little Prince* (1974). Hamshere's first Lucasfilm job was on *Indiana Jones and the Temple of Doom* (1984). He went on to do *Young Indy*, *Willow* (1988), *Radioland Murders*, and the first two prequels.

"He's the best in the business," Knoll says.

At 2:50 P.M., McGregor, Christensen, and Portman watch edited footage of the Mustafar landing platform scene. With Lucas and company, they'll soon be recording bits of missing continuity, created by changes made during editing: an over-the-shoulder shot here, a bit of dialogue there.

"You need my shoulder?" Christensen asks, incredulously.

"Well, we're going to turn around and do the emotional part, too," Lucas says. "And we need your lips to make a *w*."

"Fantastic," the actor says.

As the afternoon ticks by, Knoll remarks to Lucas that doing partial scenes isn't as exciting as shooting complete scenes.

"But when we get back to editorial," Lucas points out, "there is nothing better than patching this material into the film."

CAMERA WRAP: 19:27
SETUPS: 42

ADDITIONAL PHOTOGRAPHY DAY 4: THURSDAY, AUGUST 26, 2004

LOCATION: B Stage

SET: Mustafar volcano edge

SCENES SHOT: Anakin and Obi-Wan talk while dueling; Obi-Wan looks
on in horror as Anakin becomes toast

As crew prepare to shoot the new dialogue Lucas has written for the duel on Mustafar, the director explains to Hayden, "Basically you're arrogant–at one point I had you say to Obi-Wan, 'I could've beat you when I was ten years old.' "

Second AD Deborah Antoniou, who also made the flight from Australia, walks up to Lucas and whispers, "Just a gentle reminder about your costume fitting tonight, is that still okay?"

"No, but I'll do it anyway," he says, referring to preparations for his cameo.

"You're a gentleman," she smiles and departs.

For the dialogue sequence, McGregor and Christensen are standing on four-foot-wide blue disks, which can be rotated by stagehands. At first, however, they have a hard time judging at what speed to turn them–so when Christensen says, "You can't fight!" he also happens to be jettisoned from his disk.

"Well, you can't fly!" McGregor jokes.

In the village, someone inquires how the disks are able to float on lava.

"Does it make sense?" McCallum responds. "No. Will it work in the movie? Maybe."

Production moves on to Obi-Wan's new line just before he slices off Anakin's limbs. To prep him, Lucas shows McGregor the edited sequence on one of the monitors. "I cut out Anakin's line, 'Help me, Master,' " he explains. "I didn't want him to be redeemed."

"But the end stays like that?" he asks, referring to the sequence as a whole.

"Yeah."

"Good," says Ewan, who seems to have been impressed with the scene's quality even in its rough form.

"When you get the sound and the music in there," Lucas says, "it'll be really powerful."

CAMERA Wrap: 19:10   Setups: 52

ADDITIONAL PHOTOGRAPHY DAY 5: FRIDAY, AUGUST 27, 2004

LOCATION: B Stage

SET: Senate landing platform, Chancellor's office

SCENES SHOT: Fight up to where Palpatine changes to Sidious

"Good morning. It's good to be here," Samuel L. Jackson says to Lucas. Today's key scene, which will take a couple of days to shoot, is the end of the Mace-Palpatine fight. The Jedi Master is winning when Anakin arrives, but Palpatine, as the scene has been rethought, now seizes the occasion to exaggerate his weakness in order to force Anakin's hand–after which Palpatine kills Mace.

Although the emotional context of the scene is complex, the set is simple: just a section of the window in Palpatine's office–the niche in which Mace corners the Chancellor. McCallum is here early making sure everything is on track, while Lucas sits alone in the video village studying the already cut material.

```
                      PALPATINE
You are not one of them, Anakin. You must choose. Don't let
  him kill me [. . .] I am your pathway to power to save the
                    one you love.

                     MACE WINDU
 Don't listen to him, Anakin [. . .] I am going to end this
right now [. . .] He is too dangerous to be kept alive [. . .]

                       ANAKIN
         He must live . . . I need him . . .
```

A combination of elements show Windu's death: (above) he and other Jedi arrive in a final frame; (top right) in one of the pickup shots, fencing double Michael Byrne (Palpatine) cuts down Kit Fisto; Carney's May 7 animatic of CCM.340 (top, far right) shows the window shattering . . .

Thursday, August 26: ILM completes the first "hero" Mustafar motion control shot–an "incredibly complicated and messy process," according to Janet Lewin, "because we have to get the lava flow to look just right, especially in the wide establishing shots." Jedi Temple miniature elements are also being shot, and prep continues on the Utapau hero wall, as well as the Kashyyyk beach, hologram room, and tree.

because we're dealing with things that aren't so obvious. The audience knows Anakin is going to turn to the dark side, but the things that he's struggling with are so subtle that it may be hard for people to understand why his obsession to hold on to Padmé is so strong."

Jackson and McDiarmid join Lucas in front of the monitor to review the scene.

"It's coming together," he says. "But the only scene I hadn't thought through enough is the scene we're reshooting today."

"The fight itself was fine," Lucas says. "The problem was that the final confrontation between Mace and Palpatine wasn't specific enough in terms of Anakin, so we're working to make his story, his conflict sharper—I have what I call two sharp 'right turns' in the movie," he adds, "and they are very hard to deal with. For the audience, it's a real jerk, because you're going along and then somebody yanks you in a different direction. Anakin turning to the dark side and killing Mace is a very hard right,

"It makes it easier for Anakin to come in later in the fight," McDiarmid notes.

The actors rehearse in their dressing gowns and then adjourn for final costume adjustments, while Lucas and Knoll continue to examine the footage. When Palpatine easily strikes down Mace's three associate Jedi at the outset of the scene, Knoll says, "Look at this—Mace brought the B-team!"

"You have to be either Mace or Yoda to compete with the Emperor," Lucas says. "If Anakin hadn't got all beat-up, he could've beat the Emperor."

"But Mace was going to arrest Palpatine," Knoll says, "and a few moments later he says Palpatine's too dangerous to live. What happened?"

"Mace was going to do the right thing by arresting him, but after Palpatine does the lightning, he changes his mind."

. . . while a final frame of Palpatine (McDiarmid) and Windu (Jackson) has Yanick Dusseault's digi-matte painting of Coruscant in the background (middle). Thinking he has won, Windu winds up his death blow in a pickup shot (above).

205

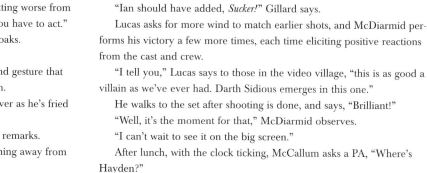

Jackson and McDiarmid return, final checks are completed, and cameras roll.

"You're under arrest, my lord!" Jackson threatens. Towering over Palpatine, he booms, "You old fool!!"

For the moment when Anakin arrives, Lucas explains the situation to Christensen: "You almost come a second too late. You're rushing over to make sure that nothing happens—but your anticipation is that they're going to hurt each other. When the lightning starts, things are getting worse from your point of view. And when Mace is going to kill him, you have to act."

Fletcher calls action and the large fans ruffle the Jedi cloaks.

"You have lost!" Jackson intones above the machines.

After a couple of takes, Lucas asks Jackson to add a hand gesture that warns Anakin to back off as he prepares to execute the Sith.

For the end of the conflict, Jackson screams over and over as he's fried by Sith lightning.

"He's pretty good at that electrocution business," Knoll remarks.

"Yeah, but I want him to do a little bit more before turning away from the camera," Lucas says.

After Jackson adjusts his performance, completing another convincing death scene, the crew applauds.

CAMERA WRAP: 18:24 SETUPS: 40

"Ian should have added, *Sucker!*" Gillard says.

Lucas asks for more wind to match earlier shots, and McDiarmid performs his victory a few more times, each time eliciting positive reactions from the cast and crew.

"I tell you," Lucas says to those in the video village, "this is as good a villain as we've ever had. Darth Sidious emerges in this one."

He walks to the set after shooting is done, and says, "Brilliant!"

"Well, it's the moment for that," McDiarmid observes.

"I can't wait to see it on the big screen."

After lunch, with the clock ticking, McCallum asks a PA, "Where's Hayden?"

"He's dressing."

"Tell him we're desperate."

Christensen arrives a few minutes later, ready for the moment in which Anakin submits to Palpatine's temptation:

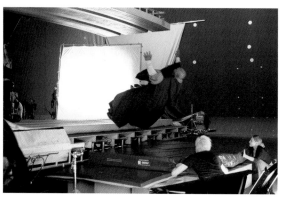

ADDITIONAL PHOTOGRAPHY DAY 6: SATURDAY, AUGUST 28, 2004
LOCATION: B Stage
SET: Naboo main square, Chancellor's office, Jedi Council
SCENES SHOT: Sio Bibble walks in Queen's funeral procession; Sidious laughs while attacking Mace; Anakin sits alone in the Council chamber

```
                    ANAKIN
      I will do whatever you ask. Just
      help me save Padmé's life. I can't
         live without her. I won't let
                    her die.
```

"It's basically *Faust* in the end," Lucas explains. "This is the one where you make a pact with the devil. And that usually leads to the same end: You cannot change the inevitable. If you try, you're basically going against the cosmos or however you want to define that."

Ian McDiarmid is in his Darth Sidious makeup as crew prepare for different angles and sections of the Mace-Palpatine-Anakin showdown. Christensen does his usual push-ups to warm up. He is staying with Nick Gillard in Brighton, so Gillard jokes about writing a book titled, *Darth Vader Is Living in My Basement.*

During McDiarmid's close-ups as Sidious, as he unleashes his pent-up fury on the doomed Jedi, the power of the actor's performance is impressive. There is applause and hoots of joy after he screams out, "Power! *Unlimited power!*" twisting his face with unmitigated delight at his sadistic victory.

After the first take, Lucas says to Christensen, "When you get to 'I won't let her die,' I need you to say it with real determination."

After the next take, Hayden asks, "It's more in that direction, right?"

As Lucas climbs up the stairs to the set, he responds, "Yeah. Also the words should be hard to get out."

Take. "Don't turn up the volume; just grit your teeth," George says.

After the next take, Lucas asks, "You want to go straight into one more?" and Christensen does another.

"Great. Really good—one more like that," the director says. "Those were at exactly the right levels"—but Christensen has to wait while they alter the lighting, so he says to Fletcher, "As soon as possible," in order not to lose the moment.

"One more right away," the actor asks after the previous one.

Take. "That was fantastic, Hayden. Fantastic," Lucas says. They do another one. "That was fantastic, too. You want to go right into one more?"

"Yes, please," Christensen says.

After the final take, McDiarmid walks over to Christensen and pats him on the shoulder.

Next on the Call Sheet is Anakin in the Jedi Council chamber, brooding on his and Padmé's destiny. While Nuttgens gets the lighting in place, Lucas and Knoll talk at length about how they're going to make Christensen fit into the already shot plate of the Jedi Council. McCallum listens for a few minutes and then says, "John, I have a great idea. Let's just shoot it and work it out later."

He continues watching and waiting, becoming slightly concerned about how long the setup is taking. "Can we do it?" he asks Fletcher.

"Yes, let's do it," Fletcher says. Twenty minutes later, however, other problems have developed.

Meanwhile, director and visual effects supervisor continue their debate,

```
                ANAKIN (cont'd)
        My loyalty belongs to both sides.
        I don't wish to join either.  I
        can't tell you any more.
                PADMÉ
        I understand.
He takes her in his arms,           ANAKIN
mostly  And I'm afraid of losing you....
        I'm afraid of my visions
                PADMÉ
        That won't happen...
She looks him in the eye.
                PADMÉ
        That won't happen   I believe you can protect me against anything.
```

with the latter pressing his point. Lucas finally asks, "What are you going to do if, after you put him in the plate, Anakin walks into the middle of a [digital] chair?"

Knoll thinks for a moment and says, "Beg for mercy."

As Christensen takes his place in the minimal set, Lucas counsels him: "Try and increase how uncomfortable you feel as the shot goes on. Try to think back on the Darth Plagueis story—run that through your head."

As they move into close-ups, Lucas says, "Take it one step further: You realize that by telling the Jedi about Palpatine being a Sith that Padmé is going to die. Basically, you just killed her."

They do several takes of Christensen effectively exteriorizing Anakin's internal pain, which will shortly push him over to the dark side.

"Showing how much Anakin and Padmé care for each other is one of my weak points," Lucas admits. "Expressing that is hard to do. It's really hard in the end to express the idea, *I'm so in love with you that I would do anything to save you; I'd give up everything—friends, my whole life—for you*, and make that real—make that stick—and say it in *two* minutes, which is all the time this film has for it. If I had a whole movie, I could probably manage it. But I can't go deep into the psyche of these people beyond a certain stylistic reality I've created for myself. It wouldn't work.

"It's also a very difficult structural issue," he adds. "And when I created it, I knew I wanted two hard right turns—it's designed to be that way—and I knew I was taking a real chance that it wasn't going to work. But you have to see if you can make it work. If it doesn't, well, then I'm going to get skewered for it. But if I can make it work, it'll be neat; it'll be good."

CAMERA WRAP: 17:45   SETUPS: 32

ADDITIONAL PHOTOGRAPHY DAY 7: MONDAY, AUGUST 30, 2004
LOCATION: R Stage
SET: Jedi Council, Kashyyyk hologram, Jedi gunship, Jedi war room, Mygeeto
SCENES SHOT: Anakin tells Mace about Palpatine; Jedi cut down by Palpatine

Because of budget constraints, the Jedi Council chamber is being shot in sections. The first group of five chairs is placed on their marks and Yoda is unwrapped—to reveal a truly deranged version of himself—which will be used only for camera reference and eye lines.

"Have you seen Yoda's expression?" Knoll asks Lucas. "It's priceless."

"Somebody has to get a photo of that," Lucas agrees, and Knoll adds, "Something's definitely wrong with the universe."

Top left: McDiarmid (Sidious) is reshot as he fries Windu with Force lightning, and Jackson (Windu) is reshot as he falls onto a blue mattress supervised by Gillard. Top right: A final frame of the hologram in which Anakin kneels to Sidious. Above right: Jackson casts a quizzical eye on a disturbed Yoda puppet. Above left: Lucas's efforts to write how much Anakin and Padmé feel for each other is evident in his script revisions.

After a week of shooting, Lucas says he feels "good." But today turns out to be trying.

While Phillip Wade (Plo Koon) and Tay Bayliss (Stass Allie) are being touched up by creatures department technicians, Silas Carson (Ki-Adi-Mundi) and Jackson arrive. "You're a hologram from Mygeeto listening to Yoda on Kashyyyk," Lucas says to Carson, who seems perplexed by the director's relatively esoteric vocabulary.

"I had no clue what George was talking about," Carson would later confess.

"Okay, the next shot is of Agen Kolar and Anakin," Fletcher says, and the chairs are reoriented. While waiting, there's a fair amount of joking that Mace Windu isn't really dead, and that, during the credits, he could perhaps crawl back through the window, with his clothes just a bit singed.

"Yeah," Jackson says, "Mel Gibson could do it: *The Resurrection.*"

During rehearsals, he asks what "Utapau" is. "It's a planet," Lucas replies.

"Oh, next to Badda-Bing?" Jackson says.

Between shots, Jackson explains that he travels with "a stack of comic books and a stack of Hong Kong movies." He also talks with Lucas about additional photography.

"There are some directors who think it's an affront to reshoot and that it makes them look stupid," Lucas says. "But it's a natural part of the process."

"Even as an actor, you know sometimes that what you're saying isn't connected to anything," Jackson agrees.

"Well, sometimes you take a risk and then you come back and fix it.

"*You* have that luxury."

"This is more like the theater, where you're constantly improving the material."

"There is only one director I know who claims to know exactly what he's doing all the time," Jackson says.

"I'd rather think of myself as not knowing what I'm doing."

It is gradually becoming very hot on stage. About 250 kilowatts are raining down on the crew, and the air conditioner has developed a problem, but Knoll says, "No matter how hot we're shooting, I always think this is nothing like Tunisia."

Another problem develops when the head of the camera crane malfunctions. Lucas instructs the crew to put the camera on "sticks," a tripod, to avoid waiting for repairs. As they set up the Jedi war room, crew measure the length of the room's table.

"Sixteen feet?" Lucas asks, incredulous.

"Yeah, that's the diameter according to ILM," Peter Russell says.

"I think that six is a zero," Lucas points out, and the table is adjusted accordingly.

Middle: Crew prepare to shoot a Jedi Council scene. Above and bottom: The doomed pair share a few tender moments in final frames of Padmé's veranda (digi-matte painting by Christian Haley) . . .

Hours later, Fletcher informs the crew that work will continue till eight. In an open electric car outside, Hayden, Jackson, and others are sprawled about, waiting.

CAMERA WRAP: 20:13   SETUPS: 46

ADDITIONAL PHOTOGRAPHY DAY 8:
TUESDAY, AUGUST 31, 2004
    LOCATION: F & B Stages
    SET: Alderaan space cruiser, Obi-Wan starfighter, Mustafar control room, Senate
    SCENES SHOT: Mas Amedda on cruiser monitor; Sidious approaches Yoda on the floor

Star Wars fans know that beneath the armor of bounty hunter Boba Fett was actor Jeremy Bulloch. Today Bulloch is on the side of the heroes, playing a pilot in Bail Organa's space cruiser—the cockpit of which is the one other complete set of this eleven-day shoot. Lucas decided to put Bulloch in the film "some time ago. We were just looking for a place to put him and this seemed like the best choice," he explains. "Now he's more than just a mysterious conundrum."

Jimmy Smits has also arrived for his one day of pickups, and he walks onto the set with McGregor, joining Lucas for a look at the animatics of the scene.

"Ben's doing his best work," McGregor remarks, referring to Burtt's valiant placeholder voice-overs.

They run through a rehearsal, but when it's time for Yoda to speak, nothing happens.

"Did Yoda die?" Lucas inquires.

It turns out that nobody had written down Yoda's dialogue for someone to read off-camera, so Lucas does so. During the first take, however, 3rd AD Eddie Thorn's reading is so . . . English, that everyone breaks up laughing.

The next bit of laughter occurs when Anthony Daniels, in the rehearsal for C-3PO's last scene, appears towing a red vacuum cleaner on wheels behind him, which is ostensibly for R2-D2 reference. After a take and a missed cue, Daniels, encased in his armor, walks up to the camera and says, "I can't hear a word anyone is saying."

The scene completed, Lucas gives the thumbs-up to Daniels.

"It's only been twenty-five years," George says.

"And we're still not getting it right," Anthony jokes.

"Thank you—thank you for everything," Lucas says and they shake hands.

CAMERA WRAP: 19:22   SETUPS: 52

. . . but the tide soon turns as (above and bottom) Palpatine ushers in the Empire, to Padmé's horror. Middle: Jeremy Bulloch as the pilot of the Alderaan starcruiser.

```
CJR Scene 127A/117

        EXT. CRUISER AND SENATE LANDING PLATFORM (JEDI RETURN)

* OBI-WAN, BAIL, TWO PILOTS, and MAS AMEDDA.

                        PILOT
            We are receiving a message from
            the Chancellor's Office.

                        BAIL ORGANA
            Send it through.

                        PILOT
            Yes, sir.

            The Pilot pushes some buttons.

                        MAS AMEDDA
            Senator Organa...the Supreme
            Chancellor of the Republic
            requests your presence at a
            special session of Congress.

                        BAIL ORGANA
            Tell the Chancellor I will be
            there.

                        MAS AMEDDA
            Very well.

                        BAIL ORGANA
            Do you think it's a trap?

                        OBI-WAN
            I don't think so.  The Chancellor
            won't be able to control the
            thousands of star systems without
            keeping the Senate intact.

* OBI-WAN, BAIL, and YODA land on Coruscant.  The elevator
  door opens, and they step out.

                        GUARD
            Welcome back, Senator.  May I see
            your clearance?

                        BAIL ORGANA
            Certainly.

                        GUARD
            Thank you, you may proceed.

                        OBI-WAN
            It would be better if we stayed
            with the Senator.

                        GUARD
            It would be better if they stayed
            with you.

            BAIL and his AIDES go into the Senate.  YODA and OBI-WAN head
            for the Jedi Temple.
```

(handwritten) IF A SPECIAL SESSION OF CONGRESS THERE IS EASY FOR US TO ENTER THE Jedi TEMPLE IT WILL BE

ADDITIONAL PHOTOGRAPHY DAY 9: WEDNESDAY, SEPTEMBER 1, 2004
LOCATION: B Stage
SET: Trade Federation cruiser, Chancellor's office, Jedi return, Senate chamber
SCENES SHOT: Jedi running down corridor; Dooku uses the Force to hurl Obi-Wan

Above left: 3rd AD Eddie Thorne's "sides" contain the lines for Yoda that Lucas hastily scribbles. Above right: Lucas and Daniels once again for the last time. Right: In a new scene Organa (Smits) and Obi-Wan (McGregor) are stopped by blue guards, but Obi-Wan does the ol' mind trick. Lee (Dooku) in final frames (top right) and in a pickup shot using the Force (below). Far right: A final frame of a new scene shot at Shepperton of Anakin leading clone troopers to the Jedi Temple (digi-matte painting by Vanessa Cheung).

210

Every morning, many of the crew—Lucas and McCallum among them—gather at the Orangery between 7 and 7:30 A.M. to eat a typical English breakfast of eggs, sausages, bacon, and baked beans. Today, waving away their electric car and driver, Rick says, "Let's walk to the stage."

"Yes. It's the first day of the rest of your life," Lucas says. "Put out that cigarette and let's walk."

Once on the set, Lucas says to Gillard per a shot in the elevator shaft, "This is your shot—but I need to get it in fifteen minutes."

"You'll get it in ten," Gillard replies.

McGregor joins Lucas in watching the dailies sent over from ILM.

"I find the filming of it gets in the way of the watching of it," remarks Ewan, enjoying the brief show. After he departs, Lucas expresses concern to Knoll and McCallum that he's not receiving enough final shots.

"We'll stay on schedule," Knoll says, "but we don't want to get into numerology."

"It's about trying to get a sense of the movie," Lucas counters.

"We need a reel by December 1," McCallum says.

"It's going to have to be the first reel," Lucas says, and Knoll promises that ILM will hit the thousand-shot deadline of October 31.

After lunch, 2nd AD Deb holds the blue curtain open so that Christopher Lee can enter. Dressed as Count Dooku, he hugs Lucas. They then watch animatics of Dooku's fight with the Jedi. "It's really that one shot," Lucas says, referring to the moment when Dooku uses the Force to bring a balcony down on Obi-Wan's leg.

They do a take. Lucas walks to the set. "That wasn't quite right, was it, George?"

"Come out a little more decisive," Lucas suggests. "It's almost in one motion: You turn and bring your hand up—and then you can push it down with energy."

Take. "Try one with a little more malice and evil," Lucas calls out from the video village. Take. After Lucas gives him the okay, Fletcher announces, "Well, that's it."

"Thanks for everything; you've been terrific," Lucas says to Lee.

" 'Farewell. God knows when we'll meet again,' " Lee replies, quoting Shakespeare.

CAMERA WRAP: 18:45   SETUPS: 52

ADDITIONAL PHOTOGRAPHY DAY 10: THURSDAY, SEPTEMBER 2, 2004
LOCATION: R Stage
SET: Utapau caves and sinkhole, Senate chamber, Mygeeto
SCENES SHOT: Anakin and clones; Sidious and Anakin after Mace is killed; Sidious robe is now on

As Christensen marches forward, simulating Anakin's walk to the Jedi Temple to massacre the Jedi, a corner of the blue carpet is blown up by the fans. Christensen stops midstride and fixes it. "He might be evil," McFarlane says, "but he's still neat."

Later, it's another key hood-donning moment, this time as Palpatine changes into the Emperor/Darth Sidious. After a failed attempt, Lucas calls out, "Don't worry—Ewan and Hayden had their hood moments, too." After a few takes, Lucas walks over to Ian and says, "For the end of this dialogue, you can become contemplative—and then stronger with, 'Do what must be done, Lord Vader.' "

"When he changes into Sidious," McDiarmid would note, "it's his Mr. Hyde moment."

CAMERA WRAP: 19:18 SETUPS: 45

ADDITIONAL PHOTOGRAPHY DAY 11: FRIDAY, SEPTEMBER 3, 2004
LOCATION: R Stage
SET: Utapau, Yoda's quarters, Mustafar landing platform
SCENES SHOT: Utapaun sidekicks; Anakin talks with Yoda; Anakin frowns
at younglings; death of Shaak Ti

Lucas is wearing a colorful, festive shirt today. "I thought I'd celebrate," he says. "My last day of shooting after thirty-five years."

After a couple of short pickups, production readies for the new Yoda-Anakin scene. The set consists of one cushion and a blue wall with slats in it to create the necessary lighting.

"No human can let go," Lucas would say of this scene. "It's very hard. Ultimately, we do let go because it's inevitable; you do die and you do lose your loved ones. But while you're alive, you can't be obsessed with holding on. As Yoda says in this one, 'You must learn to let go of everything you're afraid to let go of.' Because holding on is in the same category and the precursor to greed. And that's what a Sith is. A Sith is somebody that is absolutely obsessed with gaining more and more power—but for what?

Nothing, except that it becomes an obsession to get more.

"The *Jedi* are *trained* to let go. They're trained from birth," he continues. "They're not supposed to form attachments. They can love people—in fact, they should love everybody. They should love their enemies; they should love the Sith. But they can't form attachments. So what all these movies are about is: greed. Greed is a source of pain and suffering for everybody. And the ultimate state of greed is the desire to cheat death."

As Christensen prepares himself, 3rd AD Thorn confides, "I'll be reading Yoda, but I'm not doing the voice."

"Why not?" Hayden asks.

"Because the crew's been laughing at me the whole week," Thorn says. "Is that okay?"

"Okay," Christensen replies.

"Let's shoot it!" McCallum calls out—but crew have to work on the positioning of the chairs and getting better striped lighting on Anakin.

"Hayden," Fletcher says, "sorry. Ten minutes." And Christensen leaves the set to talk to some friends who are visiting.

About a quarter of an hour later, the first take is completed. "Can you feel the light on you?" Lucas calls to Christensen. "Try and keep that light in your eye." Take. "Bring your head down just a bit more so it's in that little shaft of light." Take—and for this last take, Thorn does the Yoda voice.

"Beautiful!" Lucas says, and there is applause for Christensen—and for Thorn.

While discussing the upcoming Jedi youngling scene with Lucas, Fletcher says, "I think with the kids, the best thing to do is to set up and shoot the rehearsal."

Lucas agrees, also deciding to shoot the scene in the Jedi Council chamber. Knoll thinks that might be too many scenes there, and suggests the Jedi Temple archives.

"I'm going to put it in the Council Chamber," Lucas says. "It has the right symbolism—and it's night," he adds, as Nutggens arrives. "So whatever light coming in is from the outside. And as the kids move, they go in and out of the light."

September 13: *Star Wars: Clone Wars* receives an Emmy Award for Outstanding Animated Program (for Programming One Hour or More) at the fifty-sixth annual Creative Arts Emmy Awards.

Left: In the last shot of the pickups, Obi-Wan (McGregor) clings to a rock face. Above left: Anakin seeks the help of Yoda, but winds up killing Shaak Ti (Oli Shosan). Above right: Fletcher coaches the Jedi younglings; McGregor, Christensen, and Lucas share a light moment, as do Ian and Hayden; Lucas and McCallum depart—the last Call Sheet reads, "To everyone on the Cast and Crew: Thank you so much for your hard work; we've had a fantastic time—it's been great working with you!—Rick, George, Brian [Donovan], Colin and Deb. P.S. Thanks for working on the Bank Holiday—sorry we couldn't pay you for it! (only joking!)"

Much later, the kids are ushered in, each outfitted in a tiny Jedi costume. Fletcher explains to them that Anakin will come into the room. "And then we'll run away?" one boy asks, while, on the other side of the set, Lucas says to Christensen, "You come in and you just smile."

The last shot of additional photography is of McGregor on a cave wall as he emerges from a watery sinkhole. McCallum smokes a cigarette while the camera crew tilts the camera to make the wall look steeper than it is—until Knoll and others say it's too much. "All right," Lucas says. "Straighten it up a little bit—the peanut gallery is refusing to accept that."

"More water on the wall, please," Rick says, and they do a take.

"Should I try one more?" Lucas asks.

"Yeah, get Obi-Wan's hair and beard wetter," Knoll suggests.

"Okay."

Take.

"Cut. Print. Wrap!" Lucas says.

"That's a wrap," Fletcher says to applause. As everyone celebrates, he adds, "Folks, it's been a great two weeks. It's been a pleasure working with you," and hugs Lucas. "Thank you, George. It was good fun."

CAMERA WRAP: 19:29   SETUPS: 44   TOTAL SETUPS: 469
NOTES: Additional UK shooting completed today.

ILM begins churning out finals, of Boga the Utapaun lizard (top left), Wookiees in battle (above left), Obi-Wan in the Jedi Temple circuit room (top right) and in the Temple control room with Yoda (above right). It's here that the two will decide on one last battle with the Sith.

TUESDAY, SEPTEMBER 14, 2004

ILM: Lucas is back in UJ after taking a week off to attend a premiere of *THX 1138* in Deauville, and things proceed as they did before. With his sense of invention unabated, he reviews Grievous once again. "We might hear little clicks as he unlocks his arms," George says, discussing how the droid general's two arms become four.

"What I kind of like is you don't know what he's doing," Knoll agrees.

"It's like he's spinning the sabers," Lucas continues, discussing how the general might use his two upper arms. "He pulls the lower two back, and pushes the other two lightsabers forward, spinning them. We haven't cut it yet, so let's see if we can expand the fight and make it more than it was."

SR: Yesterday was Lucas's last visit to the animatics department. "It felt weird, melancholy," Fay David says. By October's end, there will be only three left there. Dan Gregoire has already moved on to Steven Spielberg's *War of the Worlds*.

Though still editing with Lucas mornings, Ben Burtt is now spending afternoons at Skywalker Sound. Sitting in a fairly large office, which he shares with Matt Wood, Burtt is encircled by equipment. Every day, he consecrates at least an hour to research and development, so he's already devised 590 new sounds, including "buzz droids talking and Grievous's chariot." On Monday, when the first reel will officially be turned over to Burtt from editorial, sound editor Tom Meyers will start cutting in sounds both new and old. Lucas will begin coming over for reviews in November.

"We're doing some Artoo stuff at the moment," Burtt says. In fact, for

the first time since 1981, he is making new sounds for R2-D2. "I was a little afraid to go back. It was a moment in time," he adds. "Fortunately, I had my notes and I had my 1971 synthesizer, which I'd stored in the crawl space under my house. And through the miracle of Howie Hammerman [a Lucasfilm veteran], it now works again. My intention is to give Artoo a fresh voice."

TOTAL # OF SHOTS: 2,300   FINALS: 700
FINALS NEEDED PER WEEK: 57   WEEKS TO GO: 28
NOTE: The third rough cut is running, without end credits, at 2 hours 29 minutes 51 seconds.

FRIDAY, OCTOBER 8, 2004

SR: In his large, somewhat circular office, McCallum is having a brief consultation with Mike Blanchard. On one table, amid myriad books on cinema, is an Episode I ILM crew shot. In boxes are tapes of all formats and correspondence from around the globe. On the mantelpiece are *Star Wars* collectibles and a RICK McCALLUM PRODUCER toy, which was given to him as a joke.

Across the corridor from his office sits Ardees Rabang, who has been McCallum's assistant for nearly ten years; she handles everything from production crises to organizing the actors' menus to scheduling

McCallum's travel. "He calls me his 'little mom,' " Rabang says. "Rick used to be notorious. His assistants used to hide, because you could hear him yelling and screaming. But he's a lot more relaxed now."

"Our present cut is running at about two hours, twenty-five minutes," McCallum says of third rough cut, finished October 1, "and we want to try and get it down to two hours fifteen without losing any scenes, just by trimming. Francis has seen it, and George has talked with him. And what happens next is that on Wednesday, John Williams and Steven Spielberg are coming up to watch the film. Then Spielberg will leave, after talking with George, and the rest of that day and the next, George and John will spot the film. They'll work with music editor Kenny Wannberg, who's done all six. He's actually retired, but he's coming back to do this; he's been a good-luck charm and is a lovely guy.

"The rest of the month will be spent on really focusing on the digital stunt work, and ILM will just continue finishing shots. By November 7, George will have the picture pretty much locked down, at which point we can decide if we're going to do any more pickups. The looping will take

Yoda's duel with the Emperor in a final frame (top left), in early ILM cloth sims (right-hand strip, by Todd Widup, Scott Jones, and Greg Killmaster), and in early animatics directed by Steven Spielberg featuring giant HoloNet screens transmitting their duel across the galaxy. "Anytime a creature changes major poses," notes cloth sim supervisor Juan-Luis Sanchez, "like from lying down to standing, it is difficult." Far left: George Lucas (Baron Papanoida) and his daughter Katie Lucas (Chi Eekway) are prepared by Gillian Libbert for their cameo in the Galaxies opera staircase scene, filmed in November 2004, months after the crowd scene was shot at Shepperton. An early version of the Baron's costume is by concept artist Sang Jun Lee (left).

place in London, in mid-December, and on February 2, we start to score for approximately three weeks–and then we have the horror of doing all the foreign versions, trying to make the day-and-date release.

"Usually when you finish a movie, you get sick," he adds. "You've been running on adrenaline for so long. After we do all the press events, I'm going to say, 'I'm shattered.' And then it'll be a very strange feeling. The people you've worked with, and grown up with–everyone will move on. I've always been connected to John and Rob–and Ben, of course, I've been with for fifteen years. That's the sad part. It's emotionally wrenching.

"But the most important thing for me, personally, when the film is released, is that it's a breakthrough in terms of being visually breathtaking and emotionally powerful, so that the people involved in this–Gavin, and David Tattersall, Trisha, and ILM, and Ben, and everyone else–who have done extraordinary work and who have never been acknowledged–what I'm hoping is that their work is recognized."

TUESDAY, OCTOBER 12, 2004

ILM: In UJ, Lucas is reviewing an animation of Yoda as he surveys Dagobah from his vessel at the end of *Revenge of the Sith*. Rob asks George if he's looking too sad.

"Yeah," Lucas responds. "Yoda should bring his head up faster. He should look around because this is his new world. I think the word here is *wise*. Yoda has to have a *we will have our day* look on his face. He is going to persevere."

EPILOGUE: The Compassion of the Jedi

George W. Lucas was born on May 14, 1944, in Modesto, California. After graduating from the University of Southern California, he directed *THX 1138, American Graffiti*, and four *Star Wars* films. He has executive produced Francis Ford Coppola's *Tucker: The Man and His Dream*, Jim Henson's *Labyrinth* (1986), Ron Howard's *Willow* (1988), Lawrence

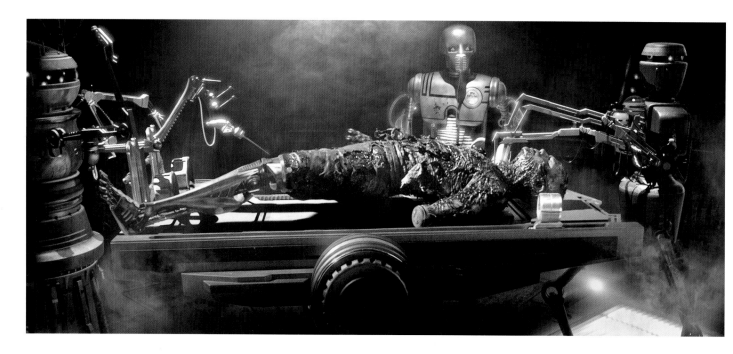

The transformation of flesh-and-blood Vader into mostly mechanical Vader, as seen in the visual script (being taken from Mustafar to the rehabilitation center, top left) and in a final frame, as droids operate on him (left).

Top: The operation continues in Markel's animatics for CRC.010 (May 6, 2004), and Vader's new life-sustaining suit is revealed in Carney's animatics for CRC.150 (April 8, 2004). The two Sith converse in a final frame (middle), and then Vader breaks free in Carney's animatics for CRC.190 and CRC.210 (above).

Kasdan's *Body Heat* (1981), Akira Kurosawa's *Kagemusha* (1980), Walter Murch's *Return to Oz*, Paul Schrader's *Mishima* (1985), Steven Spielberg's *Indiana Jones* trilogy, and of course the other two *Star Wars* films. He has helped pioneer several visual effects breakthroughs, began what became Pixar Animation, and spearheaded digital filmmaking.

With seven months of work left on *Revenge of the Sith*, though it's impossible to speak of it as complete, certain observations can be made. For three years, a nonstop barrage of art and ideas, created by an incredibly talented group of core collaborators, has gone through the filter of Lucas's mind, inspiring certain conceits and mixing with his own. The ultimate design of the movie's scripts, sets, vehicles, characters, and shots is the expression of a writer-director whose vision is at once popular and

abstract—the detached eye of the documentarian and the intensely, almost idiosyncratically emotional lens of the man.

The two *Star Wars* trilogies share many characters but have different structures. Instead of telling another heroic coming-of-age story, Lucas has crafted in the prequels a historical drama, at whose center is Anakin Skywalker. His story is tragic; that of the Republic-turned-Empire, uncom-

Top left: In this shot, Padmé's body will be delivered to Naboo, which exists here as a digi-matte painting by Yanick Dusseault, who explains, "a grayscale shading of the 3-D geometry was constructed as a base for the painting process" (inset). The following dawn a funeral is held for the former Queen (final frame, above, with digi-matte painting by Paul Huston). However, there is a new hope in her and Anakin's son, Luke, who will be cared for on Tatooine (final frame, right)—all envisioned by Lucas (above right), who began this last shot back on September 7, 2000.

fortably familiar. Anakin begins as a nine-year-old boy who is physically enslaved. He ends the prequel saga a spiritual and mental slave to the Emperor, who is his metaphorical if not biological father. First seen in Episode I as beset by a crippling bureaucracy, the Republic Senate is, by the end of Episode III, a rubber stamp for the Empire. As the locale for the duel between the Emperor and Yoda, the Senate finally becomes what it has always been: the physical manifestation of the eternal conflict between totalitarianism and democracy.

But the end of *Revenge of the Sith* is not the end of Anakin, whose story really closes when it merges with those of his children, Luke and Leia, in *Return of the Jedi.*

"It really has to do with learning," Lucas says. "Children teach you compassion. They teach you to love unconditionally. Anakin can't be redeemed for all the pain and suffering he's caused. He doesn't right the wrongs, but he stops the horror. The end of the saga is simply Anakin saying, *I care about this person, regardless of what it means to me. I will throw away everything that I have, everything that I've grown to love—primarily the Emperor—and throw away my life, to save this person. And I'm doing it because he has faith in me; he loves me despite all the horrible things I've done. I broke his mother's heart, but he still cares about me, and I can't let that die.* Anakin is very different in the end. The thing of it is: The prophecy was right. Anakin was the chosen one, and he does bring balance to the Force. He takes the ounce of good still left in him and destroys the Emperor out of compassion for his son."

Anakin Skywalker's final confrontation with the Emperor occurs during Luke's first confrontation with the Emperor, which complements his father's dealings with the same man many years earlier. Indeed, the life of the father and the life of the son are commentaries on each other. One of

Lucas's tendencies, evident throughout his films, is to tell simultaneous stories, many of which are interconnected.

"I come out of editing, and that's probably part of it," Lucas says. "I think I have a short attention span and that's probably part of it, too. [laughs] It's just my nature.

"The *Star Wars* saga is like a symphony, which has recurring themes," he adds. "You have one theme orchestrated in a particular way and place, which then comes back orchestrated as a minor theme somewhere else. There are these little threads running through things that are constantly turning events on their head. You see two people confronting the same things, with different ends. It's a rhythm. I like the idea of seeing something from different perspectives. An advantage I have in this particular situation is that I have literally twelve hours to tell a story. It has the epic quality of following one person from the time he's nine years old to the time he dies. It's Anakin's story, but obviously there are many other characters in that story—his children, his best friend—and their stories carry through. So this isn't just a tune—it's a symphony. When you do it as a symphony, I think, it actually becomes beautiful."

Don't miss the exciting online FINAL CHAPTER to THE MAKING OF STAR WARS: REVENGE OF THE SITH, detailing the work that continued even after the book was done. This exclusive material is available at www.readstarwars.com.

Creating the Visual Script

At Skywalker Ranch, on Monday, June 23, 2003, art department supervisor Fay David calls an emergency meeting. While finishing his fourth draft of the script, Lucas has decided that the corresponding visual script needs a lot more detail. The purpose of this latter reference document is to give actors, on-set technicians, and the Sydney art department a better idea of what the finished sets—post visual effects—will look like. Lucas has therefore asked for the visual script to cover every scene, and in alarming detail—given that the artists must finish paintings for the first thirty days of principal photography by Wednesday evening, with the balance due not long afterward.

To create most of these paintings—and create them quickly—the artists form an assembly line: (1) they read the scene, carefully noting all of its visual elements;

(2) Derek Thompson then composes shots in storyboard-like sketches, with black-and-white values, and places the file on a server; (3) either Michael Murnane, Robert Barnes, Feng Zhu, or Sang Jun Lee takes the file and does a character pass–i.e., putting in character details; (4) either Zhu or T.J. Frame do an ID (industrial design) pass to make the environment detailed and three-dimensional; (5) Tiemens or Church then do a composition and lighting pass, adding washes of color and checking it against the time of day specified in the script. Examples of finished visual script pages are found throughout the book.

Acknowledgments

Very special thanks to George Lucas, for his input and generosity over the past three years; and to Trisha Biggar and Gavin Bocquet, for tours and insights into their respective departments; Ben Burtt, for his refined thoughts about editing and sound; Tippy Bushkin, for her great documentary footage; Ryan Church, for many concept-art sneak previews; Rob Coleman, for a memorable Indian dinner; David Craig, for his learned help; Anthony Daniels, for a conversation about the ends and beginnings of *Star Wars;* Fay David, whose help was simply invaluable; Nick Gillard, for a talk about the character of dueling; Dan Gregoire, for letting me stand around; Pablo Hidalgo, for the mind-boggling continuity conversations in Foodles; John Knoll, for his great panoramic photos; Christopher Lee, for recalling his adventures during the making of *The Three Musketeers;* Iain McCaig, for unforgettable car-pool conversations; Tina Mills, for taking care of the thousands of images; Kathryn Ramos, for her notes on the manuscript; Erik Tiemens, for—among many, many others—the painting of Skywalker Ranch; and to everyone else who gave a helpful word or hint. At Del Rey, to Keith Clayton, Mark Maguire, Sylvain Michaelis, and Steve Saffel; and at Lucasfilm, to Amy Gary, Howard Roffman, and Sue Rostoni—for making the book readable and beautiful—and in particular to Iain Morris, who oversaw the design process with his usual skill and panache and eleventh-hour heroics! And much thanks to Hayden Christensen, for the many lucid conversations. *And very special thanks to Rick McCallum—none of this would've been possible without his unstinting support from day one.*

Top left and right: Anakin vanquishes Count Dooku, and Palpatine vs. Yoda, from the visual script. Above: Parts of the symphony: in Episode VI, Darth Vader, Emperor Palpatine, and Luke Skywalker; in Episode III, Chancellor Palpatine, Anakin Skywalker, and Obi-Wan Kenobi. Opposite page: Death droid by Tiemens. Following page: (left) Tenggren's continuity script shows the changes made on the set during the final Anakin–Obi-Wan scene in Sydney, Monday, September 1, 2003. (right) Props dresser Jeremy Fuller takes a sledgehammer to the Trade Federation cruiser hallway–the fate of nearly all the sets.

Index